Also available at all good book stores

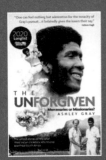

9781785315329

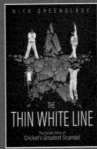

9781785317330

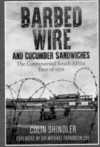

9781785316340

9781908051929

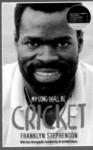

9781785315398

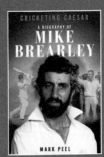

9781785316623

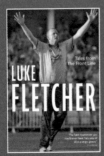

9781785316876

9781785316630

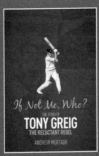

9781785316418

DO THEY PLAY
CRICKET
in Ireland?

DO THEY PLAY
CRICKET
in Ireland?

The 25-year journey to a Test match at Lord's

D A V I D   T O W N S E N D

First published by Pitch Publishing, 2021

Pitch Publishing
A2 Yeoman Gate
Yeoman Way
Worthing
Sussex
BN13 3QZ
www.pitchpublishing.co.uk
info@pitchpublishing.co.uk

ISBN 978 1 78531 840 5

Typesetting and origination by Pitch Publishing
Printed and bound in India by Replika Press Pvt. Ltd.

CONTENTS

For
John and Stella
and my son
Danny

ACKNOWLEDGEMENTS

MY THANKS to the entire Irish cricketing fraternity, even the Mooneys, for your friendship and support over the years.

Particular thanks to Barry Chambers who supplied many of the photos and permissions, along with advice and ideas; Peter Gillespie for planting the idea and Alan Lewis for insisting 'it must be done'; Mike Hendrick, Paul McCrum and Greg Molins for jogging memories of the early years; my fellow members of the Cricket Writers of Ireland; Stella Downes for her corrections and encouragement; plus editor Richard Whitehead and the team at Pitch.

Finally, a special mention for Derek Scott and John Wright, two fine men who did so much for cricket on the island and began the journey towards that Test match at Lord's.

INTRODUCTION

St John's Wood – Autumn, 1993

IT MIGHT seem a little strange that a 25-year-long odyssey with Ireland cricket should start and finish at Lord's. But all journeys have to begin somewhere, and for me the pistol was fired during a couple of post-season pints with John Carr. Guinness, as it happens. I'd introduced the recently retired Middlesex batsman to his lovely wife, Vicky, during my three years working with the county, so maybe karma was at work. 'What are you doing this winter, DT?'

'Nothing special. No plans. A few sub-editing shifts to pay for a holiday in Sydney, probably. As you know, I do like a bit of sun on my back.' Never been a fan of the English winters. Or regular work patterns, for that matter.

'Why don't you come out to Kenya and cover the ICC Trophy, then?' The World Cup qualifying tournament was being held in Nairobi and JC was going to coach Argentina.

'No one is going to be interested in that.'

'Ireland are playing in it for the first time – you might get a bit of work reporting their games. Cover your expenses? It should be a good three weeks.'

It was a good three weeks – and a fair bit more. A quarter of a century, and counting, watching a team, many of whom I count as friends, venturing forth and taking on the best in the world. From worrying about Gibraltar to worrying Australia. Countless contests in more than 20 countries. Trophies, triumphs, heartbreak, upsets and more. The best of times.

JC was right. It didn't take long to 'cover my expenses' and nudge a good few quid into profit. The Irish border has caused all sorts of problems over the years, but the beauty of partition on the island – from a selfish freelance point of view – is that there are effectively two national broadcasters, RTE and BBC Northern Ireland, and 'national' newspapers on both sides of the border. I was commissioned by both radio stations, plus *The Irish Times* and the *News Letter* – just about opposites – plus *The Times*; also *The Cricketer* magazine were interested in a preview and closing report on the tournament and, best of all, I'd get to make my debut in *Wisden Cricketers' Almanack*. The Bible.

My knowledge of Irish cricket didn't extend much beyond knowing that they had once bowled out West Indies for 20-something and that Justin Benson, a fringe player at Leicestershire, was in the squad for Kenya. So I dived into the history books for a bit of background.

Ireland's first official match was played in Phoenix Park, south of Dublin, in 1855. So they had been at it some time. Their opponents were the Gentlemen of England, who would surely have struggled to raise a side. Various challenges followed, including a couple of trips across the Atlantic to play Philadelphia, New York and Canada, and an innings victory over Scotland in the inaugural meeting of the teams in 1888.

That was pretty much how it had continued since. All very amateur: regular games against Scotland, the occasional venture overseas and, of course, tourist matches that were seen as light relief by the big beasts involved in Test series on the other side of the Irish Sea. True, West Indies were embarrassed at Sion Mills in 1969, when they were bowled out for 25, but usually it was the home side who left with red faces. Earlier that year, Australian skipper Allan Border had taken a fancy to the off spin of Angus Dunlop and hit him for five consecutive sixes. Dunlop was in the ICC Trophy squad, presumably not as a bowler.

Famous players? Well, not many since Sir Timothy O'Brien, the first Irishman to play Test cricket for England, who featured in a handful of matches in the 1880s. O'Brien also began the long association between Ireland and Middlesex, which many moons later saw left-arm spinner Dermott Monteith appear for the county. I remember watching Monty bowl at Uxbridge, a big turner of the ball. He was, and still is, Ireland's all-time leading wicket-taker with 326 wickets from only 76 matches, a phenomenal effort. Mark Cohen, who had opened the batting for Middlesex IIs, was in the squad for Kenya. He was dating a former Miss World, which was also a phenomenal effort in my book.

That was about it at the time, yet within the next two decades Ireland would supply England with three full internationals, two of them Test players, and somewhere in north Dublin a future World Cup-winning captain was running around in short trousers.

The Cricketer wanted a preview piece so I found a contact number for captain Stephen Warke and phoned him at home in Belfast. Opening batsman. Nice bloke. 'Do any of your squad have first-class experience apart from Justin Benson?' I wondered.

A pause. 'We all do.'

Ah yes, the annual three-day match against Scotland; the one where off-spinner Garfield Harrison took 9-113 to claim the best first-class bowling figures in the run-drenched summer of 1990. More research was clearly needed but I wasn't alone in my ignorance; *The Cricketer* illustrated my piece with a picture of all-rounder Junior McBrine, who had last played for Ireland in 1992 and would be spending the tournament at home in Donemana.

Two weeks before leaving, Malachy Logan, the sports editor of *The Irish Times*, called me. 'David, I hate to do this to you, but we've decided to send our own man.' Fair enough. It happens. I doubt if there is any freelancer who hasn't lost a commission at the last minute. Few have heard what followed, though: 'Would you accept half your fee as compensation?'

It was my first indication that this lot did things differently.

LAYING THE TRACKS
1994–1999

1994

Nairobi – 12 February

The first Ireland player I met was Alan Lewis, future chairman of selectors and international rugby referee, his megawatt smile illuminating a pre-tournament barbecue when the power failed. Lewie had assumed the captaincy on the eve of Ireland's first game when Stephen Warke ran into a roller during practice, and broke a bone in his elbow. The amateur nature of the set-up was immediately obvious, as was the friendliness of players drawn from all over the island. Lewie was a Dubliner, most of the squad played for clubs in and around Belfast and then there was Desmond 'Decker' Curry from the north-west, who, I was told, strangled sheep for a living.

This was new territory for all of them. After a first capped match during the Crimea War, Ireland had bumbled along playing half a dozen games or so a year without raising the consciousness, even among neighbours, that cricket was played to any great level on the island. Yet it was, and against the odds some decent players were ready to embark on their first global tournament after being elected to Associate membership of the International Cricket Council the year before.

There was ambition among the squad to show what they could do and to measure themselves against the more established Associate sides like the Netherlands, as well as their hosts Kenya who were expected to do well in familiar conditions. The challenge of trying to qualify for the 1996 World Cup was one to be relished, but if there was an enthusiasm to embrace this new world it was in a 'this is how we do it in Ireland' sort of way. They were very much innocents abroad, from the Hon. Sec. of the Irish Cricket Union in his knee-length trench coat and trilby, to journalist Philip Boylan using Perrier water to brush his teeth.

Inexperience and naivety shone through everywhere. Tips, for example. When room service delivered morning tea, we added the equivalent of 20p which seemed about right and were rewarded the following day with a complimentary plate of biscuits. Boylan, meanwhile, tipped his attendant £5 at a more upmarket establishment and the resulting misunderstanding had the poor man returning that evening wearing a pink shirt and a nervous smile.

The Nairobi hotels we encountered were all good, from the top-of-the-range Norfolk to the more basic three-star 680, where I was staying with a photographer mate. The staff at our place were top notch. A receptionist called me over as I was leaving to watch nets one afternoon.

'Excuse me, sir, a phone call for you.'

'What?' How did he know who I was? I took the receiver, expecting some sort of con.

'Hello, is that David? This is RTE radio in Dublin ...'

I'd wondered what had happened to their promise of work. No internet in those days so they would not have been able to reach me but for your man's intervention. I lashed out another 20p.

Boylan was a likeable wee fella who talked incessantly, often for the sake of it. In a reversal of tradition, he had come to cricket late through his son, Seamus, a useful club player. A chief sub-editor with the *Evening Herald*, Boylan senior had learned the Laws of his new passion and was umpiring at a high level in Leinster. Not very well, according to the Dublin-based batsmen in the squad, who ribbed him mercilessly. A lazy eye didn't help his authority. Bad enough to be given lbw, worse to see the finger raised by someone who could have been checking balls left in the over with his colleague at square leg at the same time.

For all Boylan's foibles, it was Ireland's best umpire, Paddy O'Hara, who set the cat among the pigeons early in the tournament with an outside-of-the-box ruling that was well meaning, but ultimately daft. The playing conditions set aside two days for the completion of each game, with play continuing while light allowed on the first day, but with a strict cut-off point on the second. Fair enough.

'Ah, but if there is no play on the first day, then the second day becomes the first day and play can continue,' O'Hara decreed, in his first game of the tournament. The ICC organisers enthusiastically went along with this nonsense, slapping the Belfast man on the back for his ingenuity. Those of us who understood limited-overs cricket could see the flaw and, Sod's Law, it was an Ireland game that exposed it.

Nairobi – 14 February

The first day of the Ireland campaign, a match against Papua New Guinea, was rained off although not before I'd rustled up some samosas and arranged a live radio interview for Warkie, in the Ngara club kitchen, where there was a landline phone. Remember those? The skipper was waiting to discover the extent of his injury and still hoping to play a part later on.

On the second day, which was now the first, Ireland made a decent 230/8, with Lewie stumped for 50 but recorded as run out, and were keen to bowl the minimum 30 overs to allow a result. That looked unlikely when a thunderstorm intervened with PNG on 45/4 at the start of the 22nd over. The Ireland players and supporters helped to cover the pitch and then mucked in with the mopping up. Deploying the O'Hara ruling, the game restarted after the official cut-off time. There was no chance of PNG facing their full quota and yet no set target from a reduced number of overs. The teams would play on until it was too dark.

The Pacific islanders never got close to leading on the run-rate calculation as a relieved Ireland squeezed in 32 overs. But imagine if they had? Imagine if it was so close that every ball mattered? I put this to Derek Scott, in his trench coat and trilby. Surely there has to be a cut-off point, otherwise how do you decide when the game is over?

'The umpires would decide that,' the Hon. Sec. insisted. 'That's how we do it in Ireland.'

So the umpires could come off with Team A leading, but Team B only needing a boundary from the next ball to get their noses in front?

'Yes,' said Scotty. 'That's why the umpires are neutral.'

This lot definitely did things differently.

Nairobi – 16 February

Evenings were great fun, usually starting with a couple of beers in the 680 hotel bar, which was frequented by several hospitality girls. I enjoyed chatting to 'Christine' who used to be a distance runner in her teens, she said, and still looked pretty fit. The routine was that I would buy her a Tusker, on the understanding that if a potential customer walked in – a Japanese businessman, maybe – she would abandon both me and the beer. A few minutes later she would be embracing the poor fella, winking over his shoulder and, with her small finger, indicating that he wouldn't trouble her greatly.

After a week, Christine asked me which room I was staying in? I explained that I was sharing with my photographer mate, Andy, but apparently that didn't matter. A couple of days later there was a knock on the door as we were finishing our tea and biscuits.

'What time you leave, darling?'

'In 15 minutes, or so. What's the problem?'

She wanted to walk out with us so that security wouldn't be able to tax her night's earnings, as was their custom.

A Chinese restaurant across the street was often the evening's next stop. After eating there half a dozen times, I walked in one evening with Andy, John Carr and his former Middlesex mate Simon 'Yosser' Hughes, who was covering the tournament for the *Daily Telegraph*. Our regular waiter appeared, smiling. 'Evening, Peter. Never mind the menus – just bring us four main courses and plenty of rice, please.'

He looked confused. 'What do you want to eat, sir?'

'Up to you and chef. Just bring us four dishes – we'll leave it to you.'

Peter soon returned with the food, looking very pleased with himself. A couple of our favourite dishes, and a couple we hadn't ordered before. Yosser poked at one of the new dishes. 'We don't want that!' Dearie me, leave the choice to the staff and then complain.

The Analyst and future editor of *The Cricketer* magazine didn't cover himself in glory in other areas, either, falling ill after slipping off to the Masai Mara for a few days' safari mid-tournament and then embarrassing himself when Commissioner of Sport Mike Boit dropped by the press box one afternoon. Although Kipchoge Keino had always been my favourite East African runner, now closely followed by Christine, it was a treat to meet one of the other middle-distance greats. The occasion was lost on *The Telegraph*, though.

'What was your sport, sir?'

'Athletics.'

'Were you any good at it?'

'I went to the Olympics.'

It took Yosser a while to live that one down.

What was your sport, Mr Bradman?

Nairobi was fascinating. Yes, it was poor, but most things worked, eventually, and there were signs of prosperity. The locals had smiles on their faces as they went about their various enterprises. Market traders would implore you to buy a souvenir because they hadn't eaten for three days and then produce a roll of banknotes for change. We would watch the Incredible Parking Man from our hotel balcony each morning as he ushered commuters into tiny spaces and collected a couple of bob for his efforts. A pittance, maybe, but multiply a pittance several times and it becomes a decent day's pay, as any freelance will tell you.

The trip was also memorable for the cracking company. The three-strong Irish press corps was completed by Peter O'Reilly, who had been sent by *The Irish Times*. A retired fast bowler, he had played for Ireland in the 1980s and spent time with Warwickshire, mostly injured and homesick. A good man for pints and an excellent writer. Then there was Andy Capostagno, who I had worked with at Cricketcall, the telephone commentary service, and a couple of British ex-pats who were writing for the local papers under bylines such as 'Third Man' and 'Nightwatchman'. It was rarely dull.

Nairobi – 27 February

Aided by their dubious victory over PNG, and canters against Gibraltar and Malaysia, Ireland reached the second round where their limitations were exposed by the United Arab Emirates, Bermuda and Canada. In their final game, one of the northern club pros played out a maiden 45th over, stroking five of the six deliveries firmly to short extra.

'He didn't give me anything to hit.'

Dave Houghton, hired to assist coach John Wills, managed to keep a straight face. The Zimbabwean batsman would have seen the quality in that squad, though: Lewis, Warke, Harrison and Alan Nelson, a whippy fast-medium bowler, could all have had careers in county cricket. But it was noticeable how few young players there were in a squad packed with tried and tested old soldiers, set in their ways.

Nairobi – 6 March

The ICC Trophy was won by the UAE who beat Kenya in the final by two wickets. Rumours had circulated throughout the three weeks about the origins of the Emirati side which contained only one indigenous player, skipper Sultan Zarawani. 'Their passports were all issued on the same day,' we were told by people who didn't know.

The UAE was an emerging nation then. Fast forward 25 years and no one is surprised that the majority of their team are born overseas. In 1994 it was a bone of contention, especially to the hosts who desperately wanted their name engraved on the trophy. The bad blood boiled over at the tournament dinner, held on the night of the final, where Basheer Mauladad, the chairman of the Kenyan Cricket Association, made a most ungracious speech which ended with the barb, 'We too can employ slaves to win a tournament.' Zarawani stood up and instructed his team to leave, rather proving the old boy's point.

The ICC closed ranks. Poor chap's got diabetes. Blood sugar levels too high. Didn't realise what he was saying. Nothing to see here. Move along.

The world governing body then was unrecognisable from what it has become, at least at Associate level. If no longer in name, it was still the Imperial Cricket Conference, a bastion of old-school colonialism – an organisation that allocated Gibraltar the same funding as Ireland and, crazier still, Bangladesh, and that allowed its World Cup qualifying tournament to be run by an expat from Newcastle, a former British Army sergeant who had more pies than fingers.

Nairobi – 8 March

Talking of fingers, my return home was delayed by news that my brother had been involved in a bus accident and was in casualty at the Aga Khan hospital. It wasn't the best way to end an otherwise perfect three weeks. William had flown to Nairobi to begin a round-the-world trip, and had been a great addition to the party, entertaining us royally one evening by joining an Ethiopian dancer on stage to perform a duet of jiggling breasts. Hers were covered.

Bill's tourist bus to Mombasa had veered off the road and down a ravine. Three people had died, he had nothing worse than a badly damaged hand and was waiting for a girl he was travelling with to come out of surgery with one less finger than she had going in. 'Look on the bright side, I'll be able to do my nails quicker.' Aussies, eh? Bill retained all his digits, but the world tour was delayed for another year.

I flew home with a good few quid in my pocket, some great memories, and absolutely no intention of working with the Ireland team again.

Leicester – 26 April

Except …

As a freelance, it's always good to have a specialist subject, a regular earner. A niche. From what I could see, Ireland played at least half a dozen games a summer, often on my side of the water, and they were a great set of blokes. Why not? The *News Letter* would be sending their man, Ian Callender, to cover the Benson & Hedges Cup match at Grace Road, but *The Irish Times* would take copy, as would the *Belfast Telegraph*, and both Radio Ulster and RTE wanted voice pieces. Double bubble, times two.

It was also a chance to catch up with Boylan, re-live a few of his Nairobi adventures, and see Warkie bat for the first time. He constructed a classically correct 53 from 140 balls, before Ireland lost by nine wickets. In the bar after, Lewie's eyes were twinkling.

'I've added Phil Simmons to my collection, DT!'

What collection? Having long ago given up hope of beating a county side, never mind one of the Test teams that would stop off for a tour match, Lewie had started to 'collect' international bowlers he had struck for four or six, and a much smaller list of those he had dismissed. So when he found the ropes with a glorious cover drive, the newly confirmed captain of Ireland was able to add the future national coach to his personal Haul of Fame.

Northampton – 21 June

For all the appearance of confidence, and the 'this is how we do it' approach, there was an awe of county professionals in the Ireland dressing room. Yes, Middlesex had occasionally employed the left-arm spin of Monty, while Mark Cohen was also on the staff at Lord's and O'Reilly had tried his luck with Warwickshire, but none had made a career of it. So there was little reference to this mythical world of the full-time cricketer.

During a rain break in the NatWest Trophy tie at Wantage Road, I ventured that the Ireland team – now bolstered by three-Test former India all-rounder Bobby Rao – had the beating of Northants, if they all played to their potential.

'But these guys are *professionals*,' Lewie said.

'That just means they get paid to play – it doesn't mean they're better than you.'

I pointed out Nigel Felton, who was opening for the home side: a batsman who barely averaged 30 during 13 seasons with Somerset and Northants.

'You're a better player than him, Lewie. Seriously.' His Hollywood smile was flashed in appreciation, but I could see he wasn't convinced.

The tie was carried over into its reserve day before the home side won by seven wickets. Double bubble, times two. Twice. Happy days.

Glasgow – 22 July

OK, so I was starting to get a taste for this. It was decent enough cricket, and well-paid work. More than that, it was good to be involved with a team again. I'd spent three seasons commentating on Middlesex in the late 1980s and became a quasi-member of the squad, much like the scorer or physio. It was both a privilege and a delight for someone who never rose above Oxfordshire Under-15 level to be accepted into such an elite group. It wasn't quite the same relationship with Ireland yet, of course, but there was an easy access to the players, a willingness to have a chat and trust was building.

My time with Middlesex had taught me when to contribute and when to stay quiet; to put forward an idea or opinion in the form of a question; to know when not to approach a player. There is a form of tact required. It's usually just common sense but not always.

I once found myself in a hospitality tent with Peter Such, the Essex off-spinner, who was a hopeless batsman in his early career. That day, though, he had smashed it all over the place, comfortably making his highest score and possibly doubling the runs he had made the previous season. Something like that. One of my colleagues rattled off whatever the stat was, thinking it would be well received. It wasn't. All it was doing was reminding the bloke how useless he had been.

I tried: 'Have you been working on your batting?' A smile. Yes, he had, and was more than happy to talk about it.

Lewie was always more than happy to talk about anything, but especially about Ireland being too amateur in their approach and the need to blood younger players. He spelt out a few of his ideas while Warke and Michael Rea were putting together an opening stand of 174 against Wales at Titwood – a game Ireland had to win to avoid the Triple Crown wooden spoon after losing to an England XI and Scotland on the two previous days.

'I don't want to be one of those committee men in a blazer in 20 years' time, watching us playing the same stuff at the same level,' Lewie said. 'We can do better than that, DT. We need to have more ambition. Why shouldn't we play in a World Cup? Look what someone like Cookie brings to the side. It's fresh, it lifts everyone. We need more of that.'

Lewie was right about Gordon Cooke, a greyhound lean teenage seamer from the north-west, who had bowled four maidens and taken a couple of wickets when Ireland gave the touring New Zealanders a scare at Comber earlier in the month. The Kiwis had scratched and scrambled their way to 233/6 and Ireland looked set for victory, needing 21 to win with six wickets in hand, when a panic set in and they finished six short.

While Cookie was playing his first mini-tournament, Warke was making his 100th appearance and fell five short of marking the occasion with what would have been his fifth international century – and last. He helped Ireland to 311/5 which proved 15 runs too good for Wales.

The textbook technique of the former skipper would have seen him open the batting for 15 years in the County Championship had he chosen that path. Lovely to watch from a classic viewpoint, but everything about the opener was old school, from his forward defensive to his safety-first construction of an innings, and Ireland were ready to strike out in a new direction.

1995

Stormont Hotel – January

Nairobi had shown the need for direction and drive at the top and, pressed by senior players, the ICU advertised for their first full-time national coach. After a bizarre job interview, in which one of the few questions asked was, 'What do you think of modern bowling boots?' a somewhat bemused Mike Hendrick was collared in a corridor of the Stormont Hotel by Lewie.

'We've got good players here but we need someone to show us how to compete. Can you do that?'

'I can try,' was the reply, and for the next four years the former England fast bowler threw himself into the task.

Unlike his successors, Hendrick settled north of the border, in a village on the outskirts of Belfast with three pubs. 'Don't drink in that one,' he was told by an ICU official, 'and I wouldn't recommend that one either.' Not impressed with the third, Hendo tried the second. Conversation among the other drinkers dropped when it became apparent there was an unaccounted for Englishman in their midst, three years before the Good Friday Agreement.

After a bit, a small delegation approached him. It wasn't exactly a welcoming committee. 'Who are you and what are you doing here?' Before he could frame a reply, there was a second voice. 'I know who he is – he's that cricket fella.'

The atmosphere eased, only for someone in the corner to pipe up: 'Cricket? That's a shite game, that is!' Hendo had found his local.

Dublin – 4 March

I'd become pally with Lewie in a long-distance sort of way and stayed with him in Rathgar on my trips to Dublin. His house was named 'Haynesville' after the great West Indian opener, who I knew from my time with Middlesex. The house sign was of a batsman playing an elaborate forward defensive. A black Warkie. We'd drink in town at Toners, and Doheny & Nesbitt on Lower Baggot Street, often in the company of Ger Siggins, sports editor of the *Sunday Tribune*. Ger knew both the game and the history of the game, and was a good man for pints.

I was at Haynesville for the weekend of the France rugby international. Great craic. The game kicked off early, so the drinking started even earlier. At a post-match feed near Lansdowne Road I was introduced to a Heat Detector, who turned out to be Heatley Tector, Lewie's best mate and future father of several very fine cricketers – Harry being the first to play for Ireland. I'd not encountered Heatley as a name before. Mind you, one of the ICU media officers at the time was Dexter Evans. Or was it Evans Dexter?

Kennington – 23 April

The unusual-names theme continued in the first game of Hendo's reign, an eight-wicket loss to Surrey in the Benson & Hedges Cup. Ireland were bowled out for 80, with Stratford Garfield Kenlock taking 5-15. Known as Mark, he didn't get his fellow Garfield, who batted at No.5 in a bowler-heavy Ireland team. The new coach had spoken to the Irish press for the first time before the game.

Boylan asked: 'Who will be opening?'

'Stephen Warke and Michael Rea.'

'And who will be taking strike?'

What had he let himself in for?

Ireland put up a better show at Hove two days later. Replying to a Sussex score of 261/8, Rea made 73. At one stage the visitors were 123/2 and in contention. Michael Rea did like a deflection backward of square, past gully or down to third man. Sussex quickly picked up on this, and at one stage had six fielders stationed between their wicketkeeper and cover point. Still he found the odd gap.

Owen Butler had bowled fast down the hill and taken three wickets for Ireland. Butler had enough genuine pace to worry good county batsmen, but also spindly ankles that were never going to allow more than the occasional burst of brilliance between injuries. Towards the end of an innings, team-mates would encourage him to bowl yorkers with cries of 'In the blockhole, Buttsie!' Not a gee-up you would want to get the wrong way around.

St John's Wood – 7 June

The annual MCC game, this year at Lord's, gave me a first sight of two promising youngsters: Ryan Eagleson, a 21-year-old from Carrickfergus, who bowled beautifully controlled away-swingers, and Peter Gillespie, from Strabane in the north-west, who was also seen as a medium-pacer in those days, before developing into Mr Reliable in the middle order. 'PG' claimed to be the same age as Eagy but looked decades older. He was the oldest youngster I'd ever seen. Still is.

The ritual of a two-day, four-innings match was followed – declarations, a fourth-innings run chase and on this occasion a draw. To the ICU blazers present, drinks in the MCC committee room was what the trip was really about. It was very social and on the final night I was invited to the team dinner in a local Italian restaurant. The chat was excellent.

'All it would take to get us to the World Cup is a million quid,' Uel Graham said. His theory being that for a modest salary the dozen or so players around the table could concentrate on cricket for the next two years and, without worrying about making a living, would improve sufficiently to guarantee success at the next qualifier in Malaysia.

It sounded revolutionary. I'm not sure whether Scotty was within earshot but the Hon. Sec. would have choked on his lasagne at such a blatant suggestion of professionalism.

At the end of the night we were presented with a bill that included all sorts of cheeky add-ons; cover charges, jugs of water, etc. Eyebrows were raised. Mutterings. A convivial evening was in danger of souring. It was a family-owned restaurant, we were just about the only diners and I asked to speak to the owner.

'There are 20 of us,' I said. 'What say we pay £25 a head cash: £500. None of this cover charge nonsense. You'll not have to worry about the VAT either.' I might have added: 'You weren't open tonight, eh?' with a conspiratorial wink. Alcohol had been consumed. My offer meant a discount of perhaps a fiver a head. Whether it was the lure of the cash, or the sight of 20 miffed blokes, the deal was agreed.

Then Lewie piped up: 'Will it be all right if I pay by card?'

Dublin – 14 July

On the eve of the tour game against West Indies, I found myself in a pizzeria with the new coach and his captain. Lewie was bubbling about the changes and innovations Hendo had brought to the squad, and what could be achieved in the coming seasons. 'You need to be realistic,' the old pro said, wearily. 'Ireland will never beat a county side.'

Was he downplaying expectations? Maybe. If Hendo believed what he was saying, it certainly wouldn't be for lack of effort on his part. He worked tirelessly setting up the programmes and pathways necessary to funnel talent towards the national team, and changed the policy of picking wizened old performers who could be relied on for consistency but not flair.

Youngsters like the Patterson brothers, Mark and Andy, plus Cookie and others were promoted and moulded into a winning unit. It was said that Hendrick laid the tracks that his successor Adi Birrell would drive the train along.

That winter, he literally went out of his way to get Decker playing again. A cult figure in the north-west, Curry had his ICC Trophy cut short by a family bereavement and had only been available for four B&H group matches since.

Hendo drove over to Foyle Meats in Derry to visit the big hitter at the abattoir where he worked. 'You'll find him in the third rendering shed.' A blood-splattered Decker, in elbow-length rubber gloves, approached the coach with a toothy grin. 'How'd you like this for a job then?'

The two men looked at each other for a minute. 'Do you want to play?'

A nod.

Although, in the partisan politics of Irish cricket, he was accused of not visiting the area enough, Hendo loved the north-west. 'It's a working-class game up there,' he said. 'Small grounds, big hitters, passionate crowds who know their cricket – it reminds me a lot of the West Indies.'

It was, and still is, very different to the blazer and chinos, middle-class scene in Leinster. Checked shirts and blue jeans is the dress code whether you live in Derry or Londonderry. It's a cultural as well as sartorial divide that makes for fiery clashes between clubs in the all-island Irish Cup. A trip to Donemana, the north-west village home of the McBrines, is viewed as a Deliverance-style adventure by posh southerners.

Bats instead of banjoes.

1996

Hove – 28 April

There was little to suggest this would be a breakthrough year for Irish cricket when the season-opening Benson & Hedges Cup campaign brought four more heavy defeats by Hampshire, Sussex, Gloucestershire and Surrey. The Sussex game was memorable for the home side bettering the Ireland total of 190/8 in exactly 20 overs – a more than credible T20 effort seven years before the birth of the short form. Opener Martin Speight hit a ridiculous 64 from 26 balls.

Although humbling, the defeat did give a glimpse of the spirit that the younger players were starting to bring to the side, particularly Mark Patterson. The Belfast bowler took some fearful tap in the opening overs and, muttering 'little spawny fecker', he ran through the crease and bounced

Speight from 18 yards. The illegal delivery disappeared over the ropes as well.

If the age of deference was over, the heavy defeats certainly weren't. Sussex turned up at Ormeau in mid-summer and won a 60-overs NatWest Trophy tie by 302 runs, bowling Ireland out for 80. In a game that required two days to complete, the county were 323/7 overnight; they could have declared.

South Wales – 2–4 July

Little over a week later, a first trophy was in the ICU cabinet. The Triple Crown started with a defeat but easy wins over the hosts and the England club players, in Pontarddulais, delivered the title on run-rate. Justin Benson led the team for the first time in the absence of the injured Lewie, and Andy Patterson, the younger Patto, proved the surprise attacking package when he was promoted to open in the last two games.

Champions maybe, but they still couldn't buy a win against Scotland. In a game reduced to 40 overs per side at Ynysygerwn, surely 245/6 was going to be enough? No, Iain Philip scored a century and the auld enemy won with a whole three overs to spare.

Press facilities are not always the best on the smaller grounds, and gnome-like Scottish reporter Keith Graham and I found ourselves evicted from our temporary spot in the clubhouse almost immediately after the game to accommodate a geriatric dance class. As we stood in the cold, waiting to use the one public telephone to dictate copy, music wafted out from inside.

Keith said: 'Shall we dance?' and we waltzed around the windy car park, to the amusement of the pensioners.

Brondby – July

A friend of the missus, at the time, had moved to Copenhagen. 'Anywhere near Brondby?' I wondered, sensing a night out, perhaps, during the inaugural European Championship. About half a mile away, as it happened, with a spare room and a husband with a car. Happy days.

Jurgen and Mila were great hosts. Jurgen was in his late forties, unemployed and desperately trying to find a new job despite receiving around three-quarters of his previous salary as a benefit. 'Our system is very generous, but it only works if everyone plays the game,' he said.

This grown-up Scandinavian approach to state assistance was explained again when the visiting press were given a tour of the Brondby sporting complex, which housed a professional football team, and provided facilities for hockey, cricket and a couple of other sports, plus basic accommodation for visiting teams. Small rooms with hard, single beds. Our guide was very proud of the set-up and how it was funded. 'You see this carpet? The old one was not very good so we ask the government for a new one and, of course, they paid for it.'

A pair of Scottish eyebrows shot up. 'I'll bet there's a lot of fiddling goes on, eh?'

The Ireland team were buzzing after their Triple Crown success, despite the modest nature of the digs. I found Hendo after training, attempting to stretch out on a bed that was about 30 inches wide and certainly not long enough for his 6ft 6in frame. He had stayed in worse. The spirit in the camp? Yeah, very good. There had been laughter aplenty the previous day when Paul 'Micky' McCrum had led a walk-out of the northern players. Mimicking a breakdown in the latest round of political manoeuvrings at Stormont, Micky and four others had stood up at the end of a team meeting and announced: 'We can no longer participate in these talks!'

Brondby – 15 July

The Netherlands considered themselves, with some justification, to be the top dogs in Europe and had insisted on decent opposition if they were going to be troubled to take part in this new tournament. The two groups were therefore lopsided, with the underwhelming Italy and Gibraltar in with the hosts and Ireland.

The Azzuri were led by their chairman, Simone Gambino, a bundle of energy and cricketing passion. Born in New York, he was sent to school in St John's Wood when things got a bit hot on the other side of the Atlantic – yes, those Gambinos – and had fallen for a game most Italians didn't know.

'I loved Geoff Boycott,' Simone said. 'I'm Italian, we love good defence.' His team did not show good defence, either in the field or at the crease. Ireland charged to 255/6, despite no one raising a bat, and Patto then castled the Italian top three in his opening spell. Gambino's men progressed at a Boycott-like sub-two an over to 86 all out.

Brondby – 16 July

Denmark, coached by the former Derbyshire fast bowler Ole Mortensen, were expected to provide a sterner test. After a superb breakfast of various cheeses, cold cuts, pickles and freshly baked bread, Jurgen decided he must find out what this game of cricket was all about. We arrived a few overs late, just in time to see Patto claim the first wicket. 'Ah, so the idea is to hit the three sticks?'

He didn't stay long.

The home side made 218/8, a total that would have given them confidence, but there was no stopping the Triple Crown holders and half-centuries from Angus Dunlop, fittingly in his 50th match, and Neil Doak delivered a three-wicket win with nine balls to spare. The third group match against Gibraltar was barely a contest and Ireland were in the final.

Copenhagen – 18 July

Jurgen took me to see the sights of Copenhagen on the day off, and both of them were a disappointment. I'd always imagined The Little Mermaid to be a focal point, in the harbour, obviously, but near the middle of the city somewhere. Bless her, she is stuck out in the sticks, with nothing around, no context, just plonked down there. Like a dismantled old manual scoreboard that's been 'preserved' by moving it miles away, in a setting that means nothing.

Tivoli Gardens are more central, but in the middle of summer they had all the allure of a rundown seaside promenade in November. An amusement park seemingly in terminal decline, but it's still going two-and-a-half decades later so maybe I caught it on a bad day. Or maybe it's supported by the local government. Someone has to pay for the end-of-evening fireworks.

Brondby – 19 July

The Dutch had also reached the final. Of course they had. And they would win it too, without much trouble, or so they thought. Ireland, though, were out to upset the favourites, in more ways than one. Assistant coach Bobby

Rao had a plan to throw in-form Pakistan-born opener Zulfiqar Ahmed off his game. It wasn't a very subtle plan. It involved the Ireland players learning a couple of phrases in Urdu to suggest that Zulfiqar's mother may not have had the highest sexual morals. Did it work? Well, Zulfiqar only made 14 in a total of 223/9.

Decker took 3-33 with his canny off spin and followed up with 55, but it was skipper Benson who secured the victory with a classy 79, his highest and comfortably best innings for Ireland, as they won by three wickets, with nearly four overs to spare. Benny lifted a second trophy in a month, alcohol was consumed and the balance of power in Europe had started to shift.

Linlithgow – 17 August

Lewie was back at the helm briefly for the annual first-class fixture against Scotland. The home side rattled up 380/5, with skipper George Salmond declaring soon after he was dismissed for 181; the visitors had four half-centurions in their reply of 323/6. The traditional final afternoon run chase was agreed with Ireland set 319 from 70 overs.

Lewie made 71 but Scotland looked like taking the spoils when Garfield joined Eagy with 110 still needed. The seventh-wicket pair began chipping away at the requirement. With 80 needed, it started to drizzle. The Scottish umpires played on. The target shrank to 60, and then 40. The precipitation got a little heavier, but still the umpires were unmoved. Eighteen required from the final five overs, both batsmen set. The umpires conferred and took the players off. Did I mention they were both Scottish? 'It was quite wet,' Lewie said, diplomatically.

Carlow – 23 August

Fortunately, it stayed dry the following week when the Irish cricket family gathered for the marriage of Lewie and Sharon, a few miles south-west of Dublin. I flew over on the morning with Michael Rea, who was also working in London. Garfield, Warkie and Alan Nelson had driven down from the north and there were local players there too, of course.

Team-mates formed a guard of honour with bats raised as Mr and Mrs Lewis left the church. At the reception, alcohol was consumed and Heatley gave a best-man speech about the groom scoring so many runs as a schoolboy that the only sensible option had been to join YMCA and never play against him again. He also recalled the morning after the happy couple had first met, when an excited Lewie phoned him and said, 'I think I've found her!' It must have been similar to his first meeting with Hendo.

1997

Kuala Lumpur – 22 March

My first visit to the Malaysian capital, for the World Cup qualifiers, as Boylan insisted on calling the tournament in his reports ('Nobody in Dublin is going to know what the ICC Trophy is'). It could not have started better: four seats to myself in the middle of the plane and I slept solidly for eight hours.

Arriving at the Crown Princess, where all 24 teams were billeted, I was told that my room would not be ready for another two hours, despite it being mid-afternoon. This turned out to be the best news of the trip, though, because the reward for my patience was an upgrade to an executive suite on one of the top floors, for the entire three-week stay, with an executive view and an executive breakfast. Boylan, Callender and my fellow scribes, including the Scottish tabloid bard Willie Dick, were lumped into standard rooms on the players' floors, with a very standard breakfast. Result.

The first Ireland player I bumped into, for the second ICC Trophy in succession, was Lewie, who had Mark Patterson in tow. Patto was the squad cheerleader and had developed a 'gremlin brush'. Every time the slightest gripe was raised about food, traffic or more likely the heat, Patto would brush the back of his hand across the complainant's shoulder, with a 'Let me get rid of that wee gremlin for you.' Or similar. Gremlins were an endangered species and there was a spirit and quiet confidence about the Triple Crown and European champions.

Lewie let me use his room for a shower and before long I was acquainting myself with one of the hotel bars, which had an oddly African theme. The team management could be found in here most evenings: Hendo and his assistant Bobby Rao, and various ICU committee men.

I'd enjoyed a beer or two with Hendo and interviewed him several times, of course, but the KL trip was the first time I got to know him a little. And tease him. One of the ICU officials wanted to hear more about the big games the coach had played for England, and the big characters. The 1979 World Cup Final was discussed. Straight-faced, I couldn't help myself. 'That lbw shout against Viv Richards looked close, Hendo?'

'Close? CLOSE!!!!' His voice raised an octave. Nearly two decades on and he was still incredulous that umpire Barry Meyer had not raised the finger.

Kuala Lumpur – 24 March

Getting around KL was tortuous as the Malaysian government were constructing a dual carriageway system that would be ready for the following year's Commonwealth Games, and working on it everywhere at the same time. Congestion ruled. Stuck in traffic, on our way to the opening match, Boylan stared up in awe at the recently completed Petronas Towers. 'Did you ever see anything as tall as that?'

Until the Taipei 101 building in Taiwan was completed several years later, no one had.

Strange as it may seem now, Ireland were worried Gibraltar might give them a game, and more so about the heat and humidity. Lewie answered any doubts about coping with the conditions by opening and batting through 50 overs for 127 not out, and there were half-centuries for Decker and Benny, at No.3. The islanders, who were nearly all based in Surrey, apparently, were bowled out for 86. Patto claimed four wickets but also bowled nine wides – an affliction that would haunt him throughout the tournament.

Israel were just as easily dispatched two days later, bowled out for 88. Patto managed nine wides in four overs – and a no-ball for good measure, or maybe bad measure. An unbeaten 51 from Decker saw Ireland home by ten wickets to set up a pivotal clash with the USA – the winners likely to finish group runners-up and qualify for the next stage along with Kenya. The chase was completed in 17.2 overs and Ireland might already have won by the time I told radio listeners, in a live report, that they were closing in on victory. A freelancer being paid 'per report' could get away with that sort of thing in those pre-internet days.

Kuala Lumpur – 27 March

The pre-match talk had centred on the threat of USA captain, Faoud Bacchus, who had played 19 Test matches for West Indies as a much younger man, so it was some relief when off-spinner Neil Doak bowled the 43-year-old for a fifth-ball duck. Ireland sent down 40 overs of spin, with Garfield, Greg Molins and Decker delivering their full quotas as well, and the US were bowled out for 212.

The chase began solidly, with 93/2 posted at halfway, but then stalled. Wickets fell with regularity and when Patto arrived at the crease, with a bandaged hand after dropping a catch earlier, the game was seemingly gone. Three wickets left, 54 needed off 37 balls. It was an unheard of ask in those distant days. Patto thought otherwise, lifting his fourth ball for six, and with Harrison cleverly nurdling at least a run off every ball at the other end, a glimmer of hope appeared. The 48th over yielded 15 runs, including a second Patterson six, leaving 11 to get off 12 balls. A daft call for a single to short cover saw the end of Garfield for 18 from 14 balls, leaving Molins to ease a full toss past square leg for the winning boundary from the first ball of the final over.

Caught up with the emotion – and quite possibly the prospect of an extra week's well-paid work – I ran onto the field with a dozen or more Irish fans and found myself mobbing the match-winner. The adrenaline was pumping furiously and the memory of that two-wicket win still brings back tingles. Patto, 27 not out from 18 balls, with two sixes, lost out on the man of the match award to Decker, 25 and three wickets from ten tidy overs. Judges, eh?

Kuala Lumpur – 29 March

Perhaps inevitably, the high was followed by the low of a hammering by Kenya at the Rubber Institute ground, some miles outside the capital. The top four all failed to reach double figures, chasing 247/7, including a duck for Angus Dunlop, who we had been expecting to go well on a rubber plantation. (Never tire of that one.)

Ireland would still qualify if they beat Singapore in their final group match, though, and what could have been a nerve tester turned into a formality, Decker and new opening partner Andy Patterson knocking off the 111 required in 10.2 overs. Decker hit six sixes, several of them landing in a drainage ditch at one end where the slumbering snakes would have congratulated their ancestors on having the good sense to leave Ireland.

This was Uel Graham's one match of the tournament. He should have been a key component in the campaign. Hendo saw what an excellent job Stuart Kennedy was doing for Scotland and desperately wanted his own wicket-to-wicket dobber to find the same nagging length and consistency on the artificial surfaces. I stood next to him as Uel bustled through one of his seven overs. 'For fecksake, just bowl the bloody thing!' Hendo muttered under his breath.

At that point, the coach had not settled on his best team or tactics. Patto was still troubled by wides – eight against the USA, five more against Kenya, nine against Singapore – and Eagleson was struggling with niggles, so Ireland had turned to the reliable medium pace of Gillespie to open the bowling. Lewie dropped down to No.3 against Singapore, allowing Decker to resume his successful partnership of the year before with the younger Patto, who also took the gloves from specialist Allan Rutherford. All-rounder Derek 'Deako' Heasley came into contention for the latter stages.

As he tinkered and fine-tuned, Hendo was lucky to have a number of ICU committee members on hand to impart their advice and wealth of experience. Facing up to the business end of the tournament, with second-stage group games to come against the Netherlands, Bangladesh and Hong Kong, he would often comment on his good fortune.

The ICU had no fewer than seven national selectors, at the time. In a post-tournament wrap for *The Sunday Times*, I suggested it might be an idea to add four more to the panel so they could pick a player each. Roy Torrens, one of the seven, took exception to this. He took greater exception to a mobile phone bill well north of £500 when he arrived home. He hadn't reckoned with the roaming charges when Radio Foyle contacted him for updates. 'Those calls cost three times what they were paying me, bejaysus!'

Kuala Lumpur – 1 April

In bidding to host the tournament, the Malaysian Cricket Board had written that in March and April a shower or two could be expected 'on the odd day'. It was indeed an odd day because on all the other days it had now started chucking it down each afternoon, and the relatively new Duckworth/Lewis method of calculating a winner would come into play.

In their first match of the second stage, Ireland restricted the Dutch to 211/8 and had reached 73/2 after 17 overs when the first rains fell. Hovering lakes, rather than mere clouds, were approaching and it was clear that a full game would not be completed. The teams pored over the D/L charts because, with Bangladesh clear favourites in the new four-team group, a slip of a finger on a calculator could mean the difference between joining them in the semi-finals and going home. Play resumed long enough for another six overs to be bowled, Lewie to get out, and a game to be declared (a minimum of 20 overs were required). The D/L calculation came down five runs in Ireland's favour. The Netherlands would have won under the old run-rate method and would have been ahead of the new calculation had a fourth wicket fallen.

The Orange men were a strong side, with Queenslander Peter Cantrell and county experience in Roland Lefebvre and Andre van Troost, and would probably also have won if the game had run its natural course. It was hard to feel too sorry for the Dutch, though. There was an arrogance about them and an assumption they would qualify, as they had done in Nairobi. So much of an assumption, that their board had already spent a chunk of the ICC funds that would come with qualification.

Knowing the dire financial ramifications of failure, team manager Hans Mulder, normally the most phlegmatic of characters, started to show the strain. He wanted the tournament rules changed. He wanted the rain to be taken out of the equation. He even accosted me over a line in *The Irish Times* where I described him as 'running around like a one-armed Dutch boy who had found six holes in a dyke'. Rather good, I thought. In different circumstances, he would have too, but after the Netherlands' second game against Hong Kong was abandoned as a 'no result' Hans wasn't in the best of moods.

Kuala Lumpur – 2 April

The next Ireland game was played at the Royal Selangor Club, which was still under construction, and the first time there was what could be described as 'a crowd' in attendance, with more than a thousand Bangladeshi migrant workers assembled and desperate to see their team win.

How could Ireland beat the favourites? The late-night think tank had a plan: bat first, get a good score on the board and then remind their opponents what awaited them at home should they miss out on a World Cup place. Retribution, flaming effigies, that sort of thing. 'Have you got a nice house? Will it burn easily?' As plans go, it wasn't particularly cunning, but it may have worked if only Ireland had accomplished the first part. All out for 129 is not a good score on any board.

In 6.1 overs of the chase Patto managed to send down six wides and Bangladesh were 23/0. Then the rain came; lots of it. There was no chance of a restart, or so we thought. While the pitch had been covered, the surrounds were marshy. The entire Bangladesh squad, including coach Gordon Greenidge, joined in the mopping-up exercise and so, initially, did several hundred fans. Ireland insisted the fans be removed. The sight of the great West Indian opening batsman on his hands and knees with a sponge was remarkable, though. A testament either to his dedication or, a cynic might suggest, the size of the bonus he had been promised for qualifying.

Under pressure, the umpires and Argentinian match referee decided the game would resume at 5.20, three minutes before it would have to be abandoned. PG, without spikes – they were not allowed on the artificial pitches – tentatively delivered the second ball of his fourth over. Doak moved sharply in from cover to field and theatrically aquaplaned. Two balls later an edge plopped into a puddle short of the skipper at slip who fell over to underline the absurdity, and the match was abandoned.

The Bangladesh fans were in uproar, first surrounding the umpires' quarters and then the press box, which was a Portakabin-like affair. We locked the doors only for the structure to start rocking as the furious supporters tried to turn it over. The police on duty called for back-up while, deadlines being deadlines, I banged out a few words. OK, it was scary.

Kuala Lumpur – 4 April

So, to qualify for the semi-finals, and have two cracks at a World Cup place, Ireland had to win their final group game, and did so by the comfortable margin of 51 runs. Angus Dunlop made 54 in a total of 223/7 before Hong Kong, who were already eliminated, were bowled out for 172. Patto sent down another nine wides, bringing up his half-century for the tournament. I'd begun referring to him as Wide of the Mark in copy. Sometime after the trip, it was discovered that bowling on the hard plastic surfaces had thrown his pelvis out of alignment by something like two inches. That he continued bowling at all was extraordinary. On the plus side, Micky McCrum was starting to find good rhythm, taking 3/30 from his ten overs.

Kuala Lumpur – 6 April

The Netherlands lost their final match to Bangladesh and were packing for home, just as their wives and girlfriends were arriving for the final week. We wished them well on their travels. Bangladesh topped the group and would play Scotland for a place in both the final and the World Cup, but not before Ireland had met Kenya in the first semi-final. It was a free hit. Beat the favourites and nirvana – or at least Grace Road and Bristol – awaited. Lose and have another chance three days later when the third and last spot would be up for grabs.

Ireland bowled and fielded with tenacity in the heat. Doak castled Steve Tikolo second ball, Micky took four wickets, but from 159/5, Kenya slipped the leash in the final five overs, adding 56 crucial runs to reach 215/8. Bobby Rao was a big fan of working the singles and pushing through the V, and had been preaching batting patience all trip. Keep your powder dry; there is always more time than you think. With targets never more than five an over, often less, this was sound advice.

Benny and Doak took it to extremes, the former taking 21 balls to get off the mark, the latter managing a single from his first 16. The ask rose to 83 from the last ten overs but Heasley, in for the injured Lewie, found his range, clearing the ropes four times and seemed to be taking Ireland to victory. The result – and so much else – hinged on one delivery from Martin Suji: Kenyan paceman to Lisburn fireman. Heasley jammed down on a yorker, hit it into his boot and the ball cannoned back into the stumps. So much for the luck of the Irish.

PG kept us guessing, even in the final over when two seemingly certain sixes landed feet short, as did Ireland by seven runs. Was it really that close? In runs, yes. In reality, no. It was one of those chases – like a furious dream – where the prize is always in sight but never quite in reach.

Kuala Lumpur – 9 April

The ICC had hired a large communal room in the Crown Princess for teams to use in the evening, to eat and drink, to mingle, and develop friendships; if not quite to sit in a circle and sing 'Kumbaya'. A cricketing equivalent of the United Nations, perhaps, a place where the Irish could drink, the Papua New Guineans strum guitars and the Argentinians stroke their moustaches. The reality was nothing of the sort, of course, although the Irish did drink.

By the final knockings, it was now quiet and mostly empty, but remained a good spot to relax after a busy day's scribing. The BBC World Service guys were still in town, and good company. A senior sports editor flew in to join them for the finals, and brought with her a batch of specially commissioned lapel badges to commemorate the BBC's role in covering the tournament. I've still got mine. Most were given away to Bangladeshi fans attending the final, possibly in the hope that they would cherish the souvenirs and wouldn't notice that the 1997 ICC Trophy had apparently been played in somewhere called 'Kuala Lumpar'.

On the eve of the third-place play-off, Willie Dick walked in and plonked himself down next to me. 'What do you reckon, Towny: "The Million Dollar Game from Hell?"'

It was the line he had gone with in one of the red tops, and if not the finest of his career, surely it was the finest any Scottish tabloid had ever used for a cricket preview? How accurate? Well, a small fortune in ICC funds would be coming the way of the victors, along with the TV exposure and publicity. A million Singapore dollars, maybe.

Scotland had gone about their first ICC Trophy unobtrusively, reaching the semi-finals with little fanfare where they were trounced by Bangladesh. Ireland were expected to win the showdown and, significantly given the weather, would qualify by dint of scoring more points in the second round if the game were not completed.

Kuala Lumpur – 10 April

Two days were set aside for the play-off. Darrell Hair was one of the umpires, Venkat the other. Ireland won the toss and again decided to field. The right decision? Probably. Much was made in hindsight of Ireland's poor record chasing in the big games, the win over the USA was a fluke, and the Netherlands victory courtesy of D/L. Orthodoxy, though, says bowl when there is weather around and there was weather around. Plenty of it. Scotland had reached 56/1 off 19 overs when the rains curtailed the first day. A couple of the younger Ireland players splashed around in the puddles after play was abandoned.

The second day brought sunshine, however; the Malaysians deployed a helicopter to help with drying the outfield, and despite boggy spots at long leg, play resumed soon after midday; same match but reduced to 45 overs per side. Micky, who had bowled beautifully on the first day, conceding 14 runs from seven overs, wasn't used again; Patto infuriatingly sent down 12 of the 22 wides Ireland bowled. Scotland scrambled to 187/8, and received a D/L bonus of four, leaving Ireland 192 to win.

Scotland opened the bowling with a spinner who Decker deposited over long-on for six but the big man then chased a wide one in the second over and was held a cover point, one of what was to be nine catches; plus a stumping. Hendo chain-smoked and circled the ground anti-clockwise. An old county tradition: right for runs, left for wickets. Bobby prowled the boundary with him, muttering 'Down the ground' and 'Through the V' to no avail.

Doak probably had the best head in the team, but after playing himself in, the Lisburn man lofted a sweep to deep square leg. 'Couldn't believe how well I hit that. Only meant to help it out there. No way should it have carried,' he said. Adrenaline. Angus lofted his first ball for six, but added only four more, Deako threatened briefly with 18 from 22 balls but there was to be no Patto/Harrison-inspired miracle this time. Garfield struck two fours and was last out for 16 in his final game for Ireland. Scotland had won by 50 runs.

Kuala Lumpur – 11 April

The wake was conducted by the hotel swimming pool, and continued late into the evening. Alcohol was consumed. It was convivial, but awkward at the same time, and for someone who was part of the group but not a member of the team it was difficult to know what to say.

The players all knew they had blown it. 'If only I'd …' was etched into brows. There was a party atmosphere of sorts – the campaign was over, they were going home. But the realisation of fourth place and missing out on the World Cup cast a gloom. It seemed like months since Patto was brushing gremlins off shoulders.

Inevitably, as the drink took effect, things began to get a little louder. A little raucous. Around ten there was a loud splash as Hendo was thrown fully clothed into the deep end – his glasses had to be retrieved from the pool the following day. Caught up in the jollity, I moved closer to the edge, laughing, only to feel the sensible hand of John Wright on my arm. 'Time for you and I to retire to our rooms, David.' It was my first exposure to Wee John's cool head. There were three more loud splashes as we made our way up the stairs.

The following morning, I found PG and told him: 'For what it's worth, you were my player of the tournament.' No one had been outstanding and the Strabane man was the pick of the bunch: consistent with the bat and happy to accept the responsibility of opening the bowling.

While the Irish packed to go home, I still had the final between Kenya and Bangladesh to report on for *Wisden*. It too spilled over into a second day and what should have been a thrilling finish turned into a farce. The scoreboard showed a D/L target of 166 from 25 overs. Kenya took this to mean that Bangladesh, having lost more wickets, would need to better it to win. Bangladesh correctly knew it meant they needed 166 for victory. At 165/8, with a ball to bowl, Kenya put all their close fielders back on the ring, Bangladesh pushed a single and both sides celebrated.

The final indignity for Ireland was an air-traffic controllers' dispute that led to flights being cancelled. Twice the squad left for the airport and twice they returned to the hotel. It was cruel. I made the same trip on the Sunday evening, leaving in plenty of time, in the expectation of doing the same. At check-in, I was told: 'We can get you on an earlier plane, if you like.'

Excellent, and those of us in the middle again had a row of four seats to ourselves. I stretched out and slept all the way to Heathrow.

Dublin – 27 April

No sooner had the defeated squad arrived home than it was announced Hansie Cronje would be joining them for the Benson & Hedges Cup campaign. A deal to secure the services of the South African captain was being supported by the Independent Newspaper Group and their exclusive, written by Boylan, was headlined 'Cronje to captain Ireland'. Knowing how these things work, I called Hendo. Great news about Hansie, but is he really going to be skippering the side? 'What? No. Justin Benson is the captain of Ireland.' He was, and he remained so.

Cronje was introduced to his team-mates at the Grand Hotel in Malahide, the day before the first game, and had a captivated audience. He told them he was targeting three wins from the four group games and would dye his dark hair blond if they got them. There was no doubting he meant it. Of the relationships he struck, the closest was with Micky, the two men sharing a passion both for physical training and Christianity.

'Everything about Hansie was top class,' McCrum said. 'How he carried himself on and off the field; his mindset, ideas and work ethic. He was light years ahead of us in his thought processes.'

Clontarf – 28 April

The opening match of the B&H campaign was against Middlesex at Castle Avenue. Ireland batted and a second-wicket partnership between Decker and Lewie built the perfect platform for Cronje at four. Decker powered to 75 and, according to Gus Fraser, was allowed to go about his business in relative silence. 'We'd been told he strangled sheep for a living, so there wasn't a lot of chat in his direction.' Cronje filled his boots with 94 not out in a total of 281/4.

The Middlesex reply stalled in gloomy conditions. Mark Ramprakash was lbw to Cronje, Mike Gatting lobbed a return catch to Benny, who hadn't bowled his dobbers at all in Malaysia, and when a combination of bad light and rain sent the game into a second day the professionals needed another 148 in less than 18 overs, with only four wickets in hand. Barring something unexpected, Ireland had won. Gatt was bemused. 'Does that left-armer know what he's bowling, because I'm buggered if I do. He's all over the place – you can't line up against him.' Greg Molins accepted the back-handed compliment: Ireland's first mystery spinner.

I spent the night at Haynesville and enjoyed a restrained celebration with Lewie and a couple of team-mates. None of us could quite believe they were going to beat a county side in a proper match. It would be the first time in 27 attempts. Lewie arranged to collect Hansie from his hotel the following morning, and take him for breakfast. His first choice of café was closed and we found ourselves in a well-known establishment that had finished serving but 'would rustle something up'. It was both the smallest and most disappointing breakfast I've eaten. Hansie looked at the pathetic offering of a tiny fried egg – presumably quail – chipolata and piglet rasher, plus half a slice of toast, with undisguised disappointment.

Further disappointment would follow for the South African after Ireland had wrapped up their 46-run win and the press decided to award man of the match to Decker. Boylan, outvoted, was in a huff; '94 runs and three wickets – it had to be Hansie!' Judges, eh? I bumped into Gatt.

'Would we be daft giving man of the match to Decker and not Cronje?'

'The opener? No, not at all – that start made Hansie's job easy.'

And so, barely two years after his pizza-house insistence that it couldn't be done, Hendo had overseen Ireland beating a county side.

Taunton – 2 May

The euphoria quickly ran into a dose of reality. Somerset rattling up 349/7 and Mushtaq Ahmed bamboozling his way to 7/24 in a whopping 221-run victory, while the following game in Cardiff wasn't much more of a contest as Glamorgan eased past a modest 202/9 with four wickets and nearly 20 overs to spare. Cronje top-scored with 85 at Sophia Gardens and then narrowly avoided an embarrassing moment at Cardiff airport when he found the pair of panties Micky had slipped into the pocket of his team blazer. They were relocated to Callender's bag.

Hansie left a lasting impression on Micky who, in 2005, named his son in his memory. I liked the South African too, finding him easy to approach and interview. It was only after the match-fixing revelations and his death in a plane crash at the age of 32 that other stories emerged. Wee John reckoned Hansie had arrived with £40,000 in cash to be deposited in an English building society. While there was no suspicion of him fixing, or attempting to fix, any of the three games he played for Ireland – the last against Essex was rained off – he wasn't in need of his match fees. Or a leather jacket.

The Cardiff loss coincided with Ken Doherty winning the World Snooker title, and the Dubliner's success was toasted during a late-night team curry. Bobby Rao and I tried to discover whether Lewie, maybe while playing for the MCC, had ever batted against the demon South Zone spinner Jal Freizi. Hot stuff that Jal Frezi. Alcohol had been consumed. Lewie was having none of it, but Bobby found it wonderfully amusing and has greeted me with a slap on the back and a 'How are you Jal Frezi?' ever since.

Headingley – 24 June

Hendo's charges were next in action in the NatWest Trophy, and another upset looked on the cards when Yorkshire collapsed to 55/6. Micky again found an irresistible rhythm, taking 3/26 from his 12 overs bowled straight through. But with no one to match his effort Craig White, Peter Hartley and Darren Gough revived Yorkshire to the tune of 249 all out. As the runs started to flow, I went for a walk at the Football Stand End. The skipper signalled to Lewie to warm up and a loud voice in the crowd boomed: 'Hey up! They're going to give the old fella a bowl!' Prematurely grey, but carrying it well, Lewie had just turned 33. His three overs cost 23 runs.

A win looked beyond Ireland before they batted, and even further away as the England pair Gough and Chris Silverwood crashed through the top order. The first five batsmen made half a dozen between them, and after Heasley and Eagy, the only two to reach double figures, had hauled the score to 53/7, Gough wrapped up the innings with a hat-trick.

During the afternoon, I'd chatted for the first time to a big bear of a young Irish cricket writer, Emmet Riordan. Born and raised in Dalkey, south of Dublin, his three great loves were cricket, music and drinking. What was not to like?

West Bromwich – 22 July

Watch enough cricket and you come to understand the game's rhythms and limitations. You know what to expect within certain parameters, be it a Test match or a village knock-about. Comfortingly so. Then there are those special moments. The Shane Warne 'Ball of the Century', the

Allan Donald/Mike Atherton confrontation, Freddie in 2005, that sort of thing. Sit-up-and-take-notice moments. The first game of the Triple Crown between Ireland and Scotland was unfolding in a familiar way – earnest seam bowling, workmanlike batting – when a teenager from Bray made his way to the crease, for the first time at senior level.

I was at long-on, half watching and half chatting with Alan Hill, the former Derbyshire opener, when the debutant brushed a ball off his thigh pad, dismissing it past square leg for four. Time stood still for a moment. 'Hello, what's going on here?' the old pro said. We sat up and watched intently for the next hour, or so, as Ed Joyce caressed his way to a top score of 60. It was another losing cause, but we knew something special had happened.

The following evening, after a defeat by the England ECB XI, I phoned Middlesex head coach Ian Gould. 'I think I've got an Irishman for you, Gunner.'

'Is he a bowler?'

'No.'

'We've got plenty of batters, thanks, DT.'

'Not sure you've got anyone as good as this lad.'

Fair play to Gunner, he sent Keith Tomlins to take a look the following day against Wales and, of course, it rained. Ed was offered a Second XI game later that season, anyway. Tomlins and Hendo knew each other from their playing days. 'Word gets around quick, doesn't it?' the coach said.

Derek Scott insisted that it was Hendo who had contacted Middlesex, looking for a finder's fee. This is what professionals did, apparently. It wasn't Hendo, though, and I didn't receive as much as a bottle of wine for the introduction.

Ed had to find his own way to the ground for the game against Northants, expenses would be reimbursed. A sister, who lived in London, dropped him at the Uxbridge CC ground, where Middlesex played Championship matches. He was early, but it still seemed rather quiet, and remained so. The fixture was to be played at Vine Lane, the RAF ground, about a mile away.

Ed walked it, with his kit, and arrived with 15 minutes to spare. A couple of quick introductions and he was in the middle. Where would he like to field? Anywhere on the leg side. He found himself in the gully and missed a couple of half chances in the opening overs.

Then it rained for two days. He did get to bat twice on the fourth day, and made a couple of 20s. Gunner decided there was something there, and the two parties would stay in touch.

From that first shot in international cricket, there was never any doubt that Ed Joyce would make the grade. I kept a scorecard from that game at West Bromwich; it's the only Ireland scorecard I've ever kept. His success in county cricket was an important step forward: not only could an Irishman be good enough, he could be very good indeed.

Lord's – 21 August

As Ed stepped onto the stage, Lewie took his curtain call. Was it 'Hey up! They're going to give the old fella a bowl!' that made up his mind? More likely that he would have been 36 come the next World Cup qualifiers and with a business to run, a family to start and a burgeoning career as a rugby referee, he could no longer devote the time necessary to the increasing demands of being an Ireland cricketer.

As an MCC member, he wanted to bow out at Lord's. He confided his plans and I ran an exclusive in *The Irish Times*, along the lines of, 'Alan Lewis will gather his team-mates around this morning and tell them that his 122nd cap for Ireland will also be his last.' Neither of us had reckoned on Hendo's pragmatism and hopeless lack of romance. As Ireland took the field, I looked for Lewie in vain. Fully aware of his intentions, the coach had made his former captain, and the man who had pushed for his appointment, carry the drinks as 12th man.

It meant that Lewie's final appearance was in the biennial fixture at Arundel the previous day. He almost went out in the grandest style, hitting the off spin of Greg Kennis for five sixes from the first five balls of an over, but could only manage a single from the last to take him to his 20th half-century for Ireland in 145 innings. He also made four centuries.

Benny did take his Ireland bow in the loss to the MCC. An explosive bat on his day, the skipper failed to record a century in 60 innings, although he did make nine fifties. Ed made half-centuries at Arundel and again the next day at Lord's. Out with the old, in with the new.

1998

Lord's – 5 May

At the grand old age of 39, Matt Dwyer finally got the call. By all accounts, he had been the best left-arm spinner on the island for a decade, but he wasn't a posh lad, and he didn't suffer fools gladly. A roofer by trade, Matt played for The Hills, in Skerries, not one of the fashionable clubs with a Dublin postcode. Strong, with builder's hands, he propelled the ball towards the batsman's pads when he chose to follow Hendo's instruction to 'Fire it in!' That's all the coach wanted: ten overs of monotonous negativity. Matt, though, has mischief in his soul, and could rarely resist flighting the odd little tempter. If it was hit for four, Hendo would scowl. Occasionally it would produce a wicket. Hendo would still scowl. 'Fire it in, Matt!'

The old fella made a losing debut in the B&H Cup, taking 2/40 against Glamorgan, suffered a bit of tap four days later in another defeat by Essex, but then enjoyed a fine first appearance at Lord's. After so many years toiling away in Leinster League cricket, it must have seemed like a dream to be bowling to a side containing Justin Langer and Mark Ramprakash, with Dickie Bird umpiring. His figures of 1/23 were exceptional but Middlesex still won by six wickets.

Would Matt have made a difference in Kuala Lumpur? Possibly not, but he should have been there. His ten overs at Headquarters didn't win man of the match, either; another injustice. That went instead to Angus Dunlop for his 59 not out. It's a batsman's game, as Gus Fraser, another opponent that day, is always quick to point out.

Waringstown – 5 June

After winning the ICC Trophy, Bangladesh were pushing to become the tenth Test-playing nation and paid their own expenses for a week-long tour of Ireland, with coach Gordon Greenidge in charge. It didn't go quite as they had hoped. The visitors lost a thrilling opening game at Waringstown, where PG was run out for 94 as Ireland chased down 229 with four wickets and three balls to spare, and the remaining matches were washed out.

The rain thwarted Hendo's attempts to play at least one of the games on a decent surface. He was always griping about the poor quality of pitches in Ireland; slow, low dogs where average players could lunge forward, in no danger of the ball flying past their nose. There was no incentive for bowlers to bend their backs, with medium-pacers picking up plenty, simply by hitting a length. If the international team were to improve they needed truer surfaces where back-foot techniques could be developed, and sharp, shorter deliveries rewarded. It was only a matter of better preparation, according to the coach. Cut, water and roll. Repeat. So he took a suspicious club groundsman under his wing, accepting responsibility if his methods went wrong, and between them they produced a rock-hard belter.

Greenidge took one look at the surface, rapped his knuckles on it and smiled. 'Reckon you and I could have a game on here, Hendo.'

'I reckon we could – I'll bat, you bowl!' And then it rained.

Birmingham – 24 June

Two of the great left-handers of modern times experienced different fortunes as Warwickshire won a keenly contested NatWest Trophy tie by 41 runs at Edgbaston. Brian Lara was out for a six-ball duck, bowled by McCallan, continuing his poor record against Irish spinners, having previously succumbed cheaply to Conor Hoey and Neil Doak, while Ed confirmed his promise of the previous season with a lovely 73. Nick Knight had carried his bat for 143 not out to take the home side to 302/5 from their 60 overs, but Ireland were not cowed and would have got closer but for having to face 11 overs in near darkness at the end of a rain-affected first day.

Opening the batting and oozing class, Ed stroked five fours in his 119-ball innings and the county side were just a little concerned with 139 needed from the final 20 before Ashley Giles took a decisive turn with 4/29.

The press room was abuzz; where had Ireland found this little gem. The answer was Bray, south of Dublin. There was more delight to discover he was the son of James Joyce. Although known as Jimmy. Mr Joyce senior thought cricket might be a good game for his kids to play in the back garden and ended up with five internationals: Ed and younger brother Dom, twins Isobel and Cecelia, and the pub-quiz fifth, elder brother Gus, who made three unremarkable appearances in 2000.

In the bar after play, Hendo was having a drink with a couple of players, including Eagy, when he was approached by a local fan who had clearly not gone thirsty.

'I know you, don't I?'

'Do you?'

'You used to play for England! Fast bowler. You're … you're big Dave Hendrick!'

'Yeah, that's right,' said Big Dave and signed his book.

Glasgow – 30 June

A week later the old Saab pulled up outside Willie Dick's house in the early evening, after the long drive from London. My Scottish friend was due down to Lord's later that summer and with me wanting to cover the Triple Crown in and around his home town we had decided to save a few quid by hosting each other. It was mid-summer and we sat in the garden until it turned 11, with more natural light than there had been at Edgbaston on the first evening a week ago.

The opening match was the inevitable loss to Scotland, though the margin was only nine runs. Matt fired it in to great effect, taking 3/29 while Kyle gave up a parsimonious 17 runs from his ten overs. A victory target of 161 didn't seem too many, even on a poor pitch. At 19/3, with Ed gone for a duck, it seemed harder, but at 127/4 the long wait for a win was surely over. No. PG fell for 55 and the wickets kept on tumbling until Matt was last out in the final over.

Ah well, deep breath, there was always next time.

I was still smarting from the loss the following evening when, after an equally close game, this time a narrow victory over the England XI, I got back to Willie's halfway through the first half of the England v Argentina clash in the World Cup.

'Let's watch the second half down the pub,' he suggested.

It wasn't his best idea. I was the only bloke in the bar not barracking very loudly for an Argentinian win, and even Willie was a bit taken aback by the strength and depth of the vehemence towards the England team (although he wasn't cheering for them either).

Judging the mood, I didn't open my mouth once as the game went into extra time and then penalties. As inevitably as Scotland beat Ireland at cricket, England lost the penalty shoot-out and the whole rotten place erupted in delight.

On the walk home, we stopped at a filling station. Willie wanted an evening paper to see if they had used his cricket copy. The middle-aged woman behind the counter was bubbling.

'Did you see the game? Greeet, wasn't it?'

I'd had enough. 'So you were cheering for the same lot who were shooting your soldiers a few years back, were you?'

Her face contorted. 'Aye, well you would say that, wouldn't you?'

Yes, I would, and it would be relevant.

The funny thing is, a couple of weeks earlier, I'd been in a London bar packed with English fans, watching Scotland take the lead against Brazil. No, they did, look it up. Every single one of us was supporting the underdogs and we were gutted when the world champions sneaked a win with a couple of late goals.

It was just a natural reaction, or so I thought. What sort of reaction it was that night in Glasgow, I have no idea. But I've not remotely considered cheering for Scotland in any sport since.

There was a combination of results on the final day of the Triple Crown that would have seen Ireland take the title on a combination of run-rate and wickets lost, but the parameters were very narrow. Ireland duly consigned Wales to the wooden spoon but with three teams tied on two wins apiece, the calculation went in favour of the England XI. Scotland finished third. Ha!

Downpatrick – 10 July

Micky McCrum gave Ireland a dream start in the first of two 50-over games against South Africa, having his hero Hansie caught behind in the first over and bowling Daryll Cullinan with a beauty four balls later. The match, which was abandoned, was Micky's last for Ireland. He had been unstinting in his efforts over ten years; a great servant who had many memories to savour in retirement, not least claiming Robin Smith first ball in a B&H game, and sharing a last-wicket stand of 100 with John Davy, against Scotland, that was still an Ireland record two decades later. His finest hour, though, was surely in the ICC Trophy semi-final, when he took 4/51. If a stone-cold lbw had been given against Maurice Odumbe, early in the Kenya captain's innings, then he would have gone down as the man who bowled Ireland to their first World Cup finals.

Maybe that injustice gave him a special connection with Hendo because, like the Viv Richards appeal, the ball could only have been missing if it had gone under the stumps. Hendo would also have recognised a fellow son of the toil. A wholehearted seamer who left nothing out on the pitch, except sweat. Probing, consistent and able to drop into a rhythm of line and length that could be irresistible in the right conditions.

Big Dave drove to Armagh early the following year, to buy Micky a coffee and thank him for his efforts. 'Him thank me? It should have been the other way round. I adored the man, as a friend as well as a coach.'

Hendo also asked if he might still be available 'in an emergency'? The answer was 'Yes' and McCrum would have featured against the South African Academy that summer, but wasn't able to get off work. It's sometimes forgotten that in those amateur days players relied on the generosity of employers, and others missed games because of studies.

Even those who could twist the boss's arm may have been less than wholly focused, worrying that representing Ireland may be damaging their chances of promotion. Or that they would be the first out of the door when cuts were required. There were 26 days of international cricket in 1998, not counting those rained off. Plus travelling, of course. More than the average annual holiday entitlement. Players not only needed a supportive missus, but an understanding boss as well.

The second game did produce a result, at Castle Avenue, where South Africa won by 63 runs. Cronje scored 74 against his old team-mates and Cullinan stroked a century. In reply Dunlop was 101 not out as Ireland finished on 226-9.

The Hague – 18–24 July

A first trip to the Netherlands for the second European Championships was one I'd eagerly anticipated, but it was a bit of a letdown, on and off the field. The Ireland squad were not as focused as they had been in Denmark, despite beginning with a two-run victory over the England XI, who treated the tournament like a stag jaunt, losing all their games, including the final one to Division Two winners Italy.

The Boys in Green were hammered by the Dutch, lost by three wickets to Denmark and, of course, lost to Scotland. The match to decide third and fourth was a re-match against the Scots and, despite scoring 242/4, Ireland lost again by four wickets. Not required to file copy, I couldn't bring myself to watch and instead took in the final at the wonderful, if tiny, HVV Den Haag, with its colourful awnings and pile of pushbikes discarded at the gate. The Netherlands beat Denmark comfortably to succeed Ireland as champions.

Stephen Smyth, the Brigade left-hander, had a good tournament, making a half-century against England and falling lbw for 93 in the final game; Matt did what he did, taking wickets in each of the four games he played and Cookie had success with bat and ball.

There wasn't the same cohesion and purpose about the squad that there had been in Copenhagen, though. It wasn't gelling, and Hendrick knew it as he paced the boundary. Right for runs, left for wickets. Maybe his message was no longer getting through.

I liked The Hague. A very relaxed town; great architecture and easy enough to walk around, although I kept getting shouted at for strolling in the cycle lanes. The cannabis cafés were intriguing, but not for me. Fair enough when someone gets the skins out after a night down the pub, but the idea of entering a café with the sole intention of getting stoned seemed a bit too cold and calculating. As did the infamous ladies in windows.

The visiting press were not good boys in every regard, though. One of us abused the free phone our hosts had provided to compile round-ups of Scottish club results, and I sulkily lobbied for an invite to the end of tournament dinner, knowing perfectly well I couldn't attend.

'Why no table for the media? The Danes had a table for the media.'

After a couple of days of hectoring, the organisers did a U-turn and squeezed us in. 'That's very kind, but I'll be on my way back to London by the time it starts. Sorry.' The bloke's face …

Waringstown – 26 August

A packed summer ended with a three-day match against Australia 'A', followed by five one-dayers, the first of which was abandoned. Ireland lost all the completed games despite the presence of Steve Waugh, guesting in the middle order.

The closest of the contests was a 35 overs per side affair on The Lawn, where the Aussie made a half century, along with McCallan, in a competitive 192/7. Kyle followed up with 2/22 from his seven overs but Matt had a shocker and the Aussies got home with 16 balls and three wickets to spare.

It was hard to see what either side were looking for from the tour, although the Ireland players were able to watch how one of the greats went about his preparations and game. Their opponents were far too strong. Matty Hayden, Mike Hussey, Michael di Venuto, Damien Martyn, Andy Bichel and Jason Gillespie – what good would spanking a few Irish club players do them? It wasn't even an Ashes year, so it couldn't be explained as looking to gain playing time in the British Isles, geographically speaking.

Hendo's mood would not have been improved by a string of defeats. The coach's relationship with the ICU was becoming more fractious, and instead of finding a way through the various irritations of committees and outdated traditions, perhaps by going through Wee John, he seemed ever more ready to meet his opponents head-on. The biggest of whom was Scotty, of course. The old boy had never accepted that Hendo was anything more than an employee of the ICU, there to do its bidding. The coach certainly wasn't in charge and that was made clear more than once. The devil in me used to enjoy writing 'Mike Hendrick's men …' in *Irish Times* reports, knowing the old fella would bite. 'It's the ICU's team!' he would correct me, gruffly.

The clash of cultures had met head-on at Arundel the previous year when Hendo had tried to change the Earl of Arundel's fixture to a limited-overs game. Scotty was having none of it. It would be a 'timed match'; always had been, always would be. 'What fecking use is that to anyone?' Big Dave fumed. 'Timed cricket? No one's played that since the Middle Ages!'

'Then why not just pretend it's a timed game, but play it like limited overs? Restrict bowlers to ten overs and declare after 50?' I suggested.

Hendo smiled. 'Good idea, I'll speak to Trout.' Off he went to arrange the details with John Barclay, who was coaching the home side. It didn't take Scotty long to work out what was going on and he wasn't amused. I was.

When a coach takes on his bosses, whether it be in cricket, football or any other sport, there is usually only one winner, and so it would prove. I wonder, though, if Hendo knew by the end of that summer that he had taken Ireland as far as he could? Were his frustrations as much due to that, as to Scotty and the ICU clinging grimly to the past?

1999

Jesmond – 4 May

Freelancers do some crazy things to save a few quid. It was 275 miles from Primrose Hill to Jesmond, where Ireland played Northumberland in the NatWest Trophy, and I decided to drive there and back in the day. Left the house at silly o'clock and regretted my foolishness before the old Saab had passed Watford Gap. Not quite as daft as the time I took a bus from Brisbane to Melbourne – that was 34-and-a-half hours – but close. This time I was driving.

The game was a routine five-wicket win for Ireland, noteworthy for Dwayne McGerrigle taking five wickets on debut and Ed making an effortless 37 not out. After his innings against Warwickshire the previous season, word had got around that Ireland had a classy left-handed opener and a couple of counties sent scouts to check on his progress. The problem was, Ed batted at No.6. An opener did top-score, but it was Neil Carson, a somewhat more lumpen leftie from Banbridge, who made 58. Word has it that both scouts had left, shaking their heads, before Ed emerged to speed his side home with 13 balls to spare.

My head hit the pillow sometime around 2.30 – am.

Lurgan – 20–22 July

Other than that outing, it wasn't a great year for freelance earnings. No overseas trips, either, in a miserable fixture list of only 14 games, 12 of them at home. Ireland were not included in the B&H Cup and after the Northumberland victory, I didn't bother travelling for the two NatWest rounds that followed in Comber and Clontarf: a two-wicket victory over the Essex Board side and a 136-run drubbing by Leicestershire.

Ireland then hosted the Triple Crown and lost all three matches. Again I stayed home but even from a distance, and from the odd chat with Lewie, it was obvious that all was not well. Had the players stopped listening to Hendo altogether? Was the ICU faction that had never really taken to him starting to gain the upper hand?

Six of the 14 matches were against a touring South African Academy XI, with Jonty Rhodes doing a Waugh and batting No.4 for Ireland. Daft as it may seem now, the games were capped and two were deemed 'first-class'. Rhodes scored 86 and 82 in a three-dayer at Lurgan, but the bigger story was a vicious assault in the Stormont Hotel one evening when Stephen Smyth and Cookie got into a row over a woman. Alcohol had been consumed. An affray between the team-mates led to Cooke being beaten up as he lay in bed and police being called. It was bloody and ugly.

Smyth, who had captained the side the previous year, was immediately banished. The atmosphere at breakfast the following morning was 'like there had been a death' according to one player.

What made the incident more shocking was that the two played for the same club side, Brigade, and less than a month later, they were in the team that beat Merrion in the semi-final of the Irish Cup. Greg Molins recalls standing next to Cookie at Anglesea Road during the game when his assailant stroked a cover drive to the boundary. 'Shot, Smythy!'

'You're very forgiving?'

'Ah, you have to let things go.'

Funny lot in the north-west. Decades later I made some random observation to John Mooney about it being a unique place and how did any of them live past 35 on that Derry diet? Burgers that require scaffolding and 'What potatoes would you like with your chips and mash?' He responded with a serious point that I'm still not sure about: that the obsessive behaviour is a legacy of the Troubles. 'Most of them up there are suffering from some form of PTSD, whether they realise it or not.'

I don't know whether Johnboy meant the Six Counties as a whole, or just the north-west, but it's a theory that would explain some of the eccentricities and extremes. What I do know is that the international careers of two fine left-handers, Smyth, and a couple of years later, Decker, were both cut short by violent confrontations.

Dublin – 10 August

The Stormont Hotel incident didn't help Hendo's relationship with his employers, and neither would his decision to bat on against the MCC at Lord's a couple of weeks later, instead of declaring at the end of the first day, as was the custom. Ireland gambled on spinning their way to an innings victory, but Greg Molins, winning the last of his 25 caps, failed to deliver. The match ended in a tame draw, to lots of committee-room grumbling.

Days later the coach was sacked. By mutual consent. While he had spoken earlier in the year about wanting to lead Ireland into the next World Cup qualifiers in 2001, it was probably the best for both sides. Hendo had done his bit: coaching structures were greatly improved, pathways to funnel talent to the top were in place, youth cricket was thriving and the organisation now functioned with a clear purpose. Mostly. There were still the odd pockets of resistance, usually to be found in a trench coat and trilby, but Big Dave had changed the ICU from an amateur set-up which informed players of their selection by letter, and reminded them to 'bring whitener for their boots', to the beginnings of a slick, professional outfit.

On the same day, Smyth was banned from representative cricket for five years, effectively ending the 30-year-old's international career. He was also banned from domestic club cricket for a season, but that sanction proved unenforceable without recourse to the law courts, which involved a financial risk that the ICU were not willing to take.

Smyth had been Ireland's best batsman in 1998, but discipline was always a problem for him. Originally in the squad for the ICC Trophy in Kenya, he was dropped at the last minute for playing rugby when the ICU had proscribed participation in contact sports leading up to the tournament.

Belfast – 21–23 August

Almost inevitably, after failing to beat Scotland in 11 attempts during Hendrick's tenure, Ireland won the annual first-class match barely a week after his departure. Dunlop struck 112 in a low-scoring contest at Ormeau while no other batsman made 50 and the home side nearly made a pig's ear of chasing 42 to win, losing six wickets in the process. The three-day game marked the arrival of Adrian 'Scooby' McCoubrey, who was slippery enough during his six-year international career to earn a contract with Essex for a couple of seasons.

THE MESSIAH AND A VERY NAUGHTY BOY

2000–2004

2000

Sydney – 9 January

The ICU announced Ken Rutherford would succeed Hendo towards the end of 1999, and the former New Zealand batsman gave his first in-depth interview to a dwarf from Coogee Bay. It was revealing in several ways that should have set alarm bells ringing. Rutherford would combine the Ireland role with the final two years of a playing contract with Gauteng, the South African provincial side. He didn't know whether he had what it took to be a coach. This would be the chance to find out, but he wasn't a great one for standing in the nets and telling a guy how to bat. 'If the position was simply coaching I wouldn't have been interested. I wanted a broader role behind the scenes, helping Irish cricket with good structure.' Which Hendo had already set in place, of course. Rutherford also thought it was a bonus to have no first-hand knowledge of the Ireland players.

The interviewer was Tony Munro, an Aussie fella who researched and wrote about the ICC Associate nations until his untimely death in 2016. Tony emailed me several times, looking for info on Ireland, and we became Facebook friends. A couple of drinks were proposed the next time I was staying in Randwick. It wasn't until he posted a full-length photo of himself, which obviously wasn't very long, that I realised he was a dwarf. We finally met up one afternoon in Coogee. Alcohol was consumed. I learned a lot about his work and more about his condition. 'Never call a dwarf a midget, that's a different thing altogether.'

The afternoon was a great success until we went to cross a busy road and, instinctively, I put my hand down to hold his, before snatching it back. Tony roared with laughter. 'You wouldn't believe how many people do that, mate!' He was well into his forties, at the time.

Harare – 6–13 April

If Rutherford genuinely had no idea about the Ireland players, he would have learned more about the batting than bowling during a six-team Emerging Nations tournament in Zimbabwe. Ed scored half-centuries in wins over Scotland and Zimbabwe, although the Full Member hosts played the political game of fielding an 'A' team against Associate opposition, in case they should lose. Which they did three times. Peter Davy also hit two fifties – three if you count one in a warm-up match against the Zimbabwe Academy in which Boylan umpired. Molins, Dunlop and PG showed form with the bat as well; Decker wasn't on the trip.

Matt was the pick of the bowlers, taking three wickets in a defeat by Denmark, and another three against Zimbabwe. McCallan's best figures of 2/32 came in the same game after an experiment to open the bowling with his off spin was ditched. The seam attack would have looked weak to

Rutherford. Scooby, Patto and Eagy were not available, and Cookie was out of sorts for most of the tournament. The new coach was drawn to the pace of Owen Butler, giving him seven games during the season, although he wasn't in the ICC Trophy squad a year later.

The Emerging Nations was nearly cancelled over security concerns raised by the European governments whose teams were involved. President Robert Mugabe was not flavour of the month and his torturing regime only got worse over the next few years. Zimbabwe were due to host six matches at the 2003 World Cup, but England refused to travel, and New Zealand also forfeited points rather than face Kenya in Nairobi. It's a myth that it was those two abandonments alone that enabled Kenya to sneak into the semi-finals. No doubt they helped, but the East Africans were a strong unit at the turn of the century. Steve Tikolo was at the height of his powers and scored an unbeaten century as Ireland were thrashed by nine wickets. Kenya won the tournament with victories in all four completed games. The Netherlands came second, after their match against third-placed Ireland was rained off.

Clontarf – 7 June

My first chat with Rutherford was during the Zimbabwe innings at Castle Avenue. I was sitting alone, he introduced himself and asked my opinion on a couple of players. I told him I liked the look of the whippy medium-pacer who had just sent down five overs. Who was it? Could he bat too? The coach smiled. Yes, Mark Waugh, who was contracted for the two games, could bat a bit. Seriously, though, of the players who weren't there, who would be top of my list to take to Toronto next year? Well, Ed and Decker, obviously.

If I had to pick just one other who wasn't there it would be Neil Doak, who had started playing again but was still focusing on rugby, which was further down the road of professionalism.

Rutherford thanked me and went back to reading his *Racing Post*, which he did a lot. There is a technique for watching cricket and reading a newspaper that involves getting into a rhythm of looking up just before the bowler delivers, and then back to the page. I learned it as a Middlesex fan in the 1980s and while it was hard to read while a spinner was on, you could complete *The Telegraph* crossword between Norman Cowans's deliveries. Rutherford didn't seem to have acquired the skill. Indeed, he often didn't seem to look up for overs at a time.

Talking of techniques, I'm pretty sure it was this trip that I first witnessed Callender in action at an eat-all-you-can restaurant. There have been a few occasions over the years, but Jimmy Chung's is a favourite. Scoop at a Chinese buffet is a sight to behold. You wonder if his nickname isn't to do with the speed he shovels in food, only breaking off to demand 'More rice, more tea'. A phenomenal scoffer for a small man.

Ian wasn't appreciated by the players back then; still isn't. Yes, his copy is often harsh and you can't hammer someone one day and expect an interview the next. He can lack empathy and doesn't seem to grasp that the game is played by people, not just by batsmen and bowlers. But Scoop is Mr Ireland Cricket, when it comes to reporting. More so than Ger, and far more than myself. He got hooked as a kid, scoring Ashes series in Australia under the blankets at night, and despite having met his wife on an England tour in the 1980s, he still loves the game.

Contact him on a day off and he may well be watching an obscure Test series, or some T20 nonsense. A real enthusiast, with an enormous appetite. The game in Ireland owes him a lot.

Ireland lost both matches to Zimbabwe, by 49 runs and five wickets, having already been beaten at the same ground by Shropshire in the NatWest Trophy, and defeated by the MCC on a damp couple of days in the north-west. It wasn't the start Rutherford would have wished.

Colwyn Bay – 4–6 July

The wettest few days of this entire journey were spent in north Wales, where all six matches in the Triple Crown were abandoned. The title went to Scotland who won their three 'bowl-outs', including beating Ireland, of course. Appropriately, the reigning champions became the raining champions. To pass the time, and give my newspaper something to fill a space, I interviewed the skipper. We previewed the European Championships in the Netherlands, and looked further forward to next year's ICC Trophy. Kyle knew that if Toronto went well he was in pole position to captain Ireland in their first World Cup campaign, and liked the idea. He was still feeling his way in the job, but he could read the game and as a teacher in real life he had some of the leadership skills required. The Belfast man was also developing into a very fine off-spinner, who gave himself, and the captains who succeeded him, control and consistency in the middle overs of one-day games. It would not be exaggerating to say that at this time, and until Graeme Swann began to emerge towards the end of his career, he was the best off-spinner in the British Isles, geographically speaking.

Glasgow – 21–27 July

The third European Championships did not get off to the smoothest of starts. The tournament hotel put up a large display of flags in the lobby, using a tricolour to represent Ireland. 'That's not my flag!' Cookie said, and asked for it to be taken down. He considered himself British and his flag was red, white and blue.

The traditional divisions in Ireland were rarely, if ever, an issue within the team, but sectarianism was everywhere that week in Glasgow. The new millennium was still mired in the 17th century, it seemed. Boylan decided he would visit Parkhead for a pre-season Celtic game. A more obvious southern Irishman you will never have met and he was welcomed by fans of the green hoops. What was he doing there? Cricket? Do they play cricket in Ireland? And so on. By half-time he had made friends for life, and then he mentioned he was planning to visit Ibrox the following evening, so he could experience that stadium too. The rest of the match passed in silence, without so much as a goodbye at the end.

If that passive aggression was bad, it was nothing compared to Ibrox. The two hours spent there were the most unpleasant I have endured at any sporting event. By a very long way. It was a non-stop cacophony of hatred and vile abuse, aimed mostly, but not exclusively, at the Pope and the IRA. Bit daft for Rangers to organise a pre-season friendly against an Irish side, you may be thinking. It was actually a Champions League qualifier and the opposition were from Lithuania. I was with a group of Dutch players and they couldn't believe the vitriol they were hearing, either. When I got back to the hotel, I took a long shower.

Nor were we entirely safe from tribalism at the cricket. Or at least reminders of it. After Ireland had lost to the

England XI, their second defeat in two days, Matt and I stayed behind for a couple of pints at Titwood. The old left-armer had not gone well against the Netherlands in the opening game but a couple of maidens and 1/27 was much better, and he was in good form and thirsty with a rest day to follow. It was one of those impromptu sessions of anecdotes and laughter, made all the more fun by a middle-aged, flirty barmaid. Near closing time there was just the three of us left and we were fairly roaring at each other's company. Then her husband and a mate walked in, wearing replica Rangers shirts and tattoos. 'Ah feck,' said Matt, and we were away.

Andrew White, making his debut in the month he turned 20, scored the first of six international centuries in his third match against Denmark. He was whippet-lean at the crease, upright and pale, even by Belfast standards. Whitey followed up with two wickets in a 73-run win. He didn't get much of a bat or bowl the next day, as Italy were dismissed for 74 and beaten by six wickets in Ayr. Kyle took five and Matt squeezed out 3/10 from his full quota. That just left the inevitable loss to Scotland in the final match at Linlithgow, although in a novel variation, the home side managed to score seven fewer runs and still take the points, on a D/L calculation. It was Ireland's 11th loss in 12 one-day games against the auld enemy and they would suffer three more defeats in the next four years before the sequence ended. The Netherlands retained their title, ahead of England, with Scotland third.

Ayr – 19–21 August

The season ended with the annual first-class match against Scotland, which was dominated by the batting of Angus

Dunlop, even though the home side came through on the rails to win by six wickets. The YMCA man was wonderful to watch when he stood tall and hit through the line, and hard to bowl at once he got into his stride. There was a touch of arrogance about him when he had the measure of an opponent. Not short of confidence off the field either, he once tried to avoid a speeding fine by telling a Dublin judge he had been 'late for a cricket match'.

No chance of going too fast on a fresh pitch at Cambusdoon New Ground, though. Angus had to bat most of the first day for his 150, in a total of 259/8. It was Ireland's highest individual score against Scotland, and fourth overall – although two decades later it didn't make the top 20 on the all-time list. No other batsman bettered 43 in the match as Scotland matched Ireland's first innings and then bowled them out for 121 on the final morning to set up the win.

Rutherford's first season had produced just four victories from 15 matches: one of those against Italy and another by D/L in a match Ireland would probably have lost. True, the new coach was often without his best players, but he seemed to tinker far too much. If he knew his best side for the ICC Trophy, it was a mystery to the rest of us.

2001

Shenley – 31 May

The MCC had decided that two-day friendly matches were very 'last century' and would now only be extending an invitation to play a one-day game on their hallowed sward, once every four years. This season, a three-day match was offered at Shenley, a neat ground, north of London, and sort of accepted by Ireland, who instead asked to play three one-day games as preparation for the upcoming World Cup qualifiers.

The MCC comfortably won the first two matches as Rutherford continued to experiment with different combinations from a squad of 14 already selected for Toronto. In fairness, it wasn't easy. Ed and Scooby had exams and were unavailable. Deako Heasley was injured. Mark Patterson, who hadn't won a cap since Kuala Lumpur, and Eagy were both in the squad with question marks over their fitness. Patto was a much-changed bowler after a spell with Surrey, and had lost a yard. He was restricted to two three-over spells in the first two games and rested for the third.

What was clear, is that Matt would be one of the key bowlers, and the 42-year-old set up a four-wicket consolation victory with a parsimonious spell of 1/13 from his ten overs. The little northern English voice in his head, demanding 'Fire it in, Matt!' worked a treat for once. Who would share the burden in Toronto? Eagy did his case no harm by taking 2/30, as the MCC were restricted to 167/9. Kyle would be another, but Doak had not been persuaded away from his egg-chasing and other than McCoubrey, the seam department looked fragile.

After opening with Decker and Dom Joyce in the first two games, Rutherford tried Molins and Peter Davy for the third, dropping the sheep strangler to No.6 where he hit an unbeaten half-century to deliver victory with nearly ten overs to spare. He followed up next day with what would be his only Ireland century, against the Duchess of Norfolk's XI at Arundel, also batting in the middle order. Decker wasn't happy going in so far down, though, and would let it be known to the coach in Canada.

The quality Ed was showing at Middlesex was starting to attract a few familiar faces to Ireland games, hoping to unearth another green diamond. Keith Fletcher, the former England captain, turned up for this one, with his folding garden chair and sunhat. 'Any more in the pipeline like Joyce, let me know,' he said, handing over an Essex business card.

The disconnect between the county game and the Irish boys was still very much there, though. During the afternoon, Dom Joyce told me he had been offered a Second XI trial game, but the match clashed with his end-of-year university exams. Did I think he should forego them or turn down the invite? Maybe he was just looking for a way out of revising, but I suggested that if he was good enough to play professional cricket his future career wouldn't depend on one three-day game in Worksop, or wherever. If he wasn't, it might well depend on a good degree.

Toronto – 27 June

Another ICC Trophy, another new country. Canada. Apart from a six-hour stopover in Los Angeles, on the way home from Australia, I'd not spent any time in north America; the place has never appealed to me. So a trip to Toronto for the World Cup qualifiers was more of a chore than other Ireland adventures, and it wasn't one to look back on with any affection.

We were billeted out by Toronto Pearson International Airport, a vast area of seemingly endless car parks, with no new local culture to explore, other than a lap-dancing club. The grounds used were, with the exception of the exclusive Toronto Cricket Skating and Curling Club, very functional and like park pitches run by the council, which some of them were. Everything was expensive, especially the lap dancing.

I'd booked into the hotel where most of the teams were staying, but found it so hideous that the Travelodge on the opposite corner of a massive road junction was a better option, and on the advice of Ruud Onstein, the Dutch journalist and scorer, I paid a few extra dollars for a better room, which included access to the executive lounge, and a free feed each evening.

Getting around was a challenge, too. The teams were moved about in yellow Bart Simpson-style school buses (it was the summer holidays) and public transport wasn't much help. In hindsight, we should have hired a car, but none of us fancied driving on the wrong side and trying to navigate multi-lane freeways that led everywhere and nowhere. We got by somehow.

Toronto – 29 June

The ICC had devised a four-division system for the tournament to separate the better teams and the hopefuls in the early stages, yet still give all 24 teams a chance of success (although only 22 took part; Simone withdrew Italy when the ICC blocked the registration of Joe Scuderi, a one-time 12th man for Australia, and Canadian immigration refused visas to several of the West Africa side).

Ireland found themselves in one of the top two divisions of six, from which three teams would qualify for the Super Eight stage, plus the winner of a play-off between the fourth-placed team and a side topping one of the two lower divisions. It was a clever little set-up that initially rewarded previous form among the leading Associates but also gave lesser lights a pathway to claim one of the three World Cup places on offer, as Namibia eventually did.

The campaign began against the United States in Wilson Avenue, a lovely setting where three leading clubs in different sports had amalgamated in the 1950s, to form the TCSCC, with 'Cricket' earning top billing in the title over 'Skating' on the toss of a 25 cent coin, which was on display inside the clubhouse.

As McCallan went out for his toss, Callender and I settled in the press tent, along with Clive Ellis of the *Daily Telegraph* who had nicked my *Wisden* gig. We were soon disturbed by James Fitzgerald, a young journalist from Dublin who allegedly broke Scoop's laptop within minutes, as he moved tables around. Fitzy claims he did no such thing. A less controversial arrival was Rupert Rumney, an old mate from way back, who was producing the TV pictures.

Ireland won the toss and batted. A solid start from Molins and Whitey gave way to a classy knock from Ed but wickets fell regularly, Dom was fourth-highest scorer with 12, Joyce the elder was eighth out for 80 from 87 balls and a total of 209 looked a good few under par. It was. Ireland used seven bowlers, three of whom were carted for ten runs an over or more, as the US romped home with 12 overs, or so, to spare.

Rutherford was livid. He did his presser outside, surrounded by four or five of us. Not quite sure what to make of such a lacklustre start, I tried what was supposed to be a gentle opener: 'Did you expect the US to be that good?'

His eyes blazed. 'Good? They were good were they?' Whenever anyone tells me that Rutherford didn't care and was just going through the motions for a pay cheque, I remember those eyes.

Toronto – 5 July

Ireland got off the mark against Hong Kong the following day, with Molins and Ed both making half-centuries, and another eight-wicket win followed against Bermuda. Decker, out for three against the US, didn't bat in either game. Two wins from three looked OK, but it seemed unlikely that both Hong Kong and Bermuda would qualify for the Super Eight stage, so only one of the victories would be carried through. After the US loss, Ireland desperately needed to beat Denmark and expected to, having crushed Ole Mortensen's team at the previous year's European Championships.

Rutherford was playing silly buggers with the media, not letting us know what team had been selected on the eve of a match, even though it wouldn't be in print until the following morning. Kyle was toeing the party line, apologetically. Apparently this new thing called the internet would allow the opposition to discover what Ireland were planning, and they could devise their strategies accordingly. Nonsense. I bumped into Decker and Whitey, who were room-mates.

'Any changes tomorrow?'

'Deako's in for Matt,' Decker said, showing his disapproval.

'Are you playing?'

Whitey shook his head. So there was no place for Matt, the best bowler against Bermuda two days ago, nor the lad who had made a century the last time these teams had met?

The match was reduced to 46 overs and, with no one to fire it in, Denmark slipped the leash. Ireland were not helped by Scooby overstepping six times and Patto suffering a return of his KL blues: eight wides in three overs. A total of 231/6 looked formidable. The tone for the reply was set by Peter Davy using up two-and-a-half overs for a single. Dom scored 50, but took 85 balls in doing so, and even Ed found quick runs hard to come by. Decker was more than capable of coping with a target of 132 from the final 20 overs, but looked out of sorts and was bowled for 19 attempting to clear the ropes a second time. Deako blasted 40 in rapid time, but Ireland were bowled out for 219.

Decker was promoted to open in the final group game against Papua New Guinea and, back in his comfort zone, struck 95 not out as Ireland beat the team who finished bottom of the table by nine wickets. In doing so they claimed third place in the group, avoiding a nervy play-off with Namibia, that Bermuda lost. Only the one win from three to start the Super Eight, though.

Niagara Falls – 8 July

Rupert's crew arranged the must-do tourist trip to Niagara, on a rare day off, and an invite to join them enabled us to chew over old times on the two-hour minibus ride. We had first crossed paths in Madras, as it was then, during the 1984/85 England tour. Rupert and his mate Michael Fairburn were cycling around India, from Test to Test, as you could in those days, and staying at the lovely old guesthouse, Broadlands. We hit it off and a memorable week included sitting in the wicker chairs of a VIP box, next to Peter May, the England chairman of selectors, as Mike Gatting tried to go to a double century with a reverse sweep. It was a shot May had banned but, on 197, Gatt probably thought he was allowed a little latitude.

There was a queue for the boat – you don't just look at Niagara, you experience it – and we were all issued with plastic raincoats. One of the cameramen who had recently been to Victoria Falls was underwhelmed in a Crocodile Dundee 'that's-not-a-waterfall' sort of way, but the rest of us were thrilled. The noise was deafening as we disappeared into the cascade. I tried to think of a Rutherford metaphor: pluckily steering the Irish vessel into the difficult waters of a Super Eight and getting mightily dumped on from above. But it didn't really work. Anyway, I didn't have a lot of sympathy for the coach and his keep-the-press-in-the-dark shenanigans.

Toronto – 9 July

The key qualifying game was against Scotland. Not a straightforward do-or-die as it had been in Kuala Lumpur, but the loser would find it difficult to finish in the top four of the Super Eight, especially if that loser was Ireland. Kyle decided to bat. How would Decker go, we wondered? We had to wait a while to find out because, despite his near century as an opener in the previous game, the big man was back down at No.5. And not happy. Not at all happy.

Progress was slow. Dom again outscored his brother who made 33 from 70 balls. Decker, out of sorts and chuntering, made one. There was no late surge and a total of 174/8 surely wasn't enough. 'Have they got any chance of defending that?' I asked Darrell Hair, during the break.

'You're asking one of the umpires, during the game, who he thinks will win?' Eyebrows raised. Bloody ACU. It wasn't as though there was a betting market. Although there probably was, somewhere. Stupid question, anyway – we both knew the answer.

While our cordial exchange was going on outside, a feisty confrontation was taking place in the lunch queue between an embattled coach and a messed-around sheep strangler. Voices were raised, fingers poked and there was, shall we say, a tête-à-tête, a meeting of minds ... OK, let's be specific, Decker headbutted Rutherford. Not with any great force but with sufficient to end his international career. A passionate cricketer, one with a desperate desire to play in the World Cup, had reached the end of his tether.

I learned of the episode that evening from Hendo, now the Scotland assistant coach, who was drinking with his boss Jim Love, the two of them in good spirits after a seven-wicket win. 'I shouldn't really be telling you this, but ...' Decker was sent home the following morning and didn't play for Ireland again.

Toronto – 10–13 July

In theory, it was still possible for Ireland to win their remaining three games and qualify but ... Or should that be butt ...? The last wheel of the wagon had fallen off in that lunch queue; the focus of the campaign had gone AWOL, and would not return.

Not that there wasn't focus among individuals, particularly the Joyce brothers who both made half-centuries in a tournament-best total of 283/7 the day after the Scotland defeat, only to see the United Arab Emirates ease past it with four wickets and more than three overs to spare. Ed's tournament aggregate of 359 runs – at an average of 71.8 – was only narrowly bettered by Daniel Keulder, of Namibia, who had the advantage of an extra innings.

Four defeats from the five matches that counted in the Super Eight and still Ireland were not entirely without hope. Could they beat the Netherlands? Rutherford tinkered with his line-up yet again, bringing Peter Davy back to bolster the middle order and, if only by the law of averages, nearly pulled off a masterstroke.

Molins had both a century and the Dutch total of 217 in his sights when he took on the bullet-like throw of JJ Esmeijer and was run out for 93, but the ninth-wicket pair of Davy and Matt reduced the ask to six off the final over and three from the last four balls. Matt, his 42-year-old heart racing, wanted a run off the next, was rightly sent back and run out by a distance at the non-striker's end. Silly old sod. What a time for all that experience to desert him. It was to be his last innings; he walked off having amassed two fewer career runs for Ireland than his 62 wickets. Davy could still have won it with a boundary, but was stumped off the penultimate ball for 30. Ireland were beaten by two runs and would not be going to South Africa.

The shambolic disintegration of the campaign had led to James Fitzgerald, freelance journalist and alleged laptop destroyer, being pressed into action as 12th man for a couple of overs during the Dutch innings. Rutherford only had 11 fit players to start and, when Molins went off injured, a spare kit was hastily found for a weekend cricketer to field against a team that would be World Cup-bound a few days later.

Fitzy was on for Molins again the following day against Canada, this time for around an hour, wearing one of Ed's spare shirts. Not only that, but Ireland won, with Davy scoring a century in a seven-wicket, pressure-off romp. Yet a day after they had realistically still been hoping to qualify for the play-offs on run-rate, Ireland finished bottom of the Super Eight; the Dutch took top spot and went on to win the ICC Trophy with a last-ball victory over Namibia in the final.

There was barely time for a beer in the dressing room before the squad were off to the airport. Most of the batsmen could leave with heads high, although the Dutch defeat would haunt them. The only bowler to enhance his reputation was Scooby McCoubrey, who took 13 wickets and was always a threat. Playing eight of the nine matches in 15 days was too much to ask of Matt's old bones and Rutherford's gamble on the past record and fitness of Patto, who had won his last cap, and Eagy did not produce one winner, never mind a straight forecast.

It could have been different if the coach had known his best team. Only once, when he had no choice, did he pick the same side. The two I felt for were Matt and Wee John, who had both worked so hard. The old spinner would surely have soldiered on for another couple of years of beep tests and salads with a less demanding World Cup schedule in his sights, while the Hon. Sec. would now have to wait at least another six years to see Ireland on the world stage.

Toronto – 17 July

For the second time in four years Hendo was involved in the third-place play-off to decide the final World Cup place, and for the second time he was on the losing side. A decent crowd of 1,500 or so turned up to the TCSCC, hoping to see a Canada win and they were not disappointed as Scotland were restricted to 176-9 and beaten by five wickets.

Love and Big Dave did what they could from the boundary, striding purposely either clockwise or anti-clockwise as the situation demanded, but I did wonder whether the Yorkshireman had chosen his assistant wisely. Yes, Hendo had all the experience required, but the two dour old former county pros were too much alike and maybe a livelier, more optimistic sidekick would have lifted Scotland, given them a buzz. When the coach and his mate give the impression that the world is against them, nearly everything is 'shite', and even in victory you must never forget that the next setback is just around the corner, then some of it must rub off.

I loved Hendo; still do. He was always accommodating professionally and great company in a bar, yet that continual hang-dog pessimism does him no favours. How much of it is an act only he knows, but his gruff approach didn't endear him to the ICU and perhaps his playing career would have benefitted from a lighter demeanour too. How many of those lbw shouts might have been given if the umpire didn't know that deep down he was expecting a negative response?

Is it just coincidence that two of the grumpiest bowlers – Hendo and Gus Fraser – were also two of the 'unluckiest'? Ian Botham, for example, always expected to take wickets – and did. Often with rank long hops. So does optimism and expectation of success play a role in cricket, and sport generally? Throw in a couple of pars on self-fulfilling prophesies and you're halfway to a sports science dissertation, methinks. Or not. A discussion for another day, though; right now it was time to go home.

West Sussex – 14–16 August

Matt Dwyer had ridden off into the sunset after winning his 51st and last cap against Australia – although a badly rain-affected game denied him a final chance to fire it in – so it was a weakened Ireland team that looked to get back on its collective horse in the Triple Crown. With Ed at Middlesex, Decker banned, Molins not available, Eagy suffering a long-term injury and Deako pulling out at the last minute, it wasn't a horse that even Rutherford would have backed.

If we thought Toronto was bad, here was the nadir.

I drove down from central London each day, going against the commute, and found a great spot for breakfast just off the A23. That was the highlight of the three days. What looked a gentle opener against Wales at Horsham, before the more serious challenges of the England XI and Scotland, instead saw Ireland bowled out for 149 after an opening stand of 66. Jordan McGonigle, a 19-year-old left-arm spinner, took 2/17 on debut and Ireland had a sniff at 134/8 before losing by two wickets. Mark Gillespie, the older brother of PG, also won his first cap. He was a leg-spinner, apparently, but didn't bowl.

Next day, at Stirlands near West Wittering, the writing was on the wall from the first ball when Andy Patterson was lbw to Chris Batt, and definitely from the second when Peter Davy suffered the same fate. The former Middlesex left-armer was convinced he had a hat-trick but an almighty shout against Dom was turned down. The Hon. Sec. and a couple of colleagues left at that point to attend church; a special day of some sort. Their prayers went unanswered. Ireland were bowled out for 109, with only Dom and Kyle making double figures, although John Mooney hung around for a good while on debut. As the England XI raced a six-wicket win, I contemplated a second breakfast on the way home.

Then came Scotland at East Grinstead: just what wasn't required after two defeats on the back of last place in Canada. Hold on a minute, though! Davy got a half-century and given the scores of the week, a total of 211 might just be defendable. It looked a lot more defendable as McCoubrey tore through the first three. Maybe, just maybe … McGonigle also took three. Surely not? When McGonigle's final ball produced a run out, Scotland were 88/7 from 29 overs and the Super Macs had combined figures of 6/39. Finally, I was going to see Ireland beat Scotland!

No I wasn't. Gregor Maiden was having none of it. With Ireland's best two bowled out, the ginger Glaswegian struck an unbeaten 79 from 70 balls, and an unbeaten eighth-wicket partnership of 126 with Craig Wright took Scotland to victory with nine balls to spare.

The skipper was devastated – and fuming. 'Have you got your notepad?' he demanded.

'Yes.'

'Right, get this down, because this has got to change. This cannot go on like this. We are not getting the support we need to be successful. We need more games against better opposition and that means playing inter-provincial matches too. The ICU has to change; the whole system needs changing from top to bottom.'

Kyle let rip for ten minutes, tears welling.

'Are you sure you want to say all this?'

'Yes. Every word.'

The tirade got a decent show in the *Belfast Telegraph* the next day and things did start to change. Not because of that article, obviously, although it was a fair barometer of the passion in the dressing room. Things changed because they had to. The players were too good, too ambitious and devoting too much of their time and emotions to continue the old amateur ways of the ICU into the 21st century.

Three days after the Scotland loss it was confirmed that Rutherford would not be retained beyond the end of his contract in September.

Salisbury – 29 August

The long climb back had to start without McCallan, who had school duties and missed the preliminary round of the following year's Cheltenham & Gloucester Trophy against Wiltshire. Molins skippered. The visitors were again without Ed, who had just become the first born-and-bred Irishman to score a century in the County Championship, with 104 against Warwickshire at Lord's. Another century followed before the season was out and, with his sights firmly set on playing Test cricket for England, he seemed unlikely to play for Ireland again after embarking on the four-year qualification purdah that was required at that time.

Ireland found a left-handed replacement in Andre Botha, a South African-born all-rounder who had settled in Leinster and played his club cricket with Clontarf and then North County. Botha's debut with the bat lasted one ball, though, as he was sawn off by an lbw decision that left his adopted side in a spot of trouble on 25/3. Things hadn't improved much at 78/5 when PG joined Dom. The sixth-wicket pair added a match-turning 125 and a total of 247 was 85 too good for Wiltshire.

Man of the match was awarded by Joe Hardstaff, the former Middlesex secretary, who had once stood next to Alec Stewart, in similar circumstances, and declared that the best team had won after Surrey lost a NatWest Trophy thriller in the last over at Uxbridge. The Gaffer's face was a picture that day. I'm not a lip reader, but I'm pretty sure he started to say 'Can't believe that' but stopped after one word. This time Hardstaff congratulated Dom on his innings but announced the £300 was going to 'the old man'. PG accepted with grace; he was still only 27.

A depressing season ended two weeks later in suitable surroundings at a cold, windy half-finished Rose Bowl where Ireland beat a Hampshire Board XI, not the county side, by 32 runs. Botha put on a better show with 75 and took three wickets. Here was a South African who was going to have a big impact on Irish cricket; another was about to follow.

2002

Dublin – 1 March

It was a year when very little happened except, perhaps, the most important thing of all: at the start of March, the ICU appointed Adrian 'Adi' Birrell as their third full-time coach.

Described as 'humble and genuine, with a firm approach' by a former boss, the 41-year-old was exactly what Ireland needed: an ambitious young coach who would devote himself to the job. There was no baggage with Adi; no stellar Test career behind him, and no great reputation. He had been an average leg-spinner in an unspectacular first-class career with Eastern Province in South Africa, but he could mould a squad, had a way he wanted to play one-day cricket and no one who ever met him would doubt his sincerity, honesty or work ethic.

Everyone has a favourite Adi story. Mine comes from the very end of his five years in charge when, knowing he would be unable to deliver a farewell speech in the

Caribbean without breaking down, he hand-wrote an individual copy for each of the World Cup squad. Yes, he could have written out the speech just once and used a photocopier, but that wasn't Adi. It wouldn't have been personal enough.

The new coach had a grasp of what was possible, focused on achieving it, and ended up exceeding all expectations, including his own. Adi was a great believer in the 'one-per-centers'; a theory that if each member of the squad could improve just a tiny bit, it would add up and contribute to a much larger improvement in the whole. He drummed it into his charges that, while they may not be as individually talented with bat and ball, there was no reason why they couldn't field as well as any of the top teams, and hence Ireland were recognised as one of the best two or three sides in that discipline at the 2007 World Cup.

And he removed the fear from his players. No matter who they were facing, no matter how imposing and seemingly superior, Adi insisted: 'Our hearts are as big as theirs!'

Funny thing, fate. If Ireland had found another three runs against the Netherlands in Toronto they may well have qualified for the 2003 showpiece, and Rutherford would most likely have led a largely forgettable campaign in his adopted homeland. Wee John would have achieved his ambition four years early, there would have been no Birrell input and the whole project could have meandered off into a cul-de-sac. So it's not a stretch to say that if Matt hadn't panicked and run himself out in that final over, Ireland may never have played Test cricket.

Adi's reign began with an eight-wicket defeat at home, by Nottinghamshire, and ended with an eight-wicket loss to Sri Lanka in Grenada; what happened in between was very special.

Waringstown – 25 July

The fourth edition of the European Championship was staged in the north of Ireland and brought the closest of finishes, with the hosts needing three from the last ball of the tournament to win it, two to finish runners-up and anything less to finish third. They finished third.

Adi, who had appointed Jason Molins as captain, gave a first cap to Niall O'Brien, a spiky 21-year-old wicketkeeper from Sandymount. The son of former Ireland international Brendan 'Ginger' O'Brien, he was similarly thatched and universally known as Nobby. Given his subsequent efforts, it's amusing to recall he batted at No.10 on debut. After victories over Denmark, Italy and the Netherlands, and the inevitable loss to Scotland, he was up to No.8.

The crunch game was the last against the England XI, who won the toss, batted and registered 226/8 at The Lawn. Molins led from the front with a century in reply, McCallan hit 42 but no other batsman reached double figures until Nobby accepted the challenge and took Ireland to within a whisker of the title. Seven runs were required from the final over; five from four balls when the youngster called for a two and was adjudged run out, when 'home by two feet'. A single and a less contentious run out followed, leaving Jordan McGonigle to score three or more from the only ball he faced in the tournament – his single wasn't enough.

Remarkably, it was the second game the England XI had won by one run. Earlier in the week, Scotland, needing four to win from ten balls, with six wickets in hand, had blown up spectacularly. No, it wasn't a televised match. It does happen.

Finchampstead – 29 August

Nobby had shot to No.1 in the order for the next game at The Mardyke and scored the first of his eight centuries for Ireland in a five-wicket victory over the MCC, but he was back down to No.7 for the C&G Trophy match against Berkshire and was one of only four batsmen to reach double figures in a disappointing 113 all out. Jeremy Bray, a left-handed opener from Sydney, fell for two on debut. He had been living in Ireland for four years and would be eligible as a local next season.

Former Essex batsman Paul Prichard made an unbeaten half-century to see the minor county home with four wickets to spare. It was probably no coincidence that Scooby McCoubrey, who bowled a lively six overs, was offered a contract with Essex for the following two seasons. Nobby had already been signed by Kent; the county professionals were starting to take notice of the young talent across the water.

This was the only game I saw in another season of few fixtures and I was hoping to introduce myself to this new South African in charge, but it's best not to seek out even the nicest of blokes after such a hammering. My first handshake would have to wait.

2003

Belfast – 13 June

Adi's second season began with a ten-wicket victory over Zimbabwe at Stormont. Paul Mooney grabbed two early wickets, the visitors slipped to 12/3 and did not recover as Gary Neely took 3/30 with his skiddy fast medium. The result was never in doubt. Molins scored a century, Bray supported him with an unbeaten 67 and their opening stand was Ireland's second best when the victory target of 183 was reached in the 34th over.

The local media reported that a 'massive' anti-Mugabe demonstration was being planned for the second match at Eglinton two days later. The ICU doubled down on its security and committee man Roy Torrens handed out free tickets to a dozen large gentlemen who might otherwise have spent the Sunday in church, or polishing their bowler hats.

The 'massive' demo turned up in a small car, from which four hungover students emerged with placards. PR officer Robin Walsh approached them showing his palms. 'Now lads, if I promise to get your photo in the papers, will you settle for that?'

Eyeing the security, indeed they would. They posed smiling for Robin's photographer. 'For goodness sake, you're supposed to be angry! You're protesting,' the former BBC man growled. Cue anger. Cue peaceful end of demo.

Molins again won the toss but this time chose to bowl. Zimbabwe got their revenge. Heath Streak whipped out the top three as Ireland slumped to 36/5. Gillespie made a very good half-century but a total of 196 wasn't enough as the game followed the pattern of the first and the visitors levelled the series with eight wickets and nearly ten overs to spare.

Later in the season, I overheard a couple of ICU committee men chuckling 'Zimbabwe only tried in the second match.' The realisation that their team was closing the gap on the weaker Test sides hadn't dawned, nor the importance of bowling first in both games.

Clontarf – 18 June

A one-off tour match against South Africa at Castle Avenue meant each of the major provincial unions had hosted a game inside a week. It produced a routine 132-run victory for the visitors. Captain Graeme Smith was one of three half-centurions in a total of 294/8, and Ireland were bowled out for 162 in reply. Makhaya Ntini took 3-21 and won man of the match. He was presented with ... a lawnmower. The match was sponsored by Viking who manufactured the machines and a bemused Ntini paraded his prize around the outfield for a few publicity pictures, no doubt wondering how he was going to get it home.

It wasn't the first time an appliance had been awarded at an Ireland international. A three-day match against Denmark in 1978 had offered a new washing machine for the best individual performance. Fast bowler John Elder whistled through the first six wickets of the Danish second innings and was dreaming of all ten, as well as walking away with the Whirlpool, when he was whisked out of the attack by Dermott Monteith. The skipper helped himself to a couple of tail-end wickets, to add to his four in the first innings and, with a half-century too, took the award. It transpired that the Monteith family washing machine was on its last legs and the old rascal had talked the sponsors into offering a new one as a prize.

Monty would have been confident of winning, even if he hadn't been skipper. He could bat and his left-arm spin was good enough to get him nine Championship matches for Middlesex in the early 1980s, covering for Test call-ups.

At home, he was a dominant figure, taking a record 326 wickets from only 76 appearances, and then serving on the ICU committee and as a selector. Monty knew what he was looking at, but he was a miserable sod. Nothing was good enough. Few of his peers, never mind players of later eras, met his exacting standards, and none could match his alcohol consumption. A more generous spirit and he could have given much more. But what a talent, and what an asset he would have been in his prime to Adi, or any coach.

Malahide – 10 July

A series of three matches against the ECB XI filled a gap in the calendar after the Triple Crown was scrapped. It also gave an insight into the kind of team Adi was looking to build. Along with 'one-per-centers', another of the young coach's mantras was the need to perform at least two of the three disciplines: batting, bowling and fielding. He was blessed in this respect by the arrival of Botha to boost the established all-rounders McCallan and White. Nobby, with the gloves, was another who doubled up, the Mooney brothers, Paul and John, filled the brief perfectly and, although Bray was primarily a batsman, he could fill in with a few tidy overs if required, and kept wicket in the ICC Trophy two years later.

The most significant addition arrived next year in the shape of Trent Johnston, but the two-discipline brigade kept rolling off the production line after that with Kevin O'Brien and William Porterfield, a superb fielder. In the coach's eyes you needed to be outstanding at one discipline if you didn't have a second. There were exceptions. PG had all but given up his bowling and wasn't Jonty Rhodes either. Adi needed a solid presence in the middle order, though, and the Strabane man was given a remit to score at a strike rate of at least 75. After a duck in the first-game defeat, he made two half-centuries at almost exactly the required speed. The first took Ireland close to victory at Rathmines, the second helped post a winning 212/6 in the final game at The Village. The series was lost 2-1.

The two-disciplines rule was not good news for Jonathan Bushe, an excellent wicketkeeper who could only reach double figures once in 29 matches, nor seamer Neely who won the last of his 22 caps at Waringstown the following month, in a 167-run victory over the Club Cricket Conference, a side of English amateurs and part-timers.

Arundel – 18 August

The biennial Duchess of Norfolk match was confirmed as a 50-overs-a-side contest, but didn't last even half the distance. A ruthless Ireland bowling display dismissed the home side for 61 and the runs were knocked off quickly for the loss of three wickets. Ryan Eagleson won his first cap since Toronto and took a wicket first ball. After such a long time it must have seemed like starting all over again for Eagy, who had made his Ireland debut on the same ground in 1995.

A sense of this being a serious side in the making continued the next day at Lord's where an MCC team containing former Ireland all-rounder Garfield Harrison were bowled out for 212. There was never any doubt that Ireland would win, but could Bray record a coveted Lord's century. The opener needed six more, with seven to win, when he top edged a hook and was caught.

Garfield had claimed Botha, but Ireland were home and hosed by seven wickets again, with exactly ten overs to spare. I looked for Adi after the game to say hello, but got waylaid by the near-centurion. Dearie me, can Brayso talk? If there are any donkeys with hind legs in western Sydney, I'll be surprised. Entertaining, though, and yes he knew he hit the ball in the air far too often.

Eton – 20 August

Many great men have taken their first steps towards high office and fame at Eton, so whether it was by accident or design, Adi chose the perfect place to give a 16-year-old left-hander his first cap, against the Free Foresters. Eoin Morgan had been attracting rave reviews in Leinster cricket and was already attached to Middlesex. A big future in the game was predicted for the youngster, not least by himself. On first meeting Adi, the previous year, young Eoin had told the coach that although he was keen to play for Ireland he didn't know how long he would be available, as his ultimate ambition was to represent England. 'He was actually apologetic about that,' Birrell recalls. Still 21 days short of his 17th birthday, Eoin became the youngest player to appear for Ireland, which also gave a first cap to Boyd Rankin, a giant of a 19-year-old fast bowler from farming stock in the north-west.

I'd heard about Morgan from contacts at Middlesex and was looking forward to watching him bat. I was disappointed. The youngster was in early at No.3, when Bray slapped one in the air to cover, and in the next over the skipper discovered what any parent could have told him, that it's not easy to get a teenager moving in the morning. Molins pushed to backward point and called for a dubious single. Eoin was slow out of the traps and beaten by a direct hit; he had not faced. Paul Mooney, asleep in the changing room, missed the innings. Emerging half-an-hour later, he sat down next to the teenager and asked what number he was batting.

A first visit to the 15th-century college was an eye-opener for a comprehensive school lad like myself. You could almost smell the privilege and sense of entitlement, even if the little brats were all off on summer hols with Mater and Pater. It was easy to see how the place has produced so many prime ministers; just going to school there would tell any child they were destined for great things. Self-fulfilling prophesies, and all that. It was also easy to see why Eton has produced so few top-class cricketers: rubbish pitch. Ireland only managed 170 but it was enough for a 13-run win as Johnboy, the younger Mooney, took three wickets.

I was getting to like the Mooneys. Passionate, straightforward and fierce competitors – with each other as well as opponents. One supported Manchester United and the other Liverpool. Years ago, each had received a video tape of his favourite team for Christmas. The cassettes were both smashed beyond repair before Santa was back on his sleigh. It was a family that wouldn't have been too keen on the English, either. There was some good banter.

Shenley – 21 August

We got to see what the fuss was about the following day. Eoin was run out again, but not before he had made a compact, measured 71 in a return match against the Club Cricket Conference. He faced 103 balls and struck nine fours, but clearly needed to work on both his calling and responses, as he was slow responding again with a century beckoning.

As good as his innings was, it was upstaged by fellow Fingal fella, Paul Mooney, who turned on a masterclass of happy-hour batting. Striking the ball in the 'V' with power and deflecting it fine both sides of the wicket, with an angled blade more than a sweep, he made 66 not out from 44 balls, with ten fours. It was such a good knock, so simple and so effective, it would probably be in the top five of my Ireland journey. Please don't ask for the other four, I haven't drawn up a list, but it was just so pure it has to be right up there.

The 100 runs that Mooney helped find from the final 12 overs – 42 from the final three – took Ireland to 266/7 and a victory by 124 runs as the home side were fiddled out by White and McCallan.

The match had started early because Ireland had flights to catch and were on a tight schedule to get the team bus around the M25 to Heathrow. As it was about to set off, Eoin shouted 'Whoa, whoa! Wait a minute' and asked to get off. What had the youngster forgotten? Nothing. Instead he strolled across the car park and engaged a well-dressed older man in conversation for the next few minutes, before getting back on board. 'Sorry lads, my agent.' He may have been short of his ground a couple of times that week, but he was never short of confidence.

Bishop's Stortford – 28–29 August

To describe the pitch for the Cheltenham & Gloucester Trophy clash with Hertfordshire as 'a belter' would be doing it an injustice. It is frightening to think just how many runs would have been plundered on it 15 years later, when 350 had become a par score in 50-overs games. Add a lightning-fast outfield and no bowler on either side was catching the captain's eye.

Molins cantered to 84 from 88 balls, then the South African pair of Botha and Gerard Dros piled in with centuries. Boatsie reached 139 before holing out to midwicket for Ireland's highest individual score in limited overs. Dros, the overseas gun, cleared the boundary seven times, including three off successive balls in the final over. – a brutal assault that brought him 124 from 81 balls.

The Ireland total of 387/4 obliterated their previous best one-day effort of 311/5 against Wales in 1994. At the height of the southern hemisphere barrage, Herts skipper David Ward, the former Surrey player, could be heard to wail, 'Come on boys, let's see if we can get an Irishman in here!' It was funny, to be fair.

While Gary Butcher was making 126, it looked as though Herts might get somewhere near, but Mark's brother fell to Botha shortly before a rainstorm ended play. Coming back the next day, for what turned out to be 5.3 overs, delighted no one except the freelancers among us. Despite the advances under Hendo and Adi, the set-up was still very amateur and with the captain back behind his desk in the City, the coach himself was pressed into duty as a substitute fielder. The departure of Molins gave Kyle a few minutes back in charge in his 100th game, while Mooney the elder and Eagy mopped up the tail to complete a 75-run win. Boatsie had added four wickets to his century to give the man of the match adjudicator an easy task.

As the players packed up their kit at a leisurely pace, I was finally able to introduce myself to Adi, and shake his hand. 'Yes, the boys have told me about you,' he said, with that little half smile of his that doesn't let on whether that's a good or a bad thing.

Malahide – 6 September

While the coach was putting together a very useful side, the Hon. Sec. was doing his bit in the wings. Denmark expected to be one of the three European teams in the new InterContinental Cup, on the basis of finishing above Ireland at the 2001 ICC Trophy. But Wee John worked his committee-man magic and persuaded the ICC that a best-of-three series should decide who would join Scotland and the Netherlands in the first-class competition. A coin toss decided the one-day games would be staged in Dublin. Neither was close.

McCoubrey and Nobby were made available by their counties and the Essex man took 4/41 as Denmark were pegged to 224/9 in the first match at Clontarf. Bray and Botha notched half-centuries to ease Ireland home by seven wickets. The second match at The Village was even more of a stroll as Bray completed a prolific season with the first of his seven centuries for Ireland. He belted 21 fours in a superb 143, Molins and Botha made 80s and a massive 363/5 was 159 too many for the Danes. The third game wasn't required and a 14-year love affair with the IC Cup had begun.

2004

Clontarf – 5 May

Seven years after the Middlesex victory, Ireland claimed a second county scalp, beating Surrey by five wickets in the second round of the C&G Trophy. So, name the three players who featured in both matches? Gillespie is the one everyone gets straightaway, and a bit of head scratching delivers McCallan, who opened the batting in the first game. The third? It's a trick question: Mark Ramprakash played for both counties and was on the losing side twice at Castle Avenue.

The advances of the previous season were given a boost with the addition of Trent Johnston, a genuinely fast bowler, and no mean bat, who had played a handful of games for New South Wales. The big Aussie had met and married Vanessa while playing club cricket in Leinster, and had his passport application fast-tracked. Allegedly. He made his debut against Surrey and took the first wicket as the visitors were bowled out for 261. The Ireland batting was so strong that Eoin, who was listed at No.7, didn't get in. Kyle was promoted to finish the job with his old mate Whitey, and did so with ten balls to spare.

Ireland couldn't follow up by beating Northants at home in the next round, but again made a decent score of 263/8, before losing by six wickets. They were starting to compete, regularly.

Stormont – 16 June

Nobby, when Kent allowed him time off, was now a key member of Adi's team. Few would argue that when he first followed the footsteps of his father into the national side, he was cocky to the point of bumptious – and remained so for a good while. It's hard to think of Ginger having quite the same mouth or manner on him. A sound middle-order batsman, who made 51 against the Australians in 1977, I'm told he would have been more like his youngest son Kevin in temperament.

Nobby was a law unto himself in those early days. He tells a story of sneaking into the visitors' dressing room at Canterbury, searching for what plans Worcestershire had for him and his Kent team-mates. 'There was a file with stuff like "Rob Key: plays around his front pad, lbw candidate" and "Ed Smith: doesn't like the short stuff" and so on. When I got to my name all it said was "annoying redhead".'

Brian Lara would probably go along with that. The great West Indian had an abysmal record against Ireland before the first of two tour games at Stormont, so it is perhaps understandable that he didn't walk for a nick behind. The keeper explained to him that it would have been the gentlemanly thing to do, in not so gentlemanly language. And in true Nobby style, he persisted. Lara, one of the best two or three batsmen in the world, and getting towards the end of his prolific career, was not happy. Maybe, like W.G. Grace once did, he could have explained that the Stormont crowd had come to watch him bat. Or maybe he hadn't nicked it.

The flare-up between the two inspired Brian Charles to make a century, continuing his record of never having returned to the pavilion with a double-figure score against Ireland. A West Indies' total of 242 all out was 96 too good for the home side.

Cookie did not complete the match after tearing ligaments in his leg, while fielding. He was taken to hospital in the same ambulance as his nine-year-old son Curtis who, following in the family tradition, had suffered a blow to the head. It was from a Lara six, this time, rather than a spurned team-mate. Gary Wilson, who was still at school, appeared as a substitute and held a stunning catch at long-on.

Stormont – 17 June

West Indies went bigger the following day, making 292/7, with Dwayne Bravo completing a 65-ball century in the final over. It was a massive total, but Ireland always looked like chasing it down after Molins and Bray added 111 for the first wicket. Molins, in the form of his life, made 66 from 58 balls, Bray top-scored with 71 and Nobby, batting at No.4, struck a well-paced half-century to see the job done with more than three overs to spare.

Three overs! Chasing nearly 300! There was nothing flukey or contrived about the win; Ireland had beaten a Test side with something to spare. OK, it wasn't the Calypso Kings of the 1980s, but in terms of achievement this six-wicket win was far more impressive than that oft-talked of afternoon at Sion Mills in 1969, when West Indies were bizarrely dismissed for 25.

Yes it was.

Deventer – 12 July

When I found half a dozen players in the hotel bar on the eve of their first InterContinental Cup match, it was immediately obvious that something had changed. The atmosphere was different; more confident, more up front. Brayso was there, of course, I'm guessing PG and probably Johnboy. But there was also a big bloke in the middle who was dominating both the chat and the room. This was my first encounter with David Trent Johnston. Someone introduced us. A firm handshake. 'Good to meet ya, mate.' Then back to the banter.

This wasn't like any Ireland team in a bar I knew. Not only was there a buzz and a crackle about Johnston, it was clearly infectious and his team-mates were two inches taller. Fine cricketers in their own right, you sensed they still lacked something deep down. I remembered Lewie's 'But they're *professionals*, DT!'

Now, with TJ in the ranks – and to an extent Bray and Botha – came genuine belief.

Ireland had a former Sheffield Shield man with the shamrock on his chest. He was a big character, a champion, but at the same time he was one of them. He played for Railway Union. Johnston hadn't just flown in for a couple of games, like Cronje, Rhodes or the Waughs, he was there for the long haul. And the thing was: TJ delivered. Time and time again. What a bonus to have a bloke like that sitting on the other side of the dressing room.

He didn't only change the Ireland team, he changed the Netherlands as well. The sight of the big strong quick made an instant impression on Hans Mulder, the Dutch team manager. 'Where did they find this guy!?' he asked, in awe. 'He's a proper bowler.'

How did TJ change the Dutch team, you're wondering? Well, the XI who faced Ireland in that first three-day match of the inaugural IC Cup contained ten locally born-and-bred players. A decade later, the Netherlands side was packed with imported Australians, South Africans and New Zealanders. The Dutch-born successors to Bas Zuiderent and Ed Schiferli, who played in the Deventer game, Steven Lubbers, Andre van Troost and Roland Lefebvre, were nowhere to be seen.

Should the Netherlands, the United Arab Emirates and other sides be allowed to field so many 'foreigners'? Well, people move countries. Some to play professional sport, others at a younger age as their parents look for a better standard of life. Where do you draw the line? Ireland had an unofficial glass ceiling of four 'overseas' players per team, during the Adi years. One team, I believe, contained five. But no more.

Deventer – 13–15 July

Johnston proved his worth, and Mulder's assessment, with four wickets as the Netherlands batted first in the three-day match. Ireland had another bowler in their line-up who was new to me, Greg Thompson, and it was the teenage leg-spinner from Lisburn who made the bigger impression with a prodigious amount of 'inswinging' drift and sharp turn. He was the most exciting Irish bowling talent I'd seen by some way. Still is. I wasn't the only one enjoying his skills. The coach, a leggie himself back in the day for Eastern Province, was purring over Thompson's potential and Rob Bailey, a new recruit to the umpiring ranks, confirmed what we were seeing from the boundary. Big drift. Big turn. Decent pace (an often overlooked ingredient). Good control.

Bailey was also taken with the batting of Whitey, who took Ireland past the home side's modest 200 all out and very quickly to a match-winning advantage as he found top gear. On the basis of that first of five IC Cup centuries, the umpire tipped off his former county and the Belfast man spent a couple of frustrating years at Northants, not getting a run of games and not doing enough in the Stiffs to warrant one. If he had fallen early in Deventer, who knows, Thompson could have been the recommendation.

As it was, the teenager went to Lancashire, possibly as the result of a chat with David Lloyd in a Primrose Hill hostelry. I do remember waxing on about the lad one evening and Bumble jotting down a couple of notes. Alcohol had been consumed and the details are fuzzy. Sadly, the great hope was losing it before he arrived at Old Trafford. Perhaps it was a growth spurt, perhaps it was trying too many variations. Whatever. The drift was gone, so too the control, and only four years after pipping Eoin by days to become the youngest Ireland debutant at 16 years and nine months, Thompson won what appeared would be his 14th and final cap.

Every country wants a demon leggie or a mystery spinner; a Warne or Murali. It's the holy grail of modern cricket. Ireland fleetingly had one in Thompson. Had he kicked on, he was that good at 16 he could have had a similar influence to Rashid Khan with Afghanistan, and Test cricket may have arrived years, if not a decade, earlier.

Back to Deventer, where a first-innings lead of 188 still needed to be turned into a victory and it was the efforts of a third new face, albeit a fairly old one, that got Ireland over the line. Naseer Shaukat, a veteran nagging seamer with a big reputation in Leinster cricket, ran through the Dutch second innings taking 5/30. Victory, by an innings and 47 runs, was made all the sweeter by the first-day sledging of Jeroen Smits. The Dutch keeper had loudly announced that Ireland must be a 'little team' because he hadn't seen them at the recent Champions Trophy qualifiers, for the leading non-Test sides. When two wickets fell immediately after lunch on the final day, Johnboy was under the helmet at short leg to greet Smits' arrival at the crease. 'C'mon lads, nearly there, they won't even have to reheat the food for us!'

Utrecht and Rotterdam – 19–22 July

The European Championship started a few days later, or didn't. The first Ireland match against the England XI was washed out. A bowl-out took place which England won 2-1. It was to deliver them the title. Next day the 'little team' again saw off the Netherlands, this time in Utrecht. TJ showcased his batting prowess by hitting four sixes in a rain-reduced game. A couple of the blows landed in a thick hedge, the sort of bushy affair that Homer Simpson would walk backwards into, looking to escape scrutiny. That ploy might have occurred to Smits as the Dutch came up ten runs short.

On the train back to Deventer, James Fitzgerald and myself became embroiled in a discussion – it might have been about rugby – that led to me saying something about the rock that he lived on being part of the British Isles. The *Indo* man, the most proud and vehement of nationalists, was so enraged that I could even think this, never mind say it, that he snatched my laptop and ran down a couple of carriages refusing to return it until I retracted. Given his still hotly-disputed history with Callender's computer in Toronto, this was a worry. But not enough of a worry to back down. Finally he called on éminence grise and fellow Dubliner Scotty to adjudicate. 'Well, of course, James,' the old fella began, 'geographically speaking …'

In the third game, Scotland batted, but not very quickly. Ryan Watson propped up the innings with 88 not out, but took far too few risks and it was clear as he walked off, soaking up generous applause for his efforts with a display of false modesty, that 200/6 should not be enough. And it wasn't. This time there was no Gregor Maiden-engineered escape. Almost exactly ten years since my first encounter, and more than seven years after the nightmare in Kuala Lumpur, I witnessed Ireland beating Scotland for the first time. Hallelujah!

In the dressing room, Adi berated his side, quite rightly suggesting that they had made a meal of getting the runs, even with five wickets and three overs to spare. PG cut him short. 'You need to understand the history, Adi, and how important that win was to us.' Like me, the Strabane man had been in KL and East Grinstead.

As expected, Ireland eased past Denmark in the final game, by 109 runs. TJ again showed the other side to his all-round abilities with a hard-hitting 83 off 70 balls in a total of 265/5. Kyle was unbeaten on 64 and his mate Whitey followed up with three wickets. The England amateurs also claimed three wins, though, and lifted the trophy.

Clontarf – 6–8 August

After beating the Netherlands, a draw against Scotland would have taken Ireland into the semi-finals of that first InterContinental Cup, and a tasty little trip to the UAE. The players arrived at Castle Avenue, expecting to find a placid pitch, only to discover a green mamba had been prepared. What the ...? Molins lost the toss, and probably the match with it. Ireland were six down at lunch on the first day, in a game they could not afford to lose. Gillespie battled to 44, Shaukat made 48, but a total of 193 was well short of what they would have hoped.

The ball continued to misbehave during the Scotland reply, Nas took five and Ireland had a first-innings lead of 26. Still the batting conditions didn't ease, and the top order struggled again. This time it was Whitey and TJ who mounted a rearguard, but not for long enough. Ireland all out for 176, Scotland needed 202 to win. The dented but still potent Caledonian curse was no doubt responsible for the clouds then lifting and the pitch easing for the first time in the match. Scotland cruised to 118/2 at stumps on the second day..

Not all the weather gods were on the side of the visitors, though, and it rained until 3.30 on the last day. The draw was again favourite, only for the Clontarf groundsman to enlist volunteers and move heaven and earth to get the game restarted at 5.15. The Scottish third-wicket pair made light work of the remaining runs and the winter trip was off.

Who was that idiot groundsman, you may ask? Surely he had no future in the game? Roughly 14 years later, after a spell with Hampshire at the Ageas Bowl, Karl McDermott was appointed Head Groundsman at Lord's, the Home of Cricket.

Stormont – 29 August

A season that brought victories over Surrey and West Indies could have ended with a second impressive scalp. In a game reduced to 32 overs per side, Bangladesh were set 206 to win and stuttered badly in the final straight, collapsing from 162/2 to 204/8 before creeping over the line with a single from the final ball. Here was another gauge of the progress the squad had made, against the most recent of the full ICC members. It was also a morale boost ahead of the 2005 World Cup qualifiers, which Ireland would host and where they had been placed in the easier of the two groups.

ON THE GLOBAL STAGE
2005–2007

2005

Lord's – 23 April

The World Cup qualifying campaign began months before Ireland hosted their first game. The Hon. Sec. was instrumental in securing a small but significant change in the ICC qualification rules: hopeful players from Associate countries would no longer be required to endure a four-year period in limbo before they could be selected by a Full Member. In effect, subject to other criteria such as residence, a player could now represent Hong Kong or Bermuda on a Sunday and turn out for Australia or West Indies on the Monday. While this applied universally, the obvious beneficiaries were Ireland and Ed Joyce, who had not worn the shamrock since the previous ICC Trophy in Canada, as he pursued his ambition to play Test cricket with England.

At home, and in the weaker of the two groups, alongside Bermuda, Uganda, the United Arab Emirates, the USA and Denmark, from which two teams would automatically qualify, Ireland would have been hot favourites without Ed; with him, it was hard to see how they could come up short. There was still the hurdle of Middlesex agreeing to his release, which they did for the group stage of the tournament, by which time it was hoped Ireland would have already done enough.

Kent were not so cooperative with Nobby. While, officially, the county would not stand in his way, it was made clear that taking time off would not be in his long-term interests. It's a tricky situation with wicketkeepers, as there is only the one gloveman. Kent had genuine aspirations of winning the County Championship and knew that Geraint Jones would likely miss chunks of the season on England duty. If they had to bring in a third keeper, there was no guarantee that Nobby would retain his place in the pecking order. Arm twisted, he opted to remain with his employers and was the only Ireland player missing.

Bangor – 20 June

Adi had five official one-day matches to prepare for the ICC Trophy: early season runs out against Loughborough University, where Dom, PG and Eoin all scored half-centuries; and a strong Warwickshire side; a home defeat by Yorkshire in the C&G Trophy, with PG and Eoin again raising their bats; and a couple of contests against the MCC, which allowed Ireland to gain experience on two grounds where they would play group games.

The first, at Bangor, featured a maiden century for Gillespie who galloped to 102 not out from 47 balls; the middle-order rock somewhat exceeding his strike rate of 75 remit as he soared to three figures with a sixth six off the final ball of the innings. But what was still the fastest century by an Ireland player at the end of this journey was nearly a massive anticlimax.

'The scoreboard was wrong and I genuinely thought we had another over to come,' PG said. 'If that last ball had been better I'd have just pushed it for a single to keep the strike and been left on 97 not out.'

Gary Wilson, who had played for Ireland at every age level from Under-13, made his debut as wicketkeeper, pulling off a stumping and holding four catches. There was no place for the teenager in the ICC Trophy squad of 14, though. In the absence of Nobby, the all-round skills of Brayso would be employed behind the stumps.

Belfast – 1 July

Bermuda were a shadow of the force that had gone so close to qualifying for the World Cup – and probably should have – in 1994, but were still testing first opponents. Molins won the toss and Ireland made a tentative start, relieved briefly by Brayso slog-sweeping into the scorers' booth. The tension was visible as the skipper called for a daft single and was run out. Bray was third out with only 62 on the board in the 15th over. Ed and Eoin then combined in a stand of 170 to put the game out of reach. It was a Middlesex masterclass, with the younger man not at all overshadowed by his partner, who had become the first batsman to 1,000 first-class runs in England that summer. Eoin fell seven runs short of a deserved century, Ed completed his first for Ireland, ironically on the day he qualified by residency to play for England. The relief was palpable around the Stormont ground as Ireland posted 315/8. No way were Bermuda going to get near that and the win was soon confirmed, by 97 runs.

After Ed had collected his man-of-the-match award, Emmet and myself cadged a lift back into town with Fitzy. Marching season had begun and there was some sort of bowler-hatted event planned that evening. Advised to drive the long way around the ring road and come in from the west, Fitzy was a little premature – probably not for the first time – and came off too soon.

Within a mile the kerbstones were red, white and blue, and every other house flew a Union flag. We were in a Saab, with Dublin number plates. 'It would look bad if we turned around and went back,' Fitzy said, smiling. He wound down his window and suggested Emmet did the same. 'We might be able to hear the band.'

Emmet turned to me. 'It's actually so if they shoot at us the bullets pass straight through, without damaging the glass.'

Here we were, seven years after the Good Friday Agreement, when all this was supposed to have been put to bed – or at least sent upstairs to get into its pyjamas. The 'traditions' would continue for years yet, of course. Who was to say otherwise? Wasn't it every man's right to celebrate ancient battles and sing ditties about wading in the blood of people from a neighbouring community?

If I'd been born in this part of town, would I have been any different? I'd like to think so, but how do you judge something like that when you haven't grown up with it literally being drummed into you from such an early age? Without any reference, I had no idea how much danger we were in. If any. Fitzy didn't seem at all worried but Emmet was quieter than usual. What I do know is that it was a great relief to safely reach the Europa – the most bombed hotel in the world.

Comber – 2 July

The Green was the setting for Ireland's next game, against Uganda, a charming little ground just outside Belfast, and home to North Down. It seemed that the clubs hosting matches were in some sort of hospitality contest, the tournament was so well run. The one thing no one could control, of course, was the weather, and a wind whipped across the outfield and straight into our media tent, which was on a grass bank on the opposite side to the pavilion.

Whitey top-scored with 45 in a total of 231/8 as Ireland extracted what they could from a tricky pitch that even Ed found hard work. It didn't look much of a score, but there was never any hope of the group minnows bettering it. I was telling RTE listeners this when a particularly strong gust lifted our tent from its moorings and left me sitting alone and bemused at my bench as colleagues chased after it.

In the middle, the Uganda batsmen were blown away by Paul Mooney who delivered four maidens and returned figures of 3/10 before a lively last-wicket stand of 48, featuring six massive sixes. The game's only half-century, from Frank Nsubuga, did at least get the East Africans into three figures, from the embarrassment of 56/9.

Teams like Uganda intrigue me. Keen, hungry young athletes, who field superbly. You have to wonder whether the ICC shouldn't be investing more in nurturing and developing them, instead of repeating costly and futile attempts to find a place for the United States on the global stage, and now China, for goodness sake. As if to underline the misplaced priorities, Uganda beat the USA two days later. If only cricket were a sport and not a business, eh?

Belfast – 4 July

Back to Stormont for what turned out to be the key match of the group. I'd spent the day off introducing Ruud

Onstein to the delights of a Sunday roast in one of the snug bars of The Crown, across the road from the Europa, and much later on stumbled across the 'Ten o'clock Club', an exclusive gathering of Ed, TJ and Paul Mooney, plus occasional guests, who had taken to meeting downstairs in the team hotel each evening for a pint of cider and a ciggie. It was a strange arrangement, given there was no obvious bond between the three, and not least because only Mooners was a regular smoker.

It was the Ten o'clock Club who featured prominently in a two-wicket victory over the UAE that opened the door to World Cup qualification. Ireland were floundering on 23/4, with their target of 231 to win barely visible in the distance, when TJ joined Ed. The fifth-wicket pair went about their work with cold-eyed determination; arguably it was the best innings either played for Ireland. A stand of 122 ended when TJ was bowled behind his legs for 67 from 68 balls, including a six. There was no chance Ed was going to register in the maximums column – he wasn't hitting anything in the air. The ask was comfortably less than a run a ball, but PG ran himself out for one and after nudging their way to double figures both Whitey and Kyle followed him. Ireland needed 19 from four overs when Mooners strode out at No.10.

Together the Ten o'clock Club duo steadily reduced the requirement until it was five from the final over, and then a single from the last two balls. Mooners on strike. 'You've got to love the way Ed thinks,' he said. 'He told me "Just get something on it and run. Whatever happens I'll already be alongside you and there to face the last ball, even if you're run out."' A push to point and the win was secured. Ed was 115 not out from 134 balls and again man of the match.

Amid the post-match celebrations, Brayso was bemoaning his luck. 'Did you see the catch I got out to, mate? Unbelievable!' To be fair, it was: a one-handed screamer in the covers. But then again …

'How many did Ed hit in the air?'

'Yeah, all right …'

Bangor – 7 July

The day after London was awarded the 2012 Olympic Games, Ireland were primed to claim their place on the global stage. The fourth group match against the USA at Waringstown had been abandoned earlier in the week, without a ball bowled, meaning automatic qualification for the World Cup would be assured if the hosts avoided a heavy defeat by Denmark.

The venue was Upritchard Park, the home of Bangor. Ireland batted on a grey, miserable morning, and as they were making 222 all out news started filtering through of the 7/7 bombings in London. An atrocity like that puts a game of cricket and a lot else into perspective. How many lives lost? More than 50?

Denmark needed to win in 29.2 overs to go above Ireland on run-rate, but made no effort to go for it. The crowd were informed at the end of 30 overs that Ireland had qualified. There was no more than a ripple of applause, and celebrations were muted after a victory by 73 runs. Dom, who had given the back end of the innings impetus with 50 from 37 balls, pipped his brother, who also made a half-century, to what was becoming the Joyce-of-the-Match award.

Ireland had topped the group and were going to the World Cup, but a lot of good, decent people in London would never know that. It should have been a wonderful day; it was a horrible day.

Clontarf – 13 July

Ed and I had both missed the four-wicket semi-final victory over Canada two days later: he was required by Middlesex, I also had business in London. We returned for the final against Scotland, who had beaten Bermuda in the other semi. All four sides would be going to the World Cup, along with the Netherlands who easily saw off the UAE in the fifth-place decider.

Molins was injured in training and missed the final; Kyle captained, won the toss and decided to bowl. Scotland employed Paul Hoffmann as a pinch-hitter, a tactic that had worked well for them. Mooners opened the bowling with a slower ball, which made me chuckle. Hoffmann slogged it anyway. He only hit four fours but set the tempo for a massive score; Watson made 94, Dougie Brown blasted 59 and there was little for the large crowd to cheer as Scotland powered to 324/8.

Ireland lost a couple of early wickets before a stand of 137 between Brayso and Ed briefly promised a contest. The Aussie made 70, Ed added an 84 to his two centuries and half-century – another run would have given him a tournament average of 100 – but the asking rate was always just a couple of big overs out of reach and the margin of defeat would have been many more than 47 but for an unbeaten last-wicket partnership of 55. Cookie finished 34 not out in what would be his last match for Ireland.

The draw for the World Cup had been made and the sides had gone into the final knowing what was at stake. Scotland's victory earned them a trip to St Kitts for games against Australia, South Africa and the Netherlands. Ireland's loss meant they would be based in Jamaica, in a group with West Indies, Pakistan and Zimbabwe. A silver lining, maybe? I remember thinking 'You never know ...'

It had been a splendid couple of weeks, and a superbly run tournament thanks in no small part to the organisational skills of Warren Deutrom, an Englishman working for the ICC in Dubai. It wouldn't be the last he saw of Ireland.

Aberdeen – 13–15 August

The Ashes series was dominating the summer like no other since 1981. Australia had won the first Test at Lord's easily enough, but there was a new spirit and steel about England that shone through in a thrilling two-run win at Edgbaston that levelled the series. The third Test at Old Trafford had been underway a couple of days, and was shaping to be another belter, when I caught a flight to Scotland for the first match of the second InterContinental Cup, against the holders.

There was no way I could travel on the morning of the match and arrive for the scheduled start, but overnight rain fortunately meant I didn't miss a ball of a game that was every bit as close and competitive as anything going on south of the border. Ireland, missing Ed, Eoin and Whitey who were all with their counties, chose to bat. Molins, back as skipper, hung his timber out third ball and Botha went in the second over. The pitch was lively. Dom battled two hours for 31 and Thompson top-scored with 35 in a total of 172.

Also without TJ, who couldn't get off work, Ireland laboured for breakthroughs. Scotland gained a lead of 62 which looked significant, although Botha made a useful 46 second time around and Dom again applied himself to the task with 61, the second-highest score of the match. Just as in the third Test, time was running out to force a result on the final afternoon before a clatter of late wickets left Scotland a target of 135 from 39 overs. Scoobs rocked the hosts with a superb burst of 4/17, Mooners kept the other end quiet, Botha and Kyle weighed in with two wickets each. Meanwhile Michael Clarke had finally been dismissed at Old Trafford.

It was devilishly difficult trying to stay across both matches, check Betfair by piggy-backing on the groundsman's WiFi, write the beginnings of a match report, and keep an eye on the clock with my flight home far too close to stumps for comfort. Players don't know what pressure is, sometimes.

Scotland's last pair were at the crease; as were Australia's down the road. Nineteen to win from two overs. Three came from as many balls, then Craig Wright, batting with a broken finger, smashed McCallan back over his head for consecutive sixes. My taxi had arrived; it looked like Kyle's had too, but the last ball of the over was driven back to him, the non-striker had committed himself to the single and a simple run out saw Ireland home by three runs. Phew!

An Ireland win on Scottish soil was a rare thing – the previous occurring in 1974 when the now team manager had taken a career-best 7/40. Not that Roy Torrens had ever mentioned it more than a couple of times. My female taxi driver was keen to talk about the other game that had just ended, with the Australian last-wicket pair holding out for a draw. 'It was great,' she gushed. 'I did nae have a clue what was going on – but it was great!'

Ten days later, a badly rain-affected draw with the Netherlands at Stormont, where Bray made 135 in the only completed innings, meant that a year after they should have been going to the finals, this time Ireland were off to Namibia. Where? Southwest Africa. Sparsely populated, former German colony. Mostly Kalahari Desert, apparently. It sounded a decent little trip.

Gatwick – 20 October

A touring party of 30, consisting of 13 players, coach, physio, ICU officials, Scotty, a few supporters and two journalists – myself and Fitzy – set out for Namibia, but not all at the same time. The ICU had booked the northern players on a budget airline for the first leg of the journey and, as the rest of us checked in for a ten-hour flight south, news came through that they were delayed in Belfast. Various updates on progress, or lack of it, reached us as our departure time drew closer.

Wee John, team manager for the trip, explained the situation to Air Namibia, but his charm for once failed with the young manager. I tried flattery, and a bit of ego stoking. 'Sir, you know you have the power to delay the aeroplane. The people of Ireland would see it as a very fine gesture from the people of Namibia.' He went away and came back a couple of minutes later. 'We can wait 45 minutes, not two hours.'

It wasn't enough. The Belfast flight wasn't so much delayed as cancelled and the Gatwick Five, as they became known, were rebooked onto a much later plane that took off at roughly the same time as Air Namibia. The evening didn't get any better for Kyle, Whitey, PG, physio Iain Knox and the teenager Thompson because all the local hotels were full.

Given the alternative of a trip into central London, the quintet settled down for the night on the floor of the airport. The next day they had to complete their journey via Frankfurt, finally arriving at the Windhoek Country Club, to a heroes' welcome, on the eve of the IC Cup semi-final against the UAE.

While the squad was based a little way out of town, the rest of us were housed in the Kalahari Sands, an excellent hotel with a casino attached. Stan Mitchell, the President of the ICU, and his wife Eve, were staying there, with John and Nan Caldwell, Arthur Vincent and his missus, and the North County Four, an intrepid travelling gang of middle-aged blokes from Fingal: Derek Plant, Jim Casey and Ivan Harper led by David O'Connor, who many years later would become one of Stan's successors. Evenings were not dull.

Windhoek – 23–25 October

Although still spring, the Wanderers pitch was in excellent condition for the first three-day game. Excellent that is, if you were a batsman. 'Good pitch? Good for who?' as Gus Fraser is fond of saying. Botha had a bad toe and Whitey's night on the floor at Gatwick had given him a cold, so the team picked itself. Ireland also had a new captain; TJ had now permanently replaced Molins, who wasn't in the squad. The big Aussie won the toss and batted.

Dom, Brayso and Eoin all got starts, but only Moggie went on to get a century, going to three figures with a six and hitting 18 fours as well in top-quality 151. Ireland had a maximum of 90 overs to face, but declared a couple early on 350/7 to prevent the UAE, who used nine bowlers, picking up any further bonus points. Mooners took the

OUT IN AFRICA: The 1994 ICC Trophy squad relax after a training session in Nairobi, with Alan Lewis in a sleeveless sweater and a kneeling Dermott Monteith to the far right. Photo: Paul McCrum

LOVELY BUBBLY: Lewis and Decker Curry crack open the champagne after beating Middlesex to record Ireland's first competitive victory over a county side. Photo: Inpho

HONOURABLE COMPANY: *The two great administrators of the Irish Cricket Union, John Wright, left, and Derek Scott, no doubt quizzing Paul McCrum on his missing tie. Photo: Paul McCrum*

ON THE RIGHT TRACK: *Mike Hendrick, left, is credited with putting the coaching structures in place that enabled Adi Birrell to steam ahead during his time in charge. Photo: Ian Johnston*

FIRST DAY AT SCHOOL: *Future dual internationals Boyd Rankin, left, and Eoin Morgan made their Ireland debuts in the same game, at Eton College. Photo: Ian Johnston*

ON PARADE: *The North County Four stand watch over James Fitzgerald, Arthur Vincent, Stan and Eve Mitchell, Scotty and the author at the Wanderers in Windhoek. Photo: David O'Connor*

OFF AND RUNNING: *Kevin O'Brien hugs bowler Andy White as Ireland snatch a stunning tie against Zimbabwe on their World Cup debut in Jamaica. Photo: Barry Chambers*

SPIN TWINS: *Practical jokers Kyle McCallan, left, and White had the tables turned on them in Guyana when Christopher Martin-Jenkins failed to show up for lunch. Photo: Barry Chambers*

SUPPORT STAFF: (clockwise from top left) Assistant coaches 'Bobby' Rao and Matt Dwyer, cheeky physio Iain Knox and scorer Stella Downes.
Photos: Paul McCrum/Barry Chambers

LORDING IT: A trio of great Irish left-handers, one self-proclaimed, outside the Grace Gates. Barry Chambers, between Morgan and Ed Joyce, could bowl a bit too, apparently. Photo: Barry Chambers

IN THE PINK: Brother Nobby looks on admiringly as Kevin O'Brien, with dyed hair, reflects on his match-winning World Cup century against England in Bangalore. Photo: Barry Chambers

FOREIGN LEGION: (clockwise from the top left) South African Andre Botha, and the Aussie trio of Jeremy Bray, Alex Cusack and Dave Langford-Smith. Photos: Barry Chambers

A SIX AND A FOUR: Tim Murtagh, right, explains to George Dockrell that it was never in doubt, after his final over boundaries deliver a one-wicket win against Scotland. Photo: Barry Chambers

PASSION PLAY: John Mooney celebrates one of the ten wickets that earned him the man-of-the-match award in the 2013 InterContinental Cup Final. Photo: Barry Chambers

new ball and claimed wickets with successive deliveries in his first over, including the dangerous Arshad Ali. Four wickets fell on the first evening, then TJ ripped through the tail to return figures of 5/33. The UAE were bowled out for 189 and a place in the final against Kenya was all but ensured.

The Ireland second innings featured a record second-wicket stand of 304 between Brayso and Nobby that, by coincidence, was bettered by Ed and Porty at the same ground, on its tenth anniversary. Bray got to within ten runs of becoming the first Ireland player to make a double century, while Nobby made his international best of 176. TJ declared on 444/4, setting a theoretical 606 to win in two sessions. It might as well have been 6,006. A dogged ninth-wicket partnership earned the UAE a draw, if nothing else.

The result was celebrated in Joe's Beerhouse, a Windhoek institution as much as a restaurant; a sprawling mass of annexes, alcoves and additions that has grown in size with its popularity. Despite its name it is better known for a mind-boggling variety of steaks. Except for Scotty, possibly all 30 were there, and the best of nights was had. My choice of meat was springbok, simply to see what it tasted like, but I should have gone with a more traditional steak; the T-bones looked awesome. Alcohol was consumed, and there was singing.

David O'Connor found a guitar and launched into a great rendition of 'Can you sing like Bob Dylan?' while Fitzy took his turn with a traditional refrain, no doubt complaining about what bastards the English are, especially those who claim that Ireland is part of the British Isles. Geographically speaking.

Windhoek – 26 October

There was just the one day off between matches, which was still just about time enough to explore Windhoek. It isn't the biggest capital city; more a country town. But what a nice spot, with an easy-going pace of life and plenty of green spaces. Good food, too, although probably not the best for vegetarians. It wasn't only Joe's that was meat heavy. I tried some crocodile one evening, which was a first. And probably a last.

The hospitality girls at the Kalahari Sands reminded me of the 680 hotel in Nairobi, and were similarly happy to have a natter in exchange for a glass of Windhoek beer. One snippet I gleaned was that the African population of Namibia consisted of four main tribes, with the tribe known to be best endowed forming the government. I naturally assumed this meant best endowed in terms of intellect, diplomacy and organisational skills.

The girls were just about the only similarity with Nairobi, though. Windhoek worked. The roads lacked potholes, for a start, there was internet, the pavements weren't crowded and there were few obvious signs of poverty. It was the sort of place I could happily have lived if it weren't so remote from everywhere. Perhaps because of its isolation, the locals were friendly and very accommodating towards visitors, especially Laurie Pieters, a canny spin bowler in his day, who now ran Cricket Namibia as well as running us all over town, and Jeff Luck, their best umpire.

I loved the place; I was even getting to like Scotty. There was plenty about the prickly old sod that rubbed people up the wrong way, but he was an enthusiast, a lover of the game who had an extraordinary knowledge of the history of cricket on his island. He was also deeply religious, a devout Roman Catholic, and I loved the way he would refer to the Pope as 'he', as if it were the same person, as he related different episodes from the church's long history. I'd ask the odd question then listen and learn, once during a memorable lunch, but more often in his eyrie next to sightscreen. The Wanderers had a watchtower at one end which he somehow managed to climb into in his trench coat via a vertical metal ladder that, with the advantage of nearly three decades, was a challenge for me.

Windhoek – 27 October

A three-day final on the flattest of pitches was likely to be won by the team batting first, such was the complicated system of points for runs and wickets, and TJ had to break the news that he had lost the toss and Ireland were fielding. The skipper's mood was not improved a couple of overs before lunch when, attempting to hold a fierce drive at cover, he fractured the ring finger on his bowling hand. Despite pumping the crooked digit full of anaesthetic, TJ was only able to send down two more overs in the match. In his absence, Steve Tikolo and Hitesh Modi added 277 for the fourth wicket, a record against Ireland.

Each side was restricted to a maximum of 90 overs in their first innings and Kenya just crept past 400, losing Modi for 106 at the last knockings. Tikolo was unbeaten on 177, a superb innings albeit scored on a road. Such a shame his talents were never seen in a Test match.

Windhoek – 28 October

It's been written that what happened on the second day is part of Irish cricketing folklore. There didn't look much prospect of impending folklore at the start of play, though, or anything else for that matter other than loads of runs, as the Ireland top order filled their boots, just as the Kenyans had. The match was headed for a predictable draw well before its halfway point and if Scotty was enjoying it from his watchtower – a timed match with a predictable outcome – then the rest of us were not. I was thinking, 'I can't be sitting through another two days of this.'

Something had to give – but what? During a mid-morning chat in the scorers' area, a thatched structure that was both covered and open to the elements, Wee John informed us that after winning the IC Cup, Kenya were planning to press the ICC to elevate them to Test match status. It was, after all, only two years since the East Africans had reached the semi-finals of the World Cup. His words tinkled a bell and an idea started to take shape.

Towards the end of the lunch interval, I found the skipper and said: 'You're going to have to declare behind here.'

'Why would I want to do that, DT?'

'Well, you're not going to win this the way things are going ...'

'Agreed. But how is declaring behind going to help?'

'Throw down a challenge. Try to get them to set you a run chase on the final afternoon – no matter how difficult – it's the only way you have a chance of winning.'

'Why would they want to do that? Why would they even give us a sniff?'

'Because Kenya need to show the ICC that they're ready for Test cricket. What's it going to look like if they're frightened of taking on Ireland? Tell them: "You think you're ready to play Australia and South Africa – but you're scared to have a game of cricket with Ireland?" You might have to get into their ears a bit: explain that the ICC aren't going to be impressed.'

TJ grinned: 'I think we can do that alright!'

He fairly charged around the boundary to speak to the coach and returned 15 minutes later with another big grin. 'Operation Townsend is underway!'

As the big man strode off again, Arthur Vincent approached waving his phone. 'Just had a text from Lewie asking how we win this from here?'

'Tell him to watch.'

My calculation would have been to pull out 125 behind, leave a big gap, certainly no fewer than 100. I began to wonder whether the skipper hadn't just been humouring me when Nobby went to his second century of the week and those two targets came and went.

TJ waited until Botha skied one and was out for 78 before clapping his hands. Ireland were on 313/4 – 88 runs behind – and such was the element of surprise that the Kenyan team and the umpires remained on the field for several minutes. Nobby walked off with Boatsie as the 12th man brought out drinks. It was comical. The confusion was compounded by one of the Kenyan openers being off the field having a rest at the time of the declaration and therefore unable to open. Ireland were expected to bat 90 overs; they had declared after 78.5.

The African side lost three wickets that evening and were in such mental disarray that Tikolo appealed against the light in bright sunshine, claiming the sun was too low in the sky. The umpires upheld it and Kenya closed on 104/3, leading by 192.

Windhoek – 29 October

From being overwhelming favourites at the end of the first day, Kenya turned up not knowing whether to stick or twist. Did they adhere to the original plan and block it out for a day, or should they meet the challenge and set a target? If so, what target? A sporting team is at its most vulnerable when it doesn't have a clear strategy and perhaps it was no surprise that the World Cup semi-finalists fell between the two stools.

By contrast, Ireland were crystal clear in their objectives: laying down the challenge on one hand, with Nobby particularly vocal, but also looking to take wickets. Scoobs struck a crucial early blow when he had Modi caught behind and, with the various permutations buzzing around his brain, Tikolo was disorientated to the point of being out 'hit wicket' – although it went in the book as 'bowled McCallan'. With their champion gone, Kenya collapsed from 150/5 to 156 all out. Kyle reported later that there had been 'just enough' for him in the pitch, but nothing that would explain four wickets for five runs in 28 balls.

Never mind thoughts of declarations and a run chase, Ireland now needed 245 to win, had 80 overs to get them and the result was never in doubt once Dom and Brayso had settled nerves with an opening stand of 83. Tikolo dominated the bowling; over after over – desperately trying to take wickets with sheer force of personality, while all the time – whether he realised it or not – seeing his last hope of becoming a Test cricketer ebbing away.

Like Hendo, coach Adi would pass time walking around the boundary, although he was more of a stroller than a loper and, as a keen bird watcher, would scan the skies for avian activity while missing nothing in the middle.

He completed a good few laps that afternoon and didn't look confident until well after tea when Botha and White were in the final straight of a six-wicket win.

Meanwhile, his opposite number Mudassar Nazar, the former Pakistan all-rounder, paced around muttering, 'Unbelievable declaration! Unbelievable!' It was an unbelievable declaration. The genius, of course, was not so much the idea itself, or the timing of its implementation, but that an international captain would trouble himself to listen to a journalist, never mind act upon his suggestion.

But that was TJ for you. It's also the mark of the man that not once did he try to take the credit – even name-checking me in his book two years later. During the post-match celebrations at the Wanderers, he put an arm around my shoulder and said: 'I'm always going to love you for that, big fella!'

His appointment as captain had been vindicated. It hadn't been without controversy: not only was he not Irish, but he was replacing a friend in Jason Molins who had done little wrong in the role and had helped TJ settle in his adopted country. Relationships were strained, yet in hindsight it was another inevitable step on the road from the amateur past to the professional future.

Several years later I bumped into Adi in an airport lounge, on my way back to Windhoek as it happened, and after he had kindly introduced me to a couple of Cricket South African colleagues as 'the man who once won me a very important game' we reminisced for a while. 'If I have one regret, it's the way the whole Jason/captaincy thing was handled,' he said. 'I think we're OK now, but that episode did rankle with me for a long time. It should have been done differently.'

There was no trophy for the IC Cup champions, but Laurie Pieters did present all of us, including the press, with a commemorative bottle of wine. The celebrations started in the team hotel; alcohol was consumed and a sing-song ensued. Unfortunately, David O'Connor was not there to lead the party with his guitar, the North County Four having headed for home a day early, but there were a few good choruses of 'A-Root-Chy-Cha', which had become the soundtrack for the trip.

Kyle approached me grinning, 'I hear we have to call you Brearley now?' A good few years later, well after the Pakistan game, he and Whitey told me that final in Windhoek was still the best game of cricket either had played.

Funny thing, fate. I've never really bought into that 'everything happens for a reason' stuff, but there are moments and events that do change the course of the future, and there were a couple in 2005. What if Ireland had won the ICC Trophy and found themselves in the same World Cup group as Australia and South Africa? What if Wee John hadn't mentioned Kenya's intended application for Test status and TJ hadn't listened to the reporter?

Kenya never recovered from that defeat. It began a slide that saw the World Cup semi-finalists slip way down the rankings, and they were losing to Italy and Uganda by the end of 2019. With a nod to Spike Milligan, it was tempting to call this part of the book *Kenya: My part in their Downfall*.

2006

Bristol – 30 April

Windhoek seemed a very long way away when the journey resumed at a chilly Clontarf in the C&G Trophy, with nine InterContinental Cup winners on show, plus two debutants. The first was Dave Langford-Smith, an Australian-born swing bowler known as Lanky, who began his Ireland career with a near-perfect first over of deliveries that shaped away beautifully. Unfortunately what followed was not treated with quite the same respect as Hampshire galloped to an eight-wicket win, with plenty to spare.

The other new face was Saqlain Mushtaq. The Pakistan off-spinner had been hired for the one-day games, along with countryman Shahid Afridi, who took his bow the next week in Bristol. Some bow it was, too. Best known for his hitting, Afridi was also a purveyor of medium-pace leg-breaks which, if he found his rhythm and radar, could be unplayable. He found both at Nevil Road, claiming 3/4 from eight overs, with wides accounting for two of those. Kyle took a similarly impressive 3/5 at the other end as Gloucestershire collapsed from 124/4 to 146 all out and Ireland had their third county scalp by a margin of 47 runs. The strains of 'Ireland's Call', the team song, rang out across the ground with a confident gusto.

The following day, O'Fridi, as he was nicknamed during his six games, scored a half-century in Cardiff as Ireland fell 15 runs short of a Glamorgan total of 250/9. Langford-Smith was caught on the boundary looking for a six that would have left ten needed off nine balls. Afridi did not have the same influence again and Ireland lost all but one of their remaining games, with Surrey's visit to Stormont abandoned, while Saqlain was not the influence he might have been later in the summer and took only four wickets in eight appearances.

We had strict instructions that Afridi, who attracted a throng of adoring fans wherever he played, would not be talking to the press under any circumstances. I bumped into him on the balcony at Chelmsford after Alastair Cook had celebrated his first home Test call-up with a match-winning 91 not out. 'Mr Afridi, pleased to meet you. Are you enjoying your time with Ireland?'

'Yes, I like playing here very much.'

'Can we have a quick chat?'

'Sure, no problem.'

With respect to the ICU, I kept it simple. In retrospect I should have asked him what he thought of Ireland's chances against Pakistan at next year's World Cup?

The Boys in Green ran into familiar faces at Lord's and Tunbridge Wells; Ed scored 95 for Middlesex and sledged brother Dom, while the chirpy Kent wicketkeeper took great delight in stumping Eoin. The Ireland campaign could not be labelled a success, but progress was being made, and caps were awarded to a couple of promising youngsters, William Porterfield and Kevin O'Brien, the younger brother of Nobby.

Belfast – 13 June

A record crowd for a cricket match in Ireland, estimated at around 7,000, packed into Stormont for the historic first ODI against England. Most had been attracted by the chance to watch the InterContinental Cup champions, of course, and just a few had come to see the 2005 Ashes winners as well. Joking aside, it was always a teaser in Belfast knowing which team would be best supported by the locals, as Ireland were associated with the tricolour and that lot down the road in Dublin. It was even more confusing on this occasion as one of the Pope's lot appeared to be opening the batting for Her Majesty's brave boys –

Ed being one of five players who had not featured in the iconic series against Australia the previous summer. Kevin Pietersen and Freddie Flintoff were the most notable of the absentees.

In his usually measured match notes, Scotty described it as 'in the first five, and perhaps even at the pinnacle' of Ireland's best days of cricket. He must have meant the occasion itself because the hosts were never in with a sniff once Marcus Trescothick and Ian Bell had added 142 for the fourth wicket, the former making a century. A total of 301/7 would have been more but for a tidy five overs from Paul Mooney; his brother John took three wickets but leaked 79 runs.

Botha scored a half-century on his 50th appearance, but when he was sixth out another 167 were still needed from 21 overs. Whitey, O'Brien the younger and Johnboy wagged the tail yet England were able to employ Bell's rarely seen dobbers for five overs and still ease home by 38 runs. That Scotty attributed such a high ranking to Ireland's day was more an indication of how low expectations still were. Had he forgotten that second victory over West Indies, the Zimbabwe canter, even the win at Bristol only six weeks previously?

Ayr – 5 August

After ten years and a couple of very near misses, Ireland regained the European title with three victories, plus an abandonment against the Netherlands – a game they were winning easily. In the absence of the England XI, it wasn't the toughest of tournaments.

A gentle opener against Denmark was chalked off by 99 runs, but the batting stalled the following day against the hosts and the board showed 164/7 with only ten overs left when McCallan walked out to join Eoin, who had flown up to join the squad in the early hours for the only game his county commitments allowed. Still a month away from his 20th birthday, the Middlesex youngster batted with calm assurance while his eighth-wicket partner found 46 from 35 balls to take the game away from Scotland.

Eoin's innings was beautifully paced on a tricky pitch and seemed certain to deliver him a first Ireland century on his ODI debut, before Kyle panicked at the start of the final over and ran him out for 99. The nature of the dismissal and its proximity to the milestone, no doubt allied to such an early start, saw the teenager unable to contain his disappointment as far as the dressing room and he exploded with verbal fury a few yards short of that sanctuary. Surprising, perhaps, given his renowned cool head, but understandable.

The Ireland total of 240/8 proved 85 too good for Scotland and after Eoin had flown off with both the man of the match award and a reprimand from the match referee, I heard for the first time about the career plan he had mapped out in his early teens, containing goals to achieve by a certain age with Ireland, Middlesex and England, and how he was already ahead of schedule.

Big Boyd was not making the same smooth progress, but a scary spell at Hamilton Crescent two days later helped to dismiss Italy for 79, and set up a seven-wicket victory. Running down the slope, Rankin found pace and bounce that the small Italian batsmen had no idea how to combat. It was like an overenthusiastic dad bowling to eight-year-olds, and an example of what the Bready man could offer when he found the right line and length. Still wayward and unpredictable, he had been working with Hendo, who was a firm fan of his natural ability. 'I can teach him to bowl,' he said. 'I can't teach him to be six foot nine!'

Back to Ayr for the final match, where half-centuries from Botha, Nobby and Kyle took Ireland to 274, a total that looked all the more imposing when Lanky took wickets with successive balls and then another and the Netherlands slipped to 47/5. A young Ryan ten Doeschate led something of a fightback before rain arrived at the end of the 19th over. If Ireland had been able to bowl another six balls, D/L would have awarded them a comfortable win.

As we waited for the rain to stop, I upset the Dutch scorer, a bearded Australian, who kept updating us with the latest from the second division of the championship. 'France have lost another wicket!' 'Greece are now 49/6', or whatever. Maybe it was the dismal weather, maybe it was the frustration of being denied a clean sweep, but my patience ran out.

'Nobody cares, Rod!' It was a bit harsh – and obviously he cared – but it was only what everyone else was thinking.

Ireland did complete a different and rather special clean sweep that summer: European champions at Under-23, Under-19, Under-17, Under-15 and Under-13, as well as senior level.

Lord's – 15 August

The MCC had been playing Ireland at Lord's since 1858, when 120 was enough for the visitors to secure an innings and ten-run victory, but this was the last time the teams would meet on the famous old sward. Porterfield, a former MCC Young Cricketer, chose the occasion to score his first century for Ireland, and Kenny Carroll, a postman who was in Birrell's mind for a place in the World Cup squad, made 90 in an imposing total of 341/4 from 50 overs.

I'd left the Media Centre to sit in the Edrich Stand during the Ireland assault, just a few feet away from a familiar figure at third man. 'Morning, DT!'

'Thought you'd retired, Gatt?'

The last time I'd seen the former England skipper in his whites was eight years ago when he had made his way up those pavilion steps for what we assumed was the final time: lbw to Dominic Cork for 62, playing for Middlesex. Now, here he was in his 50th year, turning out for the famous old club that would bestow its presidency on him in 2013.

Turning out rather well, to be fair. I knew he was still playing in Enfield on the ground that was almost his back garden, but did not expect him to be in the sort of nick to make 90 off 81 balls against a six-man attack who would all be going to the World Cup. A diving catch by Carroll denied the old chap a nostalgic century and, after he trudged off for perhaps the last time, again, the MCC folded to a 97-run defeat.

It's interesting how some players can give up, while others battle on, their love of the game raging against the advancing years. Boycott, who had netted every day of his adult life, refused to lift a bat again when finally sacked by Yorkshire, Nasser signed off with a Test century and made straight for the commentary box, yet Alastair Cook and Paul Collingwood were happy to return to their counties after long international careers and there was Gatt still paying his subs to a north London club side.

Ireland has its own veteran survivors, too. Fast forward to the end of this journey and Decker was still plying his trade in the north-west well into his sixth decade, Lewie hadn't definitely hung up his boots while Conor Hoey, a team-mate of both at the ICC Trophy in 1994, could lay claim to still being the best leg-spinner on the island. Me? Only played the once since 1991, but I haven't retired either.

Aberdeen – 17–20 August

Almost a year to the day after the three-run thriller, I found myself back at Mannofield for another InterContinental Cup match. The third edition of the first-class competition was the first to feature four-day games and Ireland had made a solid start to the defence of their title with a five-wicket victory over Namibia at Castle Avenue in May. Scotland would be a tougher proposition, in every way.

The home side were asked to bat by TJ who made the initial breakthrough while Lanky did further damage with three wickets, including the former England internationals Dougie Brown and Gavin Hamilton. Scotland rallied from 161/7 to make 265, a decent score on a cabbage patch of a pitch. Lanky claimed 5/65 – his maiden Michelle.

The reply started well then fell away on the second afternoon, with the last eight wickets falling for 45 to give Scotland a lead of 91 and the first-innings points. The visitors were far from beaten, though. TJ and Lanky tore in under leaden skies and suddenly at 24/4 the game was back in the balance. The skipper was convinced he had a fifth wicket, but a nick behind wasn't given. Tempers flared and bad language may have been used before poor light brought an early close.

If the atmosphere had been raw then, it was worse the following morning when water was discovered to have seeped under the covers overnight; a lot of water, causing a lengthy delay, which soon became an abandonment. Nobby was livid and questioned groundsman Ken McCurdy's competence in a vicious verbal assault that earned him a one-match ban.

Small in stature, maybe, but Nobby never shied away from a confrontation. There is a story of him, as a 13-year-old, furiously riding his little green bike 'Billy' down to Ringsend Park in Dublin to sort out three much bigger boys who had sent Kevin home in tears.

'I found them sitting on a wall. They were about 15 – and I was about three feet tall. I gave them a few digs and got a few digs back and they found out that a lad from the posh suburb of Sandymount could look after himself.'

It's just about the perfect metaphor for what followed in his cricket career, the wee scrapper taking on all-comers: West Indian legends, Scottish groundsman and egotistical England batsmen alike.

In defence of the groundsman, at the height of the storm, rivulets had flowed from the top side of the ground that were irresistible given the protective equipment at his disposal. The incident led to the Aberdeenshire club installing a new drainage system that winter, specially designed to protect the high end of the square from any such repeat damage. Fair play to McCurdy who quickly named it 'Nobby's Drain'.

Dublin – 25 August

Adi Birrell was the first of the 16 coaches to name a squad for the World Cup, enabling those with full-time jobs to arrange time off work. There were few surprises. TJ was captain, of course, and one of four players born overseas, along with Brayso, Botha and Langford-Smith.

The O'Brien and Mooney brothers provided more than a quarter of the 15-man squad. The experience of Kyle, PG and Whitey assured their inclusion, as did the form of youngsters Porterfield and Eoin. Big Boyd was perhaps a gamble, but his raw pace and bounce offered something different and there was still time to work on his rough edges. Kenny Carroll was almost certainly the 15th and final name chosen. Jason Molins was one of five named reserves.

2007

Eastern Cape – January

The World Cup squad flew down to South Africa for a three-week training camp that would prove a classic of team bonding. The coach wanted to show the team his home terrain, where he had come from and the influences that had made him who he was. To train in 'all the places I used to train', to run up and down the same sand dunes, and go skinny-dipping in Bushmans River on the Amakhala Game Reserve, east of Port Elizabeth, where his cousin owned a property.

The party moved to Kenton-on-Sea for the second week. Adi's mum and sister had bungalows there and fielding sessions were organised on the community tennis courts. Iain Knox, the bubbly physio, was in charge of fitness and doubled up as social secretary. No one better at the latter. Again, work was done in the dunes, games were played at Salem CC and there were more practice sessions at St Andrew's College in Grahamstown, the coach's old school where his father taught. Golf was on the itinerary too, although the heat was stifling.

Hendo was hired on a short-term contract and joined the squad when they moved into Port Elizabeth. More time was now spent in the nets and the middle, including a final day-night match against a strong local side at St George's Park. With the World Cricket League to follow in Kenya and an InterContinental Cup match, too, before the World Cup, Roy Torrens knew he needed to be in better shape if his team management duties weren't to get the better of him. The big man undertook a walking regime and shed kilos at a rate he usually reserved for draining glasses of Famous Grouse.

The benefits of the trip were not immediately obvious, and there were rumblings within the ICU about the cost of these 'game trips and golf outings'. Former international Ian Johnston, a volunteer at the camp, stood up at the AGM and said that he had never seen such meticulous preparation and the effort from everyone was outstanding. 'We'll never be able to repay Eastern Province Cricket for what they did for us,' he said.

Nairobi – 30 January

Thirteen years had changed Nairobi, and not in a good way. The streets were far busier, much poorer and didn't feel safe, except those close to the Hilton, where we were staying. Security everywhere. Mirrors to check under cars entering the hotel forecourt. Depressing. The only thing that hadn't changed were the roads, with the same potholes, only deeper, and the big mad roundabout, on the way to the airport, bigger and madder. Not so much welcome back as jarred back.

For whatever reason, I arrived on the afternoon of Ireland's first game in the World Cricket League, a three-wicket defeat by Scotland, at the Gymkhana Club. The pendulum had swung so far in these fixtures that this was a surprise and required an explanation when Callender got back from the match. Ah, a missed run out. Brayso had dominated with 116 and TJ had matched his four sixes in a rapid 45 not out from 19 balls to take Ireland to 280/7, which should have been enough. Neil McCallum replied with a century for Scotland, but holed out to deep midwicket, leaving 31 to get from the final three overs.

In the next, O'Brien the younger back-flicked a return from the boundary into the stumps and Craig Wright was run out by a distance. Except he wasn't. Umpire Roger Dill had his back turned and couldn't give it. The Bermudian would have been embarrassed by photos of the broken stumps that appeared later that evening. Not even close. O'Brien delivered the final over, with 15 required and, Sod's Law, after a six by Wright had tied the scores, the Scotland captain hit the final ball for four.

There were grumblings from Scotty that Ireland should have given themselves longer than 36 hours to acclimatise to the Nairobi altitude, but it didn't seem an issue the next day when Porterfield carried his bat for 112 not out and a Bermuda total of 275/8 was chased down with four wickets and eight balls to spare.

The fielding was sharp and the unit looked focused. A couple of individuals were struggling, though. Big Boyd, making his ODI debut, fired six wides in four overs, including a couple of wide wides. Adi was nervously bowling every delivery with him on the boundary. 'When he gets it right …' Boatsie also had a tough time, overstepping three times and leaking 74 runs from his ten overs.

Dean Minors was in the Bermuda side: as a young wicketkeeper he had been one of the stars in 1994. He and Scotty were just about the only survivors from that first trip. I wondered what Christine was doing? The Hilton wasn't shy of a hospitality girl in the evening, but she was probably as long retired as Lewie.

Ruaraka – 2 February

Another pub-quiz special: name three players from one country who all scored ODI centuries on the same day? No single ODI innings has yet featured a trio of centurions yet three Irishmen did all score hundreds on a super Saturday. Ed made his for England against Australia in Sydney while Porty and O'Brien the younger reached the mark against Kenya. The opener carried on where he had left off against Bermuda, and was again unbeaten on 104 from 129 balls. The fourth wicket added 227, an Ireland record for any ODI partnership. O'Brien was brutal in the final overs as a blitz of six sixes took him to 142 and gave Ireland 284/4 to defend.

The Kenya reply started well and at 139/3, just past halfway, the home side were favourites. Boatsie and Kyle then applied a stranglehold, both took four wickets as the ball started to stick in the pitch and Ireland were back in control. The ninth wicket fell on 231, leaving 54 to get from 38 balls. Game over. Or it should have been, and even when Whitey dropped a difficult low catch on the boundary it didn't seem important.

The runs began to flow again, though. Two overs left, 20 needed. Lanky to bowl the 49th, but who would be entrusted with the last? We'll never know because after a dot and a single from the first two balls, Thomas Odoyo went 6, 6, 4, 4 and the game was over.

Lanky was inconsolable. Anyone who thinks that 'foreigners' do not have the same emotional investment in their adopted teams as locally born players need only to have seen the poor little Aussie over the next couple of days. Distraught doesn't begin to cover it; he was in bits. TJ, his room-mate, was only half-joking when he mentioned being on suicide watch. I'd spent an hour the previous afternoon with Lanky chatting about everything and nothing, and had got to discover why he was so popular in the dressing room. Smashing bloke. Funny, charming and ... well ... cuddly is the best way to describe him. He needed a few hugs that week.

Later the same evening I'd met a Rwandan, calling herself Antoinette. After a few drinks, she was opening up to me about the genocide and how soldiers had taken her mother away, never to be seen again. It was harrowing stuff, which put a bowler's woes in to perspective. Life had been tough. Only two months ago, her trinket business had suffered from unofficial taxation at the border; 100 per cent taxation by the sound of it. She needed to start again from scratch, yet she was remarkably chirpy, optimistic, and had a lovely smile.

Nairobi – 4 February

Porty's unbeaten run was ended by Canada at Jaffrey's when he was caught at short extra for 21, while four of his team-mates were simply being caught short. Food poisoning had ruled out Gillespie and Rankin, and although TJ and Nobby played, neither was fit enough to fulfil their primary roles. It shouldn't have mattered after Eoin scored 115 in a total of 308/7. Lanky climbed back in the saddle with a tidy ten overs for 40, but with the skipper unable to bowl, Canada got home with two balls to spare.

A forgettable week ended the following day with a fourth defeat, this time by the Netherlands, and possibly the worst of the quartet. After restricting the Dutch to 260/7, despite the absence of TJ and Big Boyd, Ireland were romping to victory on 195/1 before Eoin fell for 95. Not a problem. Plenty of time and Porty well set. Yet somehow it all went wrong again and the Boys in Green contrived to lose by six runs.

Richard Done, the ICC Head of Development, surveyed the wreckage of a defeat by Scotland, after an umpire had turned his back, another when Kenya's last pair performed a minor miracle, a third after bettering 300 against Canada and finally succumbing to the Netherlands when needing 66 from 9.3 overs with nine wickets in hand.

'After the week you've had I reckon you might just be due something special at the World Cup,' he told Adi.

Abu Dhabi – 10–12 February

While in Nairobi, news came through that contracts had been exchanged on my apartment in Primrose Hill and for the first time in ages I would soon have a few quid in the bank. Quite a few quid. I'd cashed in my London property casino chips. Downsizing, they call it. OK, it might not be quite such a picturesque walk to Lord's in future – it might not be a walk at all – but that was a small sacrifice to be mortgage free. It really was a wonderful feeling and I quickly took advantage of my new circumstances to change travel plans when we landed in Dubai.

Bugger it, enough was enough of watching Ireland lose. I'd go home a few days early. No, I'd go to Bangkok instead, and see a friend who was getting married shortly. Turn right instead of turning left. No, I'd be seeing him next month, I'd go home. Or should I just go onto Abu Dhabi? It was great having a few quid, even if it did make a bloke indecisive.

I went home, which meant I missed the first double century by an Ireland batsman. Going into that InterContinental Cup game against the UAE, Ivan Anderson held the highest score with 198 not out, against Canada in 1973. Brayso had succumbed ten short in Windhoek a little over a year previous, but this time Eoin made no mistake and was 209 not out, with 24 fours and a six, when TJ took pity on the home side and declared on 531/5.

Boatsie made 157, adding 360 with his young partner. It is still the highest partnership for any Ireland wicket, and likely to remain so. The skipper took six wickets and Big Boyd five as Ireland won by an innings and 170 to secure a place in their second IC Cup final.

Port of Spain – 5 March

The World Cup squad reassembled in good spirits and flew to Trinidad, the home island of Phil Simmons who had been announced as Adi's successor the previous month. The former West Indies all-rounder would stay with the team throughout the tournament, offering help and observations where required. Matt Dwyer was assistant coach; Simmo was there mainly to ensure a smooth transition. He chose a hands-off, watching approach, and stuck with it for the next year or more.

Two warm-up matches at the Sir Frank Worrell stadium gave an inkling that something special was indeed brewing. In the first, South Africa were in a mess at 66/7 and then 91/8 before the top-ranked ODI side and one of the World

Cup favourites hauled themselves to a semi-respectable 192, thanks to a half-century from the aptly named Andrew Hall.

Ireland replied strongly, but perhaps left a little too much to do in the final overs, and from 139/4, with 11 overs left, fell away to 157 all out. It was a disappointing outcome but it sent a message. The Boys in Green were not going to be pushovers, and a comprehensive seven-wicket victory three days later, having dismissed Canada for 115, only confirmed that the squad could not have been better prepared.

Kingston – 15 March

Two teams would qualify for the Super Eights from World Cup Group D, and you didn't need a Brearley-sized cricketing brain to know that, with matches to follow against Pakistan and their hosts, Ireland could not afford to lose to Zimbabwe. And, with a couple of large dollops of good fortune, they didn't. There was no luck for the Irish with the toss, mind. TJ lost it and his side were a wicket down at the end of the first over, and lost another three in the first hour, as the ball swung and nipped.

It should have been five wickets because Brayso was stone-dead lbw, but not given. The big opener made the most of his let-off, carrying his bat Porty-style for 115 not out. It was probably the century of the tournament, given the circumstances. Whitey and TJ weighed in, showing the advantage of having a side packed with all-rounders, and 221/9 was posted. Just about acceptable but 20–30 short of par.

Zimbabwe were always ahead of the chase and, but for one exceptional over from Big Boyd that saw opener Terry

Duffin shelled twice in the cordon and then held off the last ball, there was little for the Irish fans in Sabina Park to cheer. By the middle of the 44th over, with two batsmen set, five wickets in hand and only 19 required, all hope had surely gone.

Kyle then deflected a drive into the stumps and ran out non-striker Brendan Taylor. The next four overs sent down by TJ and Boatsie saw another wicket fall, only six runs added, and the first signs of a panic. Nine needed off two. Good time for a wicket maiden, we thought, and that's what O'Brien the younger delivered, with the bonus of a run out as well.

Whitey to bowl the last; nine still needed, one wicket left. Two, two, one, one, two. Scores level. Stuart Matsikenyeri on strike, 73 not out and preparing his man-of-the-match speech. He had batted beautifully, only to miss the one time he just had to connect. Ed Rainsford tried to steal a bye and was run out by a distance. Match tied. Stumps grabbed. Fans on the field. Scenes.

And where was I while all this was unfolding? Where else but in Thailand at a bloody wedding! It had been a toss up: a mate's nuptials or a week in Jamaica? But my regular freelance gigs were all sending their own people to cover it and a mate's a mate. I didn't think I would ever regret missing a game more. I was wrong.

Kingston – 17 March

The match that changed Ireland cricket forever could have been over before it began. St Paddy's Day morning dawned grey and damp, and the squads arrived at Sabina to find a pitch as green as a hippie in a recycling centre. Drinking crème de menthe. If TJ had lost the toss he reckons his side would have struggled to make 40. He won it and the rest really is history.

There weren't too many places showing the World Cup in Thailand and my quest to watch the game led me to a TV set in a nightclub, surrounded by dancers. OK, it was a go-go bar. Not the easiest place to concentrate. 'Nice shape on that,' I thought more than once as Lanky and Big Boyd made a couple of early inroads.

Boatsie started well, too, yet Pakistan passed 50 with only two down and the danger seemed to have passed. Suddenly TJ removed Mohammad Yousuf and an over later Inzamam edged Botha to Eoin at second slip. The same combination also accounted for opener Imran Nazir. Game on. When Boatsie finally took a blow he had 2/5 from eight overs.

Stunning figures. Indeed they were, but I only had eyes for the scoreboard that was showing 72/6 after O'Brien the younger induced a nick to his brother. The skipper cleverly brought Big Boyd back to take two wickets just as Kamran Akmal was threatening a recovery and after another brief flurry Kyle wrapped up the Pakistan innings on 132.

Willie Dwyer and his mates in the party stand could not believe what they had seen, but Adi and TJ knew the job was only half done. The coach had his say in the dressing room then the skipper gave the speech of his life. Addressing each player in turn, he barked, 'Do you want to be back in Belfast teaching geography on Monday? Do you want to be sorting mail in Dublin?' And so on.

It wasn't going to be easy. Pakistan were embarrassed and came out determined to save face. Their response was fierce: physically and verbally. Brayso and Eoin went early; Nobby joined Porty. By his own admission, the keeper had been in no sort of form with the bat, but you wrote him off at your peril. That day in Kingston he rode to the middle on his little green bike: the big boys were going to get a bloody nose.

Porty only made 13, but hung around long enough to add 47 for the third wicket, then Boatsie got a horrible decision. Lbw or caught? Obviously neither, but no one seemed to know what the umpire had given. The O'Briens advanced the score to 81/4 and then a brief shower lopped off three overs, and four runs from the target.

This could still go either way. The press box was in turmoil with Irish newspapers holding front pages, pushing back deadlines and sub-editors digging out their cricketing lexicons. Robin Walsh, a recently retired senior BBC producer, was fretting more than most. A legend at Broadcasting House, he had put the *Nine O'Clock News* to air more than once with pictures still being edited from theatres of war, yet here he was panicking over a few pars for a niche publication in the north.

Robin wrote a column of cricket news and gossip, gathered at leisure during the week, more often than not containing 'the *Sunday Life* believes ...' which we all knew was shorthand for 'Big Roy has told me ...' He was not a reporter, but he knew enough to take a view and pen an intro on 'the greatest day in Irish cricket history'. Never one to sell himself short, he may well have left out the 'cricket'.

As the O'Briens nudged Ireland into three figures the *Life's* man was congratulating himself; more so when Nobby danced down the pitch and planted Shoaib Malik back over his head for six. Only 20 to win now, but attempting a repeat the Sandymount scrapper was stumped for a wonderful 72, exactly two-thirds of his side's runs at that stage. He stomped off, cursing. Whitey found the boundary but only lasted three balls, two more than Kyle.

As TJ walked in with 15 still needed, Robin sat down and wrote 'Oh the heartbreak! Ireland were so near ...' He sat back and tried to relax with either intro ready to go. O'Brien the younger and TJ inched closer, then one of his mischievous colleagues said, 'What if it's a tie, Robin?'

It wasn't, of course. With the scores level, the skipper heaved a massive blow over the midwicket boundary that not only gave Ireland the D/L win, but also took the Boys in Green past Pakistan's original total. For some reason that always seems important to me.

A St Paddy's Day reception had been planned for the players to meet fans in Ocho Rios, on the other side of the island. It turned into the wildest of parties. Alcohol was consumed in mind-boggling amounts. Literally mind-boggling. Beer ran out first, then vodka followed by local rum, Bacardi and all the other spirits. By five in the morning there wasn't much left of the top shelf of liqueurs that are only there for show and the janitor's store was being raided for cleaning fluid.

Kingston – 18 March

The morning after, Bob Woolmer was found dead in his room at the Pegasus hotel, where the teams were staying. The Pakistan coach, who had been gracious in defeat, had apparently died of a heart attack. An overweight Englishman in his late 50s, under pressure, it made sense.

When another Bob died in Ocho Rios three days later, Bob Kerr the 68-year-old former ICU President from Fermanagh, there was no suspicion of anything other than heart failure, yet with Woolmer the rumours began to fly.

Had he been murdered after Pakistan's unexpectedly early exit? Was he the victim of aggrieved match-fixers? And so on. Sure, the potential to make millions had disappeared with that six struck by TJ, but what was to be gained by killing the coach? Revenge? Surely not. It didn't make sense.

Neither, though, did the squeaky clean image of Woolmer portrayed in the media, especially the English press. Charming bloke I'm sure, but he was coach of South Africa during the Cronje years and then in charge of Pakistan, with their history of manipulating games. Please don't tell me he wouldn't have had an inkling of what was going on, even if he wasn't involved. It would be impossible to hide any shenanigans from a man with that level of technical and tactical knowledge. But murdered? I very much doubt it.

Kingston – 21 March

Despite the euphoria of the St Paddy's Day victory, Ireland were by no means assured of a place in the Super Eights. A win for Zimbabwe against either West Indies or Pakistan would see them tied on three points and advancement decided on run-rate. The hosts didn't slip up, winning by six wickets, but there was genuine concern in the Ireland camp that Pakistan might withdraw from the tournament after the Woolmer tragedy and Zimbabwe could be awarded the game and points. The match did go ahead, though, and a convincing, if subdued, win by Pakistan meant Kyle's school would be requiring a supply teacher.

Wapping – 24 March

It hardly mattered that Ireland lost their final Group D game to West Indies by eight wickets. The Boys in Green were in the Super Eights and everyone wanted an interview.

There was no end of good copy, with background stories about real-life jobs not usually associated with international sportsmen. Another popular feature – indeed a two-page spread in one Irish red top – highlighted those distinctive wicket celebrations: TJ's chicken dance and Lanky performing his ferret routine.

If Ireland made a mistake with their PR, it was in putting the coach and captain forward for too many interviews, particularly on TV. Vice-captain Kyle, with his Belfast brogue, should have been used far more because from a distance the team didn't sound Irish enough. This was brought home to me during a shift at *The Times*. The World Cup was being discussed and I said something about Ireland reaching the Super Eights.

'It's not really Ireland, though, is it?' said Craig Tregurtha, the assistant sports editor. 'They're all Australians and South Africans.' At that very moment, the TV above our heads was showing Ed and Kevin Pietersen steering England to victory in St Lucia.

Shepherd's Bush – 26 March

Knowledge of the Ireland team and its recent history earned me a gig on *The Times* cricket podcast, recorded in west London. Mike Gatting was one of the other guests. Host Mark Chapman introduced me as an 'Irish cricket expert'. I corrected him. 'Ireland cricket expert, I'm not Irish.' Gatt chipped in: 'Not so sure about the "expert" either.' Can't remember much else, except that I predicted, with some confidence, that Ireland would beat Bangladesh. So we'll stick with the 'expert', thanks Gatt.

Meanwhile, it wasn't only the team who were faced with the logistical problems of a welcome but unexpected extension to their stay. With hotel rooms at a premium in the Guyanese capital, Ger and Emmet were billeted in a honeymoon suite at the El Dorado Inn for a couple of nights, and with no little awkwardness found themselves sharing an impressive four-poster bed in a room named 'Love Deeply'.

'Those weren't pillows …'

Georgetown – 30 March

The first game of the Super Eights, at the new Providence Stadium, saw another stout performance before the experience of England told by 48 runs. The first wicket of the match was joyously celebrated when Ed shouldered arms and lost his off stump to Rankin. A second single-figure score against his former side. Big Boyd also removed England skipper Michael Vaughan in his opening burst and tight back-up bowling pegged England to 201/5 after 45 overs. Just as the underdogs began to sniff another upset, Paul Collingwood cut loose, lifting three sixes as 65 runs flowed from those last five overs.

When Ireland replied, Brayso went first ball, driving in the air to gully, and Eoin was run out for two. The youngster was having a poor trot and it only got worse. After two ducks in his final three innings, he had managed just 74 runs in nine knocks, with a top score of 28. There would be better World Cups for him, no doubt.

Nobby made another half-century and must have looked a threat because Pietersen started to get stuck in. 'O'Brien? You're the most selfish player in the game!'

'That's good coming from him,' said umpire Simon Taufel. It was the start of a feisty little feud that would continue for a decade or more.

Nobby was stumped off his pad for 63 from 88 balls, and while TJ and Whitey continued the fight the unlikely spin pairing of Monty Panesar and Vaughan had left them with too much to do. The Colly onslaught was the difference – and inexperience. The 2011 side would have got those runs; in 2015 they would have strolled it.

Georgetown – 1 April

During training, the skipper approached his media manager. 'Today's the day those two get a taste of their own medicine,' he said, indicating Kyle and Whitey, the infamous practical jokers of the squad. 'Any ideas?'

Barry Chambers thought for a minute. 'How about an interview with a top English journalist, at a restaurant in town?'

'Perfect,' said TJ, smiling.

Barry called the Belfast pair over a few minutes later and apologised for asking this on their afternoon off, but Christopher Martin-Jenkins of *The Times* was looking to write a feature on 'The Irish Spin Twins'. Was there any chance they were free for lunch?

Yes, of course. CM-J!

One problem, though; they had promised to take their wives out that afternoon. 'Give me a minute.' Barry walked off, pretending to make a call. 'That's fine, lads. CM-J says he'll meet you at the restaurant at two, talk to you for 15 minutes or so, and then you and the wives can have a meal on his expense account.'

A couple of hours later, a dozen or more discreet but knowing eyes were watching from the quadrangle of the Cara Lodge as, dressed up for the occasion, the McCallans and Whites left in a taxi. At 2.15, Barry received a text wondering where CM-J was?

'On his way shortly, lads. Been a development in the Woolmer story. Says to go ahead and order what you want – it's all on him.'

Still no CM-J. At three, in a coordinated blitz, the Spin Twins' phones began to ping. 'April Fool wankers' was probably the most polite text.

'The "Spin Twins" line should have rung alarm bells,' Chambers said. 'I deserved an Oscar for keeping a straight face. It didn't take them long to forgive me – only about five years!'

Georgetown – 3 April

Paul Mooney played his first game of the campaign, and his last for Ireland, in a seven-wicket defeat by South Africa. The rain-affected match isn't one he will have relived too many times after retiring and emigrating to New Zealand. Caught behind first ball as Ireland made 152/8 in 35 overs, then pounded for 40 from 3.3 overs. It was time to call it a day.

'Looking back, I should have gone at the end of the previous season, but I was selfish and thought I could get the body in half-decent nick for the World Cup,' he said.

Freed of the need to be in any sort of nick, Mooners was able to indulge in the local culture and partied away the last two weeks of the tournament.

The Guyanese leg of the Super Eights ended with another one-sided defeat, by New Zealand. Lanky and the Spin Twins took two wickets each as the Kiwis posted 263/8. Ireland were briefly in a promising position when O'Brien the younger cleared the ropes three times, only to be run out by his brother for 49 from 45 balls. Nobby soon followed – all out 134.

Bridgetown – 15 April

The squad flew to Barbados with one realistic target remaining. At the start of the Super Eights, even the most optimistic of fans would not have been eyeing a place in the semi-finals. We knew there was little chance of upsetting Australia or Sri Lanka while hopes of toppling England or New Zealand, admittedly a long shot, had slipped away. South Africa, too. That left Bangladesh, a team who had struggled constantly since becoming ICC Full Members in 2000. The Tigers were seen to be on a par with Zimbabwe and definitely beatable, even if they had eliminated India at the group stage.

The clash between the two sides at Kensington Oval should have been India versus Pakistan, one of the showpiece events of the tournament. Except sport doesn't work like that, does it?

No matter how hard the corporates try to meld it, there are no guarantees and several of the superstars and prima donnas of the world game were back home in Delhi and Karachi when TJ won the toss and elected to bat. The openers put on 92, one more than Ireland had managed when losing to Australia by nine wickets on the same ground two days before. Porty made 85, O'Brien the younger and TJ contributed 48 and 30 respectively, at better than a run a ball, and 243/7 looked competitive.

Big Boyd, who had added AB de Villiers and Stephen Fleming to his list of impressive victims, again struck early and all but settled the contest when the skipper brought him back mid-innings to remove dangerman Mohammad Ashraful for 35. TJ, Lanky and Kyle also took two wickets, as did Boatsie, if you count his run out, and Bangladesh ended well short on 169.

Adi claimed it was the most complete performance of his time in charge and, back in London, I was able to point out that Ireland's record of two victories over Test teams, plus a tie, was better than England's. I may have pointed this out more than a couple of times. It also helped the perception of it being an Irish victory to have Porty named as man of the match, even if his rapid delivery in that broad north-west accent had some Indian journalists openly wondering what language he was speaking.

St George's – 18 April

I needed to witness at least a small part of this great adventure and booked a flight to Grenada, via Barbados. Awake early and excited about my first time in the Caribbean, I joined Robin Walsh for a beach walk, had a wonderful breakfast of fruit and saltfish, and then took a taxi to the team hotel where I was greeted like a long-lost friend by Lanky. The skipper was busy scribbling another chapter of a book he was writing with Ger.

'Don't forget to mention Kenya and Windhoek.'

'You've had enough praise for that already.' But he did, there in print, a couple of months later when *Raiders of the Caribbean* was published. Top man.

The rest of the squad all looked pleased to see me too, even the Mooneys. Eventually I found Adi pacing the hotel grounds; brow furrowed. 'Do I play Kenny Carroll tomorrow, DT? He's the only one who hasn't had a game.'

'Will playing him, or not, affect the result?'

'Probably not.'

Back at our hotel, Robin instigated a game of beach cricket, involving at least seven different nationalities, although I've forgotten most of them. An American guy was there. He was attached to the tournament from the UN, or similar, to promote AIDS awareness. A worthy cause, but what exactly did sexually transmitted diseases have to do with a cricket World Cup? Apparently the tournament had 'global reach' and that was important to his message. It still didn't seem appropriate.

Nor were the locals happy with the way the ICC had descended on their islands and imposed globalism in the form of ticket pricing, plus their over-officious brand purity inside the stadiums. If a logo did not belong to an Official Partner it had to be covered or removed. Sensible enough in sight of the TV cameras, maybe, but the taping over of the manufacturer's name on a toilet cistern in the Gents? Really? The event had been sanitised and corporatised at the expense of Caribbean colour and flavours, and was the poorer for it – if not in financial terms.

The real match the next morning was an anticlimax. Put into bat, Ireland started OK, with Porty and Brayso adding 28, but then three wickets fell in an over and the innings faded rapidly to 77 all out. Kenny played, but the postman could not deliver. He was bamboozled and bowled second ball by Murali and an eight-wicket defeat was suffered well before lunch. Sri Lanka were on their way to a second final, where they would lose to Australia, while the Boys in Green had won their final a few days earlier.

All that was left was for Adi to say goodbye to his men, and hand out copies of the farewell speech he couldn't deliver. That evening Ger, myself and a couple of others discovered an al fresco restaurant in what appeared to be a gravel-covered car park. Huge chunks of spicily seasoned chicken were being barbecued over pits of charcoal, in sawn-down oil drums. Bottles of beer were for sale from an ice bath and there was live music beneath the stars. It was OK.

The next few days in Barbados were OK, too: a great stay at Gatt's villa on the Westmorland estate, the chance to meet Sir Garfield (Sobers not Harrison) on a Bajun legends cruise, the discovery of a cool beach bar, some barracuda steaks, all topped off by VIP seats for a thrilling ODI at the Kensington Oval. I've had worse weeks.

Belfast – 29 April

The heroes of the Caribbean were quickly brought back to earth when only a few hundred fans braved the cold of Stormont to see them lose their opening match of the Friends Provident Trophy to Kent by 58 runs. RTE dispatched a reporter from Dublin who didn't know a lot about cricket, but enough to think that after the past month or so something special was required.

'Is there going to be a guard of honour? Fireworks?' No, the World Cup warriors just trotted out to a smattering of polite applause. It was a massive anticlimax and the hangover continued the following week when Ireland were trounced by Somerset, at Taunton.

On the way over to the next game, at the Rose Bowl, I stayed a night with Ivo Tennant, a writer for *The Times* who had ghosted books for Woolmer. No way would his friend have been involved in anything underhand or betting-related, he insisted. Did Ivo think the coach had been murdered? 'I really have no idea.' Neither did the Jamaican police, who were still investigating. Eventually it was officially decided that he had died of natural causes.

Southampton – 7 May

An eight-wicket victory for Hampshire was finished off by Pietersen who appeared to tweak a hamstring with the winning post in sight. Did this mean he would miss the first Test of the summer which was ten days away, or just Hampshire's upcoming four-day match? I joined the players for a post-match beer. Hampshire skipper Shane Warne was fuming. 'I've just asked him: "Do you want to fecking play, or don't you?"' He may well have been referring to KP who would miss the upcoming Championship game but luckily enough was fit to play the Test.

TJ introduced me to the legendary leggie who shook my hand. 'Pleased to meet you mate, Shane Warne.'

'I had rather guessed that.'

'Don't believe everything you've read, eh?'

It's hard not to be impressed by someone that famous who doesn't assume that you know who he is. I had a similar experience in a largely deserted Mumbai press area after the 1987 World Cup semi-final. 'Are you alright, son?'

'Ah, I've been sick for a couple of days, and now I'm struggling to start this report.'

'Just write down anything and after a bit the words will come.'

It was great advice, and something I've done many times since. The 400 words flew off the keys. Still it was just the two of us sitting there. 'Thanks for that,' I said. 'Worked a treat.'

'I'm actually better known for playing the game than writing about it – I'm Geoffrey Boycott.'

'The Geoffrey Boycott?' His extended hand was joined by that famous lopsided grin.

Without Eoin, Nobby and Big Boyd, who had been recalled by their counties, and now lacking any element of surprise, Ireland were well beaten in all six completed games. The skipper voiced what many were thinking when he questioned Ireland's continued participation if they couldn't field their best side. Not that TJ didn't do everything within his powers to conjure a win, including taking a hat-trick against Gloucestershire. It was only the second time an Ireland bowler had performed the feat; the first since Thomas Hanna in 1877.

The new coach, Phil Simmons didn't appear to throw himself into the job, either, and his first overseas signing flopped spectacularly. Jesse Ryder, an unknown at the time, totalled three runs in two innings and then failed to turn up at Hove for a game against Sussex that was abandoned. The New Zealander was not seen again.

The difference in style between Simmo and his predecessor was marked, and a row with Johnboy saw the younger Mooney follow his brother into 'retirement'. Officially, the 25-year-old wanted to finish his apprenticeship as an electrician; unofficially, he was banned from the national side for two years.

Simmo did cap Alex Cusack and Roger Whelan during the competition. Whelan, a young quick from Dublin, made his debut against Essex and won two more caps in the defeats by India and South Africa the following month. He took a wicket in each of his three appearances: the not unimpressive trio of Ravi Bopara, Sachin Tendulkar and AB de Villiers.

Leicester – 22–23 May

After the FP Trophy, the final of the InterContinental Cup came as a blessed relief. Ireland were back among their peers and dominant. The third final was staged at Grace Road and lasted two of its scheduled four days, which wasn't great news for the freelancers present, even those who had recently cashed in their London property casino chips.

The skipper continued his rich vein of form claiming 4/12 as Canada were dismissed for 92 in 31.4 overs, shortly after lunch, and the rest of the first day belonged to his old mate Brayso who clattered 146 to all parts.

An opening partnership of 202 with Porty, who made 54, had all but ended the contest by stumps. Canada did briefly fight back when Umar Bhatti produced a burst of four wickets in five balls, the last three a hat-trick. The left-armer's victims were all palpably lbw and it probably should have been five in six because another inswinging beauty hit TJ plumb in front too, but umpire Paul Baldwin had run out of fingers.

Eoin, who watched the mayhem from the other end, was last out for 84 in a total of 352. The Canada second innings lasted marginally longer than the first, but only just. Kyle was the destroyer this time with 5/34 and by 5pm the champions had won by an innings and 115 runs to retain their title.

Clontarf – 10 June

The penultimate FP Trophy game found me sitting in front of the pavilion at Castle Avenue, summarising for Kevin Hand on BBC London. The long-time Middlesex commentator is another to be added to the connections between the county and Ireland. The son of immigrants, he clings to his Irish heritage and passport like any other young bloke born and raised in south London. Few work harder at the mic than Handie, particularly back in those days when he regularly had to talk his way through 100 overs or more without assistance.

Knowing how tough that was I'd started to sit in with him for no more reward than a Lord's lunch or two, and the partnership clicked. Now here we were commentating on Ed catching his brother Dom, a relatively young Tim Murtagh picking up a wicket and Eoin batting Middlesex to a six-wicket win. It was all too brief, but I think Kev enjoyed his first visit to Dublin.

A rained-off final match against Glamorgan followed, or rather didn't, at Stormont. The couple of days were not wasted, though, as Emmet and myself discovered the Ardshane Country House, a glorious bed and breakfast in Holywood. A big imposing building, set back from the main road, run by a big, imposing woman. To be fair, Valerie was only big in the character sense. A proper matriarch, probably in her late 60s, who ran a superb establishment: big rooms, comfortable beds, fresh fruit every morning, and a fry cooked to order. It was also within walking distance of Ned's, a no-nonsense pub that served superbly poured Guinness and had been recommended to Emmet by the dad of some young golfer he had recently interviewed. A future star, apparently. Rory something-or-other.

What a joy that B&B was. It became our Belfast home-from-home for the next two or three years until Valerie finally retired – after threatening to do so from the moment we first walked through her massive front door. The world would be a better place if every town had its own Ardshane, but that would mean cloning Valerie, and she was very much a one-off.

Belfast – 15 June

A reception was held for the World Cup squad at Stormont Castle enabling local politicians to belatedly pay tribute and associate their names with the success. Ian Paisley, the First Minister of Northern Ireland, and his deputy Martin McGuinness were both there; the Chuckle Brothers, as they had become known during their unlikely alliance.

The Rev. Paisley, reading from a prepared script, congratulated the team on their efforts although it was clear that he wouldn't have known the difference between cricket and croquet if his continued ability to shout NO! had depended on it.

Then McGuinness got up to speak, without notes, and dropped a jaw or two. 'You might be surprised how many cricket fans there are in the Republican movement,' the former IRA commander said. He went on to recall how his wife had demanded to know what the hell was going on when she caught him watching an Ashes Test on TV in the wee hours a few years back, and how he regularly played beach cricket with Sinn Fein chairman Mitchel McLaughlin and his family.

McGuinness concluded by saying how much he was looking forward to meeting Roy Torrens 'a legend of the north-west'. The Ireland team manager, a contemporary but firmly from the other tradition, nudged a neighbour and said, 'I'd be surprised if we haven't met in the past – on opposite sides.'

Belfast – 15 July

A quadrangular tournament featuring West Indies, Scotland and the Netherlands offered an early return to the Ardshane and a chance to rise early and sit in Valerie's large garden, drinking in the summer scents. Ireland had ten of their World Cup squad available and a painstaking half-century by Eoin, who had been scoring a lot quicker for Middlesex, helped the hosts to somehow squeeze to a one-run victory over the Netherlands.

With the Nairobi roles reversed, the Dutch made an even bigger Horlicks as they got within 20 runs with seven wickets in hand before fading. With seven needed from the final over, O'Brien the younger held them to a single and four dots from the first five balls.

A rained-off match against West Indies followed, meaning the tournament would be decided on run-rate. Ireland missed out after beating Scotland by a modest 23 runs at Stormont, when Nobby had posted another 72, while West Indies were crushing the Netherlands without losing a wicket down in Dublin.

It was during the afternoon of this game that the Cricket Writers of Ireland was formed. Emmet and I had discovered a cracking bistro in Holywood and suggested we book a large table and have a gathering of scribes – which could lead to an annual event. Nothing too formal.

Ger ran with the idea. Why limit it to a meal, let's have an organisation along the lines of the Cricket Writers' Club. 'The Irish Cricket Writers' someone mooted, but that would have excluded the Englishman and Jon Coates, who was Scottish.

Callender was soon envisaging a black tie annual dinner, but that was knocked on the head too. A very loose association was formed and we arranged several get-togethers, presenting Player-of-the-Year awards, and the like. The CWI also initiated a Hall of Fame that was subsumed by Cricket Ireland. Several excellent meals were enjoyed over the years, but we never did have a night in that bistro.

Belfast – 9 August

A very special year ended with two InterContinental Cup matches, the first of the fourth edition that would feature a round robin of eight teams with the top two meeting in a final. In the first, Scotland batted most of the first two days at Stormont, crawling to 314 from 148.4 overs, then had the champions in bother at 59/4. Nobby and Boatsie steadied the ship with unbeaten half-centuries and when the third day was washed out it was simply a question of who would get the first-innings points.

Nobby fell on the final morning for 84 but there was no shifting Boatsie, who powered on to 186, adding a record sixth-wicket partnership of 234 with Cusack that secured the points. The relative new boy scored what would prove to be his only century for Ireland.

Funny thing with cricketers. Some you take one look at and say, 'Yep'. Ed at West Bromwich, for example. Others don't catch the eye and you wonder how they caught the coach's. Cusie fell into the latter category. A wiry all-rounder. Busy. Effective. What was his background? Decent Dublin club player, maybe? Even after I'd discovered he was from Brisbane, with an excellent pedigree, I still wouldn't have put money on him winning 50 caps. How wrong you can be; he was the nuts and bolts of the team for the next eight years.

Two weeks later, Botha went big again, and shared in another hefty partnership of 221 with fellow centurion Porty, against Bermuda at Castle Avenue. O'Brien the younger and TJ piled in with half-centuries in a total of 524/8 declared and, after Lanky had claimed career-best figures of 5/45, victory by an innings and 146 runs was wrapped up inside three days.

PEERLESS AMONG PEERS
2008–2010

2008

Malaysia – 17 February–2 March

Statistically, most of us meet our best friends in our early 20s. University, maybe. Leaving home, sharing a flat. My best mate Mike falls into that category, but I got to know my other best mate during the Under-19 World Cup in Malaysia, at a ripe old age.

I'd been aware of Barry Chambers for a couple of years, of course, not least as a key player in the Spin Twins meet CM-J prank. He had taken over as Cricket Ireland media manager when it couldn't be decided which of the two part-time officers in Belfast and Dublin should have the full-time role, and they gave it to a third bloke – from the north-west. The Ardmore Express, as he was widely known by no one other than himself, had bowled a bit of military-medium, pursued his talent for cricket photography, fallen in with the founder of the *CricketEurope* website and always seemed to be in the right place at the right time. He was a good man for pints and a very bad man for appearing with a round of double Jack Daniel's at the end of a night out.

Whether Malaysia was the right place at the right time is debatable. The Ireland campaign was a mess, hijacked by one parent who wanted too much say, and several others who treated it like a school tour. You had to feel sorry for coach Brîan O'Rourke, who dashed around, doing his best to hold things together, but his resemblance to a young John Cleese didn't help. 'Basil!'

O'Rourke had some very good players. Captain Greg Thompson was a full international, Paul Stirling would be within weeks, future Test captain Andy Balbirnie was there and so were Shane Getkate, Stuart Poynter and James Shannon who all went on to win senior caps. It was clear the lads weren't focused, though, from the first game against England when Stirlo and his opening partner walked out 20 metres apart. Parents wandered in an out of the team area, until physio Iain Knox arrived mid-tournament, took one horrified look at what was going on, and coned it off. Batsmen who were out strolled off to sit with family members. Shambolic.

By contrast, Barry and I had a very successful trip. Beers most evenings, usually outside. A bar across the road had a live band, which was fine until the singer produced a python one night. 'Check bin!' The two of us had that in common: scared to death of snakes. At the previous Under-19 World Cup, Knoxy had warned Barry to be on the lookout at one particular ground in Sri Lanka, waited a couple of overs, then crept up behind and pinched his calf. Poor bloke leapt in the air and ran like a cartoon character. Horrible trick. Wish I'd been there to see it.

The quality in the Ireland squad shone through in the final two games as they beat Bermuda and Zimbabwe to finish 13th of the 16. Andy Britton took 4/14 against

Zimbabwe and a very young and quiet Getkate bowled beautifully, but the campaign was probably summed up by Thompson's last ball which long-off settled under, to give the skipper a record 28th wicket in his third World Cup – and dropped.

The trip had an amusing postscript when I found myself on the same flight back to Gatwick as young Stuart, and behind him in the queue for immigration. Poor lad was given the full works.

'How old are you?'

'16'

'Travelling on your own?'

'I've been playing cricket for Ireland,' his quite clearly English voice getting higher and squeakier, face redder.

'Oh you have, have you. Ireland, eh?' It was tempting to see where it would lead, but I stepped forward to vouch for him.

Abu Dhabi – 6–9 March

The year's curtain raiser for the senior side was an InterContinental Cup match at the Sheikh Zayed Stadium, where Stirlo won his first full cap at 17-and-a-half and contributed a sharp run out as the home side were bowled out for 228. The Belfast boy's first innings lasted 18 balls, but only produced two runs and Ireland didn't gain first-innings points until a record seventh-wicket stand of 163 between Nobby and TJ took them into a healthy lead. Nobby went on to 174, only two short of his career-best, and the visitors were on course for a three-day victory when the UAE lost their seventh wicket an hour from the close.

Funny old game. Saqib Ali found a willing partner in Zahid Shah and the eighth-wicket pair sat down for lunch unbeaten on the final day. Ireland already needed to bat again, and were fast running out of both overs and ideas before Thompson had Zahid lbw and bowled his replacement next ball. Buses. When Cusack finally found an edge from Saqib, five short of his double century, Ireland needed 61 and got them with an hour to spare.

Mirpur – 22 March

A third heavy loss to Bangladesh in five days nearly killed TJ. Or so he will tell you. The heat was beyond oppressive, oven-like; the pitches dustbowls. For a proud man and such a fierce competitor, enough was enough. The strains of holding down a job with Agricultural Hardware and raising a young family had taken a toll, and Mirpur was the final straw.

The showman in him had Johnston announcing the end of his captaincy in the dressing room, stripped to the waist, after the final ODI. No longer confident that his 34-year-old body was up to the demands of one-day cricket, he would take a break from the international game. Time to hand the reins to young Porterfield.

The eagerness, bordering on desperation, to play more against top sides had led the ICU – which had been dissolved and formed afresh as Cricket Ireland in February – to throw their team into an ill-conceived series played in 40°C-plus heat, with little preparation and less acclimatisation. Still smarting from the previous year's World Cup defeat, the home side couldn't believe their luck. Face would be restored – and how. Eight wickets, 84 runs and 79 runs. No game was close.

Another contributing factor to Johnston's decision was his relationship, or rather lack of one, with Simmo.

The new coach was maintaining his watching brief of the previous season, and was yet to bond with the team. At the launch party for Ed Leahy's book *Green Wickets*, a year after the World Cup adventure, TJ said: 'You're a long way from London, DT?'

'I was invited over and thought it might be a chance to have a chat with Phil, try to get to know him a bit.'

'Good luck with that, mate.'

Clontarf – 27 April

Porty's reign did not start well. Without the senior county-contracted players, a resting TJ, and Rankin, who was injured, Ireland were bowled out for 161 on a cold day at Castle Avenue, and lost to Nottinghamshire by 56 runs. Four more 50-overs games against county opposition went much the same way before the return game at Trent Bridge saw Ireland chase 241/6 and fall short by one run. O'Brien the younger finished 93 not out from 75 balls after a canny penultimate over from Mark Ealham had left just too much to do. Porty himself was missing, having been recalled by Gloucestershire. This was ever the problem with taking part in English domestic competitions, but experience was being gained. Kyle captained in his absence, and for the final game of the campaign – a home defeat by Northants.

Dublin – 24 June

John Wright passed away in St. Vincent's Hospital, after a short illness. For someone known as Wee John, he was a giant of a man for what he achieved with Ireland. Not much of a player himself, a crafty second XI spinner at best I'm told, he was a champion in administration and nothing less than a genius in the politics of getting things done.

It was said that the Malahide man could lead sworn enemies into a meeting room or, indeed, a bar, and emerge with smiles, handshakes and a deal done. He succeeded Scotty as Hon. Sec. of the ICU in 1997, and was instrumental in setting up Cricket Ireland as well as overseeing the first footsteps on the road to Test cricket, which would not have happened as quickly, if at all, without his tireless dedication.

Wee John even chose and anointed his perfect successor in Warren Deutrom, leaving his life's work in good hands. He lived to see Ireland play in the World Cup and beat Pakistan, and he would have been looking down and smiling five years later when 10,000 fans packed into his beloved Malahide for the visit of England. It was fitting that Ireland played their first Test match at The Village too.

On top of all that, he was just a lovely man. A twinkle in the eye and a smile always playing at the corner of his mouth. Only 65. Trying to do my bit, by way of respect, I arranged for an obit in *The Times*. Ger Siggins wrote a fine tribute and, by some quirk of production, it appeared everywhere except in the Dublin edition. That would have had the little fella chuckling.

Aberdeen – 1–2 July

The summer of woe continued with heavy defeats in back-to-back ODIs in Scotland. Ireland gave an ODI debut to Manawatu-born Peter Connell against his New Zealand compatriots. PC was quick and not short of self-confidence. Asked in a pre-match interview which bowler he would least like to face, he named himself. His countrymen had no such qualms and smashed 95 off his nine overs. The stattos were busy as openers Brendon McCullum and

Hamish Marshall added 274, both passing 150 in a total of 402/2. Ireland lost by 290 runs, another unwanted record.

A less emphatic defeat followed when Scotland chased 210/8 to win by five wickets. In fairness, it was a much weakened side at Mannofield on those two days. No Porty, Eoin or Nobby, who had not been released by their counties. Rankin was injured, as was O'Brien the younger, while Cusack had broken two fingers the week before and TJ was still brooding as he drove round Dublin selling lawnmowers, or whatever. So Ryan Haire, who had played a handful of internationals in 2000 and none since, was recalled for the two games and scored a half-century in his last innings for Ireland.

Rotterdam – 9–12 July

Connell went better on his InterContinental Cup bow against the Netherlands. Far better. I'd arrived in the team hotel on the eve of the game to find Botha complaining about his creaking body and wondering how much longer he could go on. In typical Boatsie style he scored 172 over the next three rain-interrupted days before Kyle declared on 400/6, at least 50 runs later than he should have done. 'I saw you getting agitated,' he grinned.

PC had one for plenty after his first four games, but his natural length suited the longer form and he claimed four wickets in an extended opening spell, either side of lunch. Kyle weighed in with a couple and Ireland had made up for the lost time when the home side were dismissed for 127 and asked to follow on. Three more wickets fell that evening and the only worry now was the weather.

I may have reminded Hans Mulder about Kuala Lumpur and how this time the rain could come to the aid of the Dutch. He wasn't really bothered. It wasn't a tournament his side prioritised. The stoppages had also offered another chance to break the ice with Simmo. Still nothing. Even mention of being at the SCG when he took 4/3 in ten overs against Pakistan, an ODI record that is likely to last for eternity, elicited no more than a raised eyebrow. Mr Inscrutable.

The rainclouds were closing in after lunch on the final day, with Ireland still requiring three wickets. Connell started his 18th over and took the new ball after one delivery. The fourth of the over located the stumps, as did the fifth and the third hat-trick by an Ireland bowler was recorded when Eddie Schiferli was hit in front. PC had match figures of 10/69 and I headed home thinking Ireland had unearthed another Antipodean gem. Sadly, though, control of his length proved a recurring problem and consequently the Kiwi played fewer games than might have been expected.

Skerries – 25 July

My first visit to The Vineyard, the home of The Hills, and Matt and his brother Willie Dwyer, where the catering is as good as you'll find. Maybe not the oysters and seafood that used to be served at the SCG, or the opulence of the media lunches during a Test match at Lord's, but wonderful beyond expectations for a club ground north of Dublin. Big hunks of chicken, a choice of spuds, mounds of salad, if you're that way inclined, and proper puddings. Teas just as good. Way better than the fare on offer in the middle as Ireland thrashed Norway by eight wickets at the start of another successful European Championship campaign.

Ireland also chased successfully against Denmark, the Netherlands and Italy before beating Scotland in the final at Castle Avenue. Porty lifted his first trophy after a Gary Wilson half-century had spearheaded an eight-wicket win, in another rain-affected game. Kyle had bowled beautifully. A real master of the off-spinning art by now, he had lanky wicketkeeper Colin Smith stumped for the third time in a couple of years. 'It's got to the point where I just know when he's going to run past one,' he said.

Belfast – 2–5 August

Rain was becoming the feature of the summer and made a nuisance of itself again at Stormont during the World T20 qualifiers. TJ had been persuaded to make himself available for the four days and was back in the fold, although he was still reluctant to play ODIs. Rankin was injured, but otherwise Ireland were at full strength and eager to claim one of the three places available for the finals in England.

In a three-team first-round group, the Boys in Green beat Scotland on the first day with more in hand than the bare stats of four wickets and one ball to spare would suggest. Bermuda should not have presented too much of an obstacle either, but the Ireland innings spluttered and, when heavy rain fell, the scoreboard read 41/4 from eight overs.

The match could have been carried over to the next morning or abandoned: one giving Ireland a chance to recover, the other ensuring they would progress as Scotland had already beaten Bermuda. Instead, the ICC officials at the ground decided the game would resume and conclude that evening.

Simmo greeted the news phlegmatically for someone whose contract may well have been 'reviewed' had Ireland failed to qualify. Waiting to be called in to the committee room to discover just how many overs would be lopped, he told his skipper: 'We're going to be shafted, and there's nothing we can do about it. So we'll go in there with a smile on our faces, accept the decision and get on with it.' Porty recalls those words with something approaching awe; it was a defining moment for the coach.

The committee decided it would be a nine overs per side match. Ireland, possibly in shock, managed only a couple more and shed three wickets in the extra over. Only TWO runs were added for the loss of play, making the D/L calculation 46 to win, which Bermuda would have to get in eight overs to qualify for the semi-finals on run-rate. All ten wickets available, of course.

It seemed horribly unfair and it wasn't only the Ireland camp who were complaining. Umpire Darrell Hair stormed out of the pavilion, muttering: 'These boffins might understand maths, but they don't understand cricket.'

What followed was one of the most exhilarating hours I've watched, roared on by a Belfast crowd who for once got right behind the team. What should have been impossible was never in doubt from the first over when Connell struck with his first ball and third. PC was man of the match for his 3/8 while Kevin O'Brien, Botha and Cusack all bowled superbly on a pitch and conditions ideally suited to their wobblers and nibblers.

Adi Birrell, who was freelancing as a coach with the Scotland team, stood next to me for a couple of overs. 'I just don't see anywhere they can score off Botha,' he said, excitedly. His heart was still green.

The player who caught my eye was Nobby: immaculate in his glovework, busy, bright, chirpy and directing everyone and everything. He claimed a stumping off Botha and a run out. It all went through the keeper that evening; he set the tempo and the standard for what I would rate as one of the best five wins of this journey. Please don't ask for the other four, as with best innings, I haven't drawn up a list of contenders. It was just such a good performance that it has to be top five, if not right at the top.

There was a late scare when TJ was hit for six in the crucial eighth over, but with nine needed to qualify from three balls, PC held a catch at deep midwicket and Ireland were in the semi-finals on run-rate. Four singles and two dots off the final over meant they had also won by four runs on D/L as Bermuda finished two short of the original 43/7.

Ireland dismissed Kenya for 67 and beat them by four wickets in the first semi-final the following morning, creeping home with five balls to spare. Those Stormont pitches were not the best. The Netherlands beat Scotland later, but the final was rained off. It didn't matter too much because both sides had already qualified for the 2009 finals in England.

Before I could leave, the Netherlands manager Rob Kemming insisted on buying me a beer for making him a hero in the Dutch dressing room. On the first day his side had been fretting that having won their opening game, much like Ireland, they might lose their second and be eliminated.

'Just get within ten and you'll go through on run-rate,' I told him.

'How can you possibly know that? The other two don't play until tomorrow.'

'If you lose by fewer than ten you'll finish the group with a positive net run-rate, yes?'

'Sure, but the other two …'

'Mate, how is it possible for three teams in a group of three all to have positive run-rates?'

Malahide – 7–10 August

More rain frustrated Ireland's hopes of beating Canada in their final home game of the 2007/08 InterContinental Cup. Only one completed innings meant a meagre return of three points, from a possible 20, against a team destined to finish second bottom of the eight-team round robin. In the play that was possible, Whitey continued his love affair with competition, notching another century, but Canada had only lost five wickets replying to 326/6 declared when a deluge ended the match.

While the Ireland squad had busily joined in the mopping-up work and were desperate to play, across the water Scotland and Kenya sat and watched the rain for four days in Glasgow and received ten points each for not bowling a ball. Richard Done, who helped devise the points system for the ICC, explained that statistically it was proven to be the fairest way of doing things. I wasn't convinced.

Kenya had better luck with the weather in Amstelveen the following week and dispatched the Dutch by an innings, while Namibia won in Bermuda in early September to strengthen their position at the top of the qualifying ladder. So the double champions would travel to Africa in October knowing they had little margin for error, and would probably need to beat both Namibia and Kenya if they were to reach a third successive final.

Windhoek – 3 October

It was good to be back at the Wanderers for the first time since *that* game but the warm feeling soon departed as Ireland slumped to 23/4 after losing the toss. White and Cusack promised something of a recovery, but not for long, and the visitors were all out for 69 before lunch.

Even more unbelievably, Ireland were briefly favourites to take the six points on offer for a first-innings lead. Namibia lost their top seven for 37, but the tail wagged and, although an eighth wicket fell with the scores level, the home side stretched away to an advantage of 50 runs.

This wasn't the only disappointment of the afternoon. As the players walked off for tea, Nobby marched alongside one of the not out batsmen. A red mist had descended and the keeper started ranting: 'Fecking in-bred farming chap' or words to that effect and length.

Over and over. Call it what you will: indiscipline, passion, overwhelming desire to win – it was wholly unacceptable. The recipient of the abuse did well to keep his cool because with a bat in hand he could have done some damage and pleaded justification.

Ireland were in again well before stumps and lost another five batsmen on a remarkable day of 25 wickets. Botha, looking fluent, was stupidly run out for 29, the top score in the match, the skipper battled to 25 and the old firm of Johnston and White saw it through to the close.

In the calm of an evening beer, we realised that, although the Boys in Green had already bettered their first innings score by eight runs, they were effectively 27/5 in match terms. Nobby was advised to stay in his hotel room as it was believed a number of large Namibian farming chaps were looking to have a word. And their relatives.

Windhoek – 4 October

TJ and Whitey doubled the overnight lead to 54, then both fell in the space of a run. The spinners, McCallan and Regan West, who bowled two overs between them in the match, cobbled together 47 for the eighth wicket. West went and PC followed five balls later. The lead was 102. McCallan and Rankin added another 12 – crucial as it turned out. The home side needed 115 to end the champions' reign.

The Namibia top order chased the ball as though they had 20 overs to get the runs, not two-and-a-half days. A bit of pace in the wicket. Rankin and Connell took a couple each; TJ held a slip catch above his head at full stretch: 31/4. The momentum swung again as Gerrie Snyman hit Big Boyd for consecutive sixes. The converted train-carriage bar in the corner of the ground roared their side on, jeering PC when he spilled a tough chance at long leg. I may have taken issue with them. Snyman fell for 28. 64/6.

Then, glory be, some sensible batting reduced the ask to 24, still four wickets in hand. The skipper threw the ball to Boyd to break the stand, and he did. TJ followed up with two more: 99/9. Enter Kola Burger, with 16 needed to win, a bear of a man who had clattered four boundaries off as many balls in the first innings. Ireland cranked up the pressure. Namibia nudged closer. Nine to win. Rankin to Burger, a lofted shot to third man. McCallan moved in and took the catch at knee height falling forward.

Pandemonium. Boyd had 5/39 and Ireland had won by eight runs.

'This team never know when they're beaten,' Callender wrote, and my heart-rate returned to normal about 20 minutes later.

Windhoek – 5 October

A four-day game finishing in two isn't ideal for a freelancer. There were three storylines to follow up, though. Namibia doyen Laurie Pieters was telling anyone who cared to listen, namely me, that Ireland were ready to play Test cricket. The players were moaning about the overnight flight arrangements to Nairobi that would see them kicking their heels for six or seven hours in Johannesburg airport. Plus, what sanctions would Nobby face for his 'farming chap' outburst?

In retrospect, I should have run the pieces in that order, building up a bit of goodwill. Instead I went with the horror flight first, combining what everyone was saying into a 'senior player said' moan. A perfectly justifiable moan, mind. Callender and I were making the same journey and had arranged a night in a nearby hotel. If we could do it, there was no reason something similar could not be arranged for the players. It was ridiculous to expect them to pitch up at Jomo Kenyatta at seven in the morning, after a 13-hour trek, and start a key match the next day.

The article was sympathetic to the squad, but it didn't go down well in Dublin. Instructions were passed to the manager and Big Roy summoned me. 'Which player said this?'

'You don't expect me to tell you that?'

'Was it Trent?' TJ had given up a full-time job to go on the trip and that was mentioned.

'No. It's actually what's been said to me by four players, and none of them is Trent.'

'This has caused all sorts back home – they're trying to get the flights changed now.'

'You're getting a new schedule?'

'We don't know yet,' Roy said, a little twinkle in his eye. He knew my intentions were positive but his serious demeanour returned. 'Anyway, the team have been told they can't speak to you again without going through me first.'

'For feck's sake, Roy! You're joking? That piece could get you all a proper night's sleep!'

'Journalists do their job; managers do theirs,' was his final word on the matter.

When an edict like that is issued, you'll get some adhering to it, apologetically, some who will give you hard stares from a distance, and others, well ... That afternoon I bumped into Big Boyd in the shopping mall beside the hotel. We exchanged a couple of sentences, I probably checked on his fitness, then we chatted a while longer. Eventually I reminded him he wasn't supposed to be talking to me. 'Ah, feck that!'

The second piece was nearly as bad, but for a different reason. With a one-match suspended sentence still hanging over him for ranting at Ken McCurdy in Aberdeen, it was reasonable to assume that Nobby would be banned for at least two matches for his latest outburst, so I wrote 'Niall O'Brien is set to be banned for two games following his, etc. ...' with an explanation of why in the succeeding paragraphs. It's what newspapers call throwing the story forward. The sub-editors at the *Indo* headlined the report 'O'Brien banned for two games'.

Dearie me, even an enjoyable return to Joe's Beerhouse wasn't going to resurrect this trip. As it turned out, David Jukes was refereeing the game remotely, for budget reasons, and the report of the incident did not reach him until it was too late to impose any sanction and, to be fair, the subs at the *Indo* have saved me more times than not.

The third article had a much better reception. Laurie was emphatic. Ireland were good enough to play Test cricket and the ICC should make them Full Members immediately. It was the first time in print that anyone had proposed Test cricket for Ireland. The *Indo* gave it a good show, but Callender scoffed at the idea. 'Way too soon for that! Ridiculous!' Moustache bristling.

Except it wasn't. Ireland were a better team at that stage than Zimbabwe and had the measure of Bangladesh too. If the ICC hadn't made them wait so long then McCallan, Johnston and Botha would all have retired with the Test cap or two their talents and hard work deserved.

It was a shame then, and still is, that the ICC pathway to Test cricket is so cumbersome and inflexible. Surely the aim should be to get the best players competing at the highest level, at any given time, based on merit. Why is it not possible to elevate the best of the second-tier nations, via the IC Cup, to play Test cricket for a period of four or five years, with the worst of the 12 Test sides dropping down? Simple. Exactly what is the problem with that?

Nairobi – 11–15 October

Kenya's star had fallen a long way, even from 2005. Steve Tikolo was still there, but starting to show his age, whatever it was, as were the other stalwarts of the team that reached the World Cup semi-final only five years previously. Where was the new blood?

Ireland's poor luck with the weather earlier in the tournament meant that Kenya needed only a draw to join Namibia in the IC Cup final, and they had been playing for one at least a week before Simmo's squad touched down after their long trek (the itinerary wasn't changed despite Roy's efforts). The pitch at the Gymkhana Club had been rolled into submission. And then rolled some more. Flat only started to describe it.

Ireland batted and while the skipper missed out, and Cusack only managed 42, the O'Briens and Botha tucked in to make centuries, and Whitey was 92 not out when Porty clapped his hands and waved them in on 578/4. It would be a reasonable assumption that Ireland batted on after tea on the second day to give Whitey a chance to become their fourth centurion. But that wasn't the thinking. The idea was to force the Kenyans to walk out to field for a sixth time, even if it was only for ten minutes. Simmo's psychological warfare. O'Brien the younger finished on 171 not out, having cleared the ropes 12 times.

So, 20 wickets in the best part of seven sessions was the requirement and three fell that second evening, including a first to McCallan. Kyle and West, the classical right and left-arm spin duo, claimed the next seven as well, as Kenya were dismissed for 186 and asked to follow on. It had taken 85.1 overs of toil in the sun, though, and the second innings was even harder work.

TJ was immense. Perhaps drawing on the granite-hard experience of playing grade cricket in New South Wales, the big Aussie seamed new depths of willpower and sheer bloody-mindedness. After claiming the first two wickets, he bowled a wonderfully probing spell to Tikolo on the final morning. Ireland's champion to Kenya's. The game would be won or saved here, because if Tikolo put down roots he could – and would – bat all day. The Kenyan cracked, driving a half chance back to Johnston that was snapped up at ankle height on his follow through. The big man roared, but the home side were still a long way from beaten, even at 164/5 when TJ removed opener Seren Waters for a top score of 75.

To the growing frustration of myself and Roy, as we prowled the ground looking for lucky spots to sit in the slatted wooden stands, only one more wicket fell before tea. On reflection we were walking anti-clockwise, which was a mistake.

With Thomas Odoyo well set and Jimmy Kamande giving determined support, it seemed likely that Kenya would see out the draw. Westie finally had Odoyo caught at slip, after he had resisted for 168 balls, but it wasn't until the skipper turned to an eighth bowler that the game finally swung decisively. Botha, who wasn't 100 per cent, claimed an lbw with his fifth ball, then clattered the woodwork. After another 22 balls of defiance from last man Peter Ongondo, it was Westie who wrapped up the innings in his 74th over of the match. Ireland had won by an innings and 65 runs, with 25 minutes to spare.

What a victory! And what a feeling of elation along with the mental and physical exhaustion. I'm sure the players felt it as well. We were all off to Port Elizabeth.

Nairobi – 17 October

A tri-series of ODIs had been scheduled to follow the four-day game, with Zimbabwe making up the three. As the first match got underway, I began my usual stroll around the boundary. Left for wickets, this time. Big Boyd's opening spell was taking a bit of tap. He was chuntering between overs at long leg. I'd save him bending for his water bottle, hand it to him, he would take a swig and then hurl the bottle back onto the ground. I knew better than to speak at those times.

When I got back to the press area, Richard Done was waiting. 'What the hell do you think you were doing!?' I frowned. 'David, this is an ODI! A one-day international! We can't have journalists talking to players during the game. You shouldn't be anywhere near the boundary.'

The ICC man was right, of course, but to me it had seemed a natural thing to do. At least in the past; times were changing.

After Ireland had lost heavily to Zimbabwe and beaten Kenya the next day, the rest of the series was washed out. Back at the hotel, I saw a familiar smile one evening.

'Hey, Antoinette! You're still here then?' It was the Rwandan girl I'd met at the Hilton during the World Cricket League the year before.

'Still here,' she said. The rain didn't matter so much after that.

Port Elizabeth – 30 October–3 November

Emirates used to have a ridiculously generous frequent-flier programme. It's too long ago to remember the details, but they almost paid me to travel down to South Africa for the final. Sitting in the lounge at Gatwick, enjoying a third glass of a very nice white before departure, I decided it might be an idea to buy a case to drink at home. Google informed me I would have to part with close to £40 a bottle. Ah, well … I did have a fourth glass, though.

What was awaiting? I wondered. A couple of decades earlier, it would have taken a lot more than a ridiculously cheap flight and complimentary wine to get me to South Africa. I'd been in the vanguard of anti-apartheid campaigning in the 1980s. Not going quite as far as marching, or anything like that, but I had religiously, without fail, checked all the labels on the oranges in Sainsbury's and boycotted any grown in the Cape.

So it was fair to say I'd done my bit in bringing about the birth of the Rainbow Nation. Would my diligence and sacrifice have been worth it? The first thing I encountered were two female immigration officials singing a two-part harmony as one of them stamped my passport. I was going to enjoy this place.

Before bed, I knew this wouldn't be my only visit to Port Elizabeth. Super spot. Excellent family-run hotel, near to where the team were staying; long stretches of sand, if a bit windy; good bars, if a little edgy at times; mix of restaurants, many overlooking the ocean, and cheap! Dearie me, everything was so cheap. I shuffled into breakfast the next day.

'Good morning, sir!' The serving staff in Sullivans were the sort that have been in the job for decades and do an impersonation of being a great waiter, as well as being one. He could see I was struggling. 'Everything OK, sir?'

'Ugh … Your alcohol is too cheap!'

'No sir, your pound is too strong.'

The final was scheduled for five days at St George's Park, the Test match ground. Lovely little venue. Only holds about 12,000, intimate atmosphere and famous for the brass band that plays at the back of one stand during the big games. Not this one, though.

Namibia won the toss and batted. Big Boyd followed up his winning spell in Windhoek with the first wicket, the other seamers probed and chipped away before Connell took two in three balls that should have seen Namibia dismissed for around 220. Instead, last man Kola Burger again cut loose with a few meaty blows that lifted his team to 250 all out. Namesake Louis, one of four Burgers in the XI, was unbeaten on 74 when PC bowled Kola to return figures of 5/54.

So far so good, we thought, but it all went horribly wrong on the second morning as Snyman found a good line and some very late swing on a full length to rip through the Ireland top order. Three of the first five failed to score: Nobby, much to the delight of the farming chaps, Boatsie, bowled first up on his 100th appearance, and O'Brien the younger suffering the same fate two balls later. Chaos. I'd gone for a walk around the ground with Big Roy, when Mr IC Cup himself, Whitey, became Snyman's fifth victim: 37/5. The manager's chin hit his chest. 'Long way back from here, DT!'

Cusack and Johnston led the recovery with a stand of 141 for the sixth wicket, but after TJ had gone for 58, Sarel Burger bored out the tail by bowling an ultra-defensive line, two feet wide, to a packed off-side field, which the impatient so-and-sos just had to have a go at. Poor old Cusie was left stranded on 95 from 230 balls when the innings ended at 195. It was a more important knock than his maiden first-class century against Scotland the year before, and only surpassed by that crucial supporting role to come in Bangalore.

Despite the deficit of 55, momentum continued in Ireland's direction as Namibia batted poorly the second time. Again it was the seamers who did the damage. PC added another three victims, taking his tally to 28 for the five games he had played, at the very impressive average of 11.67. Rankin took 4/39 and when Kola fell for a third-ball duck Ireland needed 201 to win.

Quite a turnaround. We wondered if some of the Namibians had been less than professional on their Saturday night away from home. If so, their hangovers would not have been improved by the sight of Nobby taking Ireland to within 65 runs of victory on that third evening, for the loss of the skipper. The formality of a nine-wicket win was completed without fuss, along with Nobby's century, the following morning. Two centuries in his two finals for the keeper; Cusie added 39 not out to his first-innings effort and was man of the match.

The celebrations started early with beers in the dressing room, and went on late. Alcohol was consumed. In vast quantities. In David Boon on a flight to England-like quantities. Well deserved too, after a month away from home and a job very well done. I bumped into TJ, walking on the beach the following morning.

'Bit dusty, DT.' He wasn't talking about the sand. 'Three-times champions, though. You don't get that very often – in any sport.'

2009

Primrose Hill – 18 February

I'm not sure where the idea of 'Antoinette in South Africa' came from, but the seed was sown on a rainy day in Nairobi when she told me that her ambition was to move there, or to Dubai. Maybe it was the 'Enry 'Iggins in me, or maybe Ruud Onstein was the inspiration.

My Dutch friend and his missus had, many years ago, privately sponsored a couple of boys from underprivileged backgrounds in Cape Town and spoke glowingly of how well 'David' was doing: a good education, a university degree and now a job in banking. They visited him and his family every year. What about the other one? 'We don't talk about him.' Still, a 50 per cent success rate for their philanthropy, and they had made a small difference.

So, if I was going to spend three weeks in South Africa covering the World Cup qualifiers, why not fly Antoinette down from Kenya? She could take it from there.

'Are you serious?'

'Yes, why not? It'll be fun and when I've gone you can stay on.'

'You're crazy!'

'So you don't want to come?'

'Of course I want to come!'

Sandton – 30 March

What would Johannesburg be like? I'd enjoyed my first trip to South Africa but from what I'd read this was going to be very different to the Eastern Cape; one of the most dangerous cities on the planet where it was impossible to stray more than a few feet outside your hotel without being robbed or murdered. Probably both. But that was Johannesburg. We were staying in Sandton, an upmarket suburb where businesses had decamped, leaving the increasingly unsafe city centre.

Top spot, Sandton. Safe to walk around, with a huge shopping and restaurant complex set around Nelson Mandela Square. We even got to see the great man himself one night in the Butcher's Shop. Well, almost. It was Morgan Freeman, who has played Mandela. The American actor had eaten and was drawing a crowd of fawning middle-aged white folk looking to shake his hand as he left. The same people who wouldn't have allowed him in the steakhouse two decades ago. My Don't-Buy-the-Oranges hackles were still easily raised. Perhaps they thought it was Mandela.

Without venturing into the city itself, we only encountered one unsettling situation when James Fitzgerald, who by now was working for the ICC media department, contrived to again lose his way driving home and suddenly we were in Alexandra. Shacks, not much street lighting and scary. Up to that point, the townships had always been 'over there', now we were over there as well. Hairs on the back of the neck time. Again.

Fitzy, knowing what to do, would slow some 100 metres short of a red light and drive slowly towards it, not stopping. On one occasion when the light didn't change he drove through slowly. Apparently it's the accepted way to minimise the chance of a car-jacking. Second only to knowing where you're going.

Benoni – 1 April

Twelve teams took part in the qualifiers: two initial groups of six, followed by a Super Eight and a final, plus placings play-offs. A total of ten games in 19 days for those who got through the first round. An opening match against Scotland would have been seen as tricky only a couple of years previously, but not now.

Funny thing, momentum. Hard to come by, easy to lose and a bugger to get back again. Scotland found themselves 24/4 before the end of the powerplay with the match effectively over. A one-man rearguard from Neil McCallum, who hit an unbeaten 121, lifted his team to 232/7, but Porty responded with a century of his own, from

89 balls, and Ireland were home and hosed in the 38th over, with seven wickets to spare.

A post-match interview with Ryan Watson wasn't to be missed. Callender, moustache bristling, opened up with 'Well, that was pretty one-sided?'

After a defensive reply from the Scotland captain about the toss and early movement, I waded in. 'The gap between the two sides has obviously been growing in recent years, does this result make it even wider?' It was almost cruel.

Johannesburg – 5 April

O'Brien the younger hit an unbeaten century against Oman the next day and Ireland had also eased past Uganda before I found myself heading back to Oliver Tambo airport to see whether Antoinette had managed to catch her flight. I'd heard nothing from her for over a week, but given the state of the internet in Nairobi that wasn't unusual; the digital pigeon was probably still somewhere over Lake Victoria. The flight she was booked on had landed. I waited. And then waited some more. I was just beginning to think she'd cashed in the ticket, or died, or something, when her familiar smile appeared through Arrivals.

Boy was she happy to be in South Africa. 'I can't believe it!' We went back to the hotel and, equipped with a local SIM card, she spent the rest of the afternoon calling her many friends, and in a variety of languages – she spoke French and some Italian as well as English, Swahili and her native Kinyarwanda – proceeded to tell them where she was. Every conversation proudly contained 'Antoinette in South Africa' at least once.

Barry and I were sharing a two-bedroomed suite, with a kitchen and large living room. A few other journalists, including Callender and former BBC man Robin Walsh, were in the same hotel, which was just as well for evening socialising as the Ireland team were on the other side of Sandton and, apparently, banned from drinking alcohol. A prohibition that applied to the support staff as well. I'd believe that when I saw it.

Sandton – 6 April

The following day we media men went off to Benoni to watch Ireland dispose of Canada by six wickets, with Eoin scoring 84 not out and O'Brien the younger bettering him by five runs in an unbeaten partnership of 181. Meanwhile Antoinette set about exploring her new surroundings. She ventured into the centre of Johannesburg and reported back that, as we thought, it wasn't safe for *mzungu*. Nor was her cooking, mind. After that first evening we had to keep her well away from the meat. Antoinette had many skills, but grilling steaks wasn't one of them.

On the next day off, we visited the team in their hotel. Alcohol was not consumed. The stories of Simmo's ban were true. The coach was taking no chances, and no prisoners either, with everyone having to pass a breathalyser test each morning on the team bus, including himself and the rest of the support staff.

No one could work out how the manager kept passing, as Big Roy's consumption of Famous Grouse seemed as prolific as ever. It transpired he was palming the breathalyser in those big mitts, making a great show of blowing into his mobile phone, and then passing the original instrument back.

Antoinette was greatly taken with Roy, far more so than any of the younger, fitter players. Was it a cultural thing

– the big man of the group? Female fascination with the Alpha male, maybe.

A regulation seven-wicket victory over Namibia at the University of Witwatersrand completed a clean sweep of the five group matches. Ireland had chased in four games and not been taken past the 45th over, and had won the other match by 116 runs. All going to plan. No celebrations yet, though, and definitely no alcohol.

Krugersdorp – 11 April

The longest trek of the tournament took us into Afrikaner country again, on to the high veldt, to play Afghanistan. It was a noticeably different place, not least when I asked to book a taxi back to Sandton after the first game against Oman and was told there was no local firm. At least, no local white firm. It took all sorts to arrange transport.

The Afghanistan team were still something of a novelty. Amazing journey, we thought, from learning the game in the refugee camps of Pakistan to actually reaching a World Cup qualifying campaign. It was a lovely yarn but no one could see it going much further. Sure, didn't this lot struggle to beat Jersey by two wickets only the previous summer? Yet here they were with Mohammad Nabi, Asghar Stanikzai and Mohammad Shahzad, the nucleus of the team that went a lot, lot further over the next decade.

Future star Rashid Khan would only have been ten at the time – a very mature ten, mind. And then there was Hamid Hassan, who could bowl yorkers to command in the death overs and was that impressive before injury that Middlesex tried to sign him.

Hamid was responsible for inflicting Ireland's first defeat. A competent bowling performance had restricted

Afghanistan to 218/7, including two overs from Eoin that cost five runs. 'Is there anything you can't do?' I asked him, during a walk around the boundary. Old habits die hard and anyway it wasn't an ODI. Whitey took 2/27 from ten overs; he was not the first whitey to prosper in these parts.

Ireland struggled in reply and after a couple of poor shots and a stupid run out they were 73/5. A century stand between White and O'Brien the younger took them within 33 runs of victory, order appeared to be restored, then Hamid started firing in his toe-crushers and the last five wickets went down in a heap. The upstarts had beaten the favourites by 22 runs.

We all still thought it was a flash in the pan, and a few bad-taste jokes flew around along the lines of 'I'll bet the pitches in Kabul are minefields, eh?'

A decade later the two sides were playing a Test match, featuring five of the players that day in Krugersdorp.

Pretoria – 15 April

After crushing the UAE by eight wickets, qualification would be secured with a victory over the Netherlands. Porty won an important toss and Ireland kept the Dutch batsmen on a tight leash. The LC de Villiers Oval was in the middle of a park, with no stands or seating. I went for a wander and found myself sitting on the grass next to Barry who was happily snapping away on the boundary. I helped with his running log, jotting down which shots he wanted to keep. Digital photography has taken a lot of the chance out of the job; few important moments are missed these days with ten or more images captured every ball, but the earlier you discard the chaff, the better. Hence the log.

Next thing I knew, an armed security guard was trying to move me on. My accreditation did not allow me to sit on this particular piece of grass, apparently. There were, at best, a dozen people watching the game, other than players and officials. I ignored him, he persisted. Short of telling him to feck off, I told him to feck off. He was having none of it, though, and you can't argue with a gun-toting minimum-wager.

Rankin and Cusack took three wickets each to dismiss the Dutch for 222 before the skipper and his little ginger mate broke the back of the chase with a second-wicket partnership of 117. Ireland won with six wickets and more than five overs to spare. Eoin's 76 from 62 balls was 'a little gem of an innings by a little gem of a player' as I told RTE radio that evening. It was also his last for Ireland, after 63 matches and 2,075 runs. He sat alone on the pitch for a while at the end. A few thoughts, no doubt. No regrets, though.

Pretoria – 17 April

A return to LC de Villiers for the final Super Eight match saw Porty choose to bat first against Kenya. You wondered if sometimes he plumped for the tougher option just to challenge his team. Ireland struggled against the moving ball first thing and despite a gritty half-century from Nobby and a rapid 34 from Johnboy towards the end a total of 208/9 wasn't enough.

When Steve Tikolo fell at 96/4 there was an opening, but that was the last success as the Africans eased home with two overs to spare to claim one of the last World Cup places. Scotland missed out as a result. An ironic rendition of 'Flower of Scotland' was later heard coming from one of the dressing rooms.

Ireland had rested TJ and omitted Eoin, who wanted to fly home now qualification had been secured. There seemed to be a standoff between the little fella and the management. It wasn't possible to change his flights, he was told. This was patently nonsense given that Johannesburg is an international hub. He was on his way in one sense, but Simmo and Roy were not going to help him on his way. It was all a bit unnecessary.

Someone else on their way was Antoinette. Pretoria was the town for her and she would stay on there after the game, which was the first cricket match she had been to. 'When is Roy going to throw?' she kept asking, refusing to accept 'He isn't' as an answer. She joined the Kenyan celebrations after and told us that they were in awe of the Ireland team and hadn't expected to win. It was interesting feedback.

A little hug and we said 'Goodbye.' She would be fine, I thought. A survivor. Would I see her again? I hoped so.

Centurion – 19 April

After Ireland had qualified, Daniel James wrote a report sympathetic to Eoin and got me in hot water with the rest of the squad. Danny, as he liked to be known, was an old rogue. Indeterminable age, rheumy eyes, cravat; he followed Ireland with a passion he only mustered otherwise when studying the horses, or GeeGees as he called them, and playing golf. He had sustained a decades-long feud with Scotty over an unpaid drinks bill and always referred to the former Hon. Sec. as 'a rum cove'. He would travel between games in an open-top sports car or fly his Tiger Moth to the more remote locations. A splendid fellow; filed a few pars for the *Irish Examiner* and unfailingly called the first interval 'luncheon'.

Daniel James didn't exist, of course. He was an invention of Ger and myself. Freelancers will often use an alias, or COD, when writing for a different publication and I'd chosen to utilise my son's given names for *Examiner* pieces. Fitzy had a much better one for cricket reports: Brian Charles. It was Ger who helped me put the flesh on Daniel's old bones, creating a marvellously romantic character over several pints.

Anyway, TJ and several other players took exception to the old boy's jottings and found out that I was the author. It was nothing terrible, but just as the group had joined ranks when Eoin wanted to leave early, so they also ostracised the bloke who wrote a supportive piece.

'You made it sound as though he was responsible for us qualifying,' TJ said. 'It was a team effort, DT.'

Indeed it was.

At the qualifying final, I had no idea I was being ignored, although TJ failed to acknowledge me at fine leg between overs. I put it down to concentration as he delivered one of his best spells for Ireland. The big fella had a new trigger movement to start his run – a distinctive stamp of his right foot – and whether it was that which helped retain his focus, or a simmering grievance against a fictional journalist, his pressure was relentless. Ten superb overs gave him 5/14 and the man of the match award as Canada were bowled out for 185 and beaten by nine wickets.

Primrose Hill – 29 April

Back in London, I texted 'Happy Birthday' to TJ and got a stroppy reply. He was still angry with the bloke he was 'always gonna love' after Operation Townsend. I'd had enough of this nonsense. Feck it, I thought, and announced my retirement. After 15 years the magic wasn't the same, and the soft sods weren't even allowed a beer in the evenings now. I'd given it a good run and deserved better than this. It was time to take a back seat. I would watch from the boundary without having to worry about deadlines and super-sensitive, balding Aussies. I already had a blazer. A few egg stains and I'd fit in with the other old boys.

The *Indo* begged me to stay on. Couldn't I just file them a few pars, even if I was going to fewer games in the future? They were happy for me to watch the matches on TV and write a report 'off tube', as it became known. While I was considering this, TJ got in touch to say he hoped he hadn't influenced my decision. He appreciated all my efforts over the years and had been having a bad day.

Ah, go on then. I told the *Indo* that I'd continue to send copy on the understanding that if I wasn't in attendance they wouldn't use my byline. Retirement had lasted less than a week, although I did give up most of the radio work and Daniel James had filed for the last time.

Leicester – 4 May

What was to be the final year in English domestic competitions produced several of the usual one-sided contests in the Friends Provident Trophy, but also another victory as PC fired out Worcestershire for 58 at New Road, and nearly a second when Nottinghamshire scraped home by two wickets at Clontarf. There were fine individual performances, too, not least Stirlo making 80 at Grace Road. Still only 18, he already had three cracking half-centuries against county opposition and was one of the cleanest and most exciting strikers of a cricket ball I'd seen. Yet there seemed a reluctance to accept that here was another gem from across the Irish Sea.

An opponent dismissed Stirling's runs against Leicestershire as all 'stepping away and hitting it over gully' while an experienced broadcaster described him as the 'little Irish slogger'. Despite the World Cup and increasingly competitive efforts in county competitions, the English didn't want to believe that Ireland could keep producing top-quality cricketers. Yes, there was Ed and Eoin, but what were the odds on a third star batsman?

Stirlo's problem was not being South African. County sides were, and still are, dotted with very average Boks, who are revered for little more than their place of birth. Had he been Stirlo from Stellenbosch he would have opened the batting for a decade in the Championship and been compared to Virender Sehwag. Instead, when he did get a four-day game for Middlesex, it was somewhere down the order and then back in the Stiffs the following week.

'Why don't they open with him?' TJ would moan, as the years wore on. 'You might be one down in the first over occasionally, but other times he'll have won you the game before lunch.'

It never did happen. For a decade, Middlesex failed to get the best out of their man and Stirlo was far too nice a bloke to kick up a fuss.

Nottingham – 8 June

The only surprising thing about Ireland's six-wicket victory over Bangladesh, which saw the Boys in Green qualify for the Super Eight stage of the World T20, is that people were still surprised. I listened to 'expert' summarisers on the radio and it was all plucky little Ireland against the big boys of Bangladesh, despite having beaten them comfortably at the World Cup.

TJ took three wickets, Kyle conceded 17 from his four overs and there was nothing big about the big boys' total of 137/8. Nobby settled nerves with 40 from 25 balls and his brother hit two sixes to see Ireland home with ten balls to spare.

There were no further 'upsets' in the Super Eight, which was actually two groups of four. Ireland ran Sri Lanka close, losing by nine runs at Lord's, but lost heavily to New Zealand and eventual winners Pakistan. For the second global tournament in a row they had reached the last eight, though, and those who had scoffed at the *Indo* article calling for Test status were starting to wonder whether Laurie Pieters wasn't on to something.

Derry – 3–6 July

The little Irish slogger made his first international century against Kenya, as the champions began their InterContinental Cup defence at Eglinton. It was a controlled, mature innings of 181 balls, which featured patience and a great awareness of off stump. On 94, he might have been forgiven for nudging his way to the landmark but typically launched the ball over midwicket and out of the ground. There was no outlandish celebration. Just a handshake and an almost apologetic raising of the bat. That was Stirlo, too. He had a shy, ah shucks, manner to him; holding conversations with his hands deep in pockets and chin on chest. One of the most likeable young men you'd ever meet. But not South African.

Cusack made a half-century in both innings and was looking more and more like the long-term replacement for

Botha, whose body was screaming louder by the month. It said something for the all-round depth in that Ireland side that Cusie, Boatsie and O'Brien the younger only sent down six overs between them in the two innings. McCallan, captaining in the absence of the county players, set Kenya 298 to win in 70 overs on the last afternoon and, after threatening briefly, the East Africans clung on for a draw, eight down. Ireland had collected first-innings points but it wasn't the most dynamic start to a campaign.

Back in London, I heard from Antoinette for the first time since leaving her in Pretoria. The new life in South Africa hadn't gone quite how she hoped it would. It was hard to earn money without a visa and it was really, really cold. She had decided to return to Nairobi. I've wondered since whether I should have done a bit more to support her in those first months; whether that would have made a difference. She would always get by, though.

The last I heard she was married to an Italian.

Aberdeen – 17–20 August

Back to the Granite City, on the train this time, for the next IC Cup match. Porty, who had lost his place in the Gloucestershire red-ball side, scored 77 and 118, but didn't receive the support he would have expected in the first innings, as a very strong batting line-up subsided from 140/2 to 202 all out. Regan West found turn in the Mannofield pitch on the second morning and took a career-best 7/88 as a similar collapse almost saw Ireland claim the first-innings points. The home side's last pair stumbled over the line, though, to gain a lead of six.

The skipper looked a class apart, second time around, but rain was forecast on the final day. Heavy rain. What to do? Declare early and push for the win, or hope that the forecasters might be wrong? Porty could have declared with a lead of 257 when he was eighth out, but batted all the way down. Scotland needed 298 to win and were 72/5 at stumps. The forecasters were not exaggerating. Match abandoned, and only three points to Ireland. The odds on a fourth title were lengthening.

Another bucket-list box was ticked when I returned home on the Caledonian Sleeper. Those Highlands politicians who kept the anachronism subsidised are to be commended. What a great way to travel. A cabin to myself, bed, head down for a few hours, and woken with a cup of tea and biscuits. Shortbread, obviously. Wait a minute, though? That's weird. We were definitely going the other way last night? What's going on? Are we going back to Scotland? Did we forget something? No. Apparently the engine pulls into the buffers at Preston sometime in the early hours and exits again with the front end now the back. They might have warned us.

It was the only time during my Ireland journey that I wasn't sure which direction we were going – apart from the Rutherford years, of course.

Belfast – 27 August

An ODI that Ireland were twice winning comfortably was decided by a stunning piece of fielding from Eoin – unfortunately in an England shirt. The Ashes winners sent over a strong side, led by Paul Collingwood, and were restricted to 203/9 from their 50 overs. TJ was superb; probably at the peak of his powers he moved Ravi Bopara and Jonathan Trott for ducks at the top of the order, on his way to figures of 4/26 from ten overs. I was pretty sure I hadn't written anything to upset him in the past few days, but it was that sort of performance.

Then it rained, as it often does at Stormont. The ominous, almost inevitable clouds took the next over from the Dundonald End, and a good few overs after that. The grumpy England skipper thought that the match should have been abandoned. A large crowd probably swayed the umpires because the outfield was on the 'not' side of playable. Three hours later, Ireland were asked to get 116 from 20 overs, the minimum to constitute a match. Colly was far from amused and didn't disguise it.

It's funny how professional cricketers are rarely happier than when not playing, and I can't throw stones because the same inclination to an early finish is found in most press boxes, as well. Callender is an exception; he always wants to be watching cricket. Generally, though, those paid to be there are the least concerned by an abandonment, giving little thought to supporters who have had the date ringed for months and used up holiday from a proper job to be there, or the kids we all used to be, wanting to see their heroes and hear that gorgeous sound to young ears of grown-up bat on hard ball, echoing around the ground.

In the ninth over of the chase, Ireland were 64/2 and cruising, but then Botha was lbw and Stirlo followed in the next over for a cracking 30 from 26 balls. England cleverly took the pace off, the pitch was sticky, runs dried up and wickets fell. Owais Shah, of all people, removed Mooney, West and Cusack, batting at ten, with his part-time whatever they were.

While there was TJ there was hope and with nine needed from the final two balls the big man might just have kept the game alive with a massive heave to long-on. The fielder was a familiar little ginger fella who leapt and knocked the 'six' back into play, a metre inside the rope. Johnston crashed the last ball for four, but it wasn't enough to mark his 100th appearance with a win. At the other end, Kyle was unbeaten on five in what would be his last match for Ireland.

The crowd filed away, discussing that penultimate ball. The Irish contingent were more divided than ever between those who understood Eoin's reasons for swapping allegiance and his personal need to always perform to the very highest level, whatever the situation – and those who thought he was even more of a wee bollix.

2010

Sydney – 6 January

The fourth and final day of the Sydney Test was the most depressing I've spent at a cricket match. It became clear, almost immediately, that Pakistan were no longer trying to win the game. The tourists had bowled superbly to dismiss Australia for 127 and then took a first-innings lead of 206. At the end of the third day, the home side were eight down and only 80 runs to the good. I wasn't expecting much more than a couple of hours' play, but the SCG press lunches are not to be missed.

The Aussie ninth-wicket pair of Mike Hussey and Peter Siddle must have wondered what was going on when Pakistan posted four or five fielders on the boundary from the start and declined to test Siddle with anything short, which was a known weakness. Runs accrued, the lead stretched past 100. Then leg-spinner Danish Kaneria found an edge from Hussey and the 'catch' was taken by keeper Kamran Akmal. Neither appealed.

A former Australian captain joined a few of us in the seating area outside the media centre in between TV commentary stints. 'Bet you didn't expect this after an hour?' someone ventured, as Hussey and Siddle remained unbroken.

'Mate, with these fields this is exactly what I'd have expected after an hour.'

Pakistan were eventually set 176 to win, after the ninth-wicket pair had extended their stand to 123, and, as wickets began to fall with sickening regularity, a mood that mixed disbelief, gloom and anger settled on those former players who could see what was going on. One sat, head in hands, muttering, 'This shouldn't be allowed to happen.'

'You never know, they might still win,' Peter Roebuck said, trying to cheer him up.

'How fecking naive are you?'

At the press conference, half an hour after Australia had won by 36 runs, there was no sense of a stunning victory; no buzz in the air. Pakistan skipper Mohammad Yousuf went through the ritual of being disappointed to lose after being in such a strong position. No one hinted at what most of us were thinking, of course. I racked my brains for a neutral question that would also suggest the skullduggery and, Sod's Law, it came to me as I was leaving the ground. 'Skipper, is there anything valuable you can take away from a defeat like that?'

I walked back towards Randwick, gutted. You always want to believe what you're looking at is genuine. OK, we knew, or strongly suspected, that Pakistan messed around with ODIs, and weren't the only ones. But a Test match? And so blatantly?

It got me wondering about that World Cup defeat by Ireland. A year or more earlier, in the press tent at Stormont, a Scottish journalist from one of the Glasgow tabloids had forcefully insisted that 'of course' Pakistan had let Ireland win. It was obvious. He wasn't alone in that thinking, but he was wrong.

I was, and still am, 100 per cent sure the St Patrick's Day game in Jamaica wasn't fixed. Why? Because the defeat sent Pakistan home. If you are cheating, you don't lose a match that puts your side out of a tournament and thereby denies the opportunity of fixing at least another six matches. That's just logic.

The Sydney Test did have a silver lining, though. One of the regulars on the balcony outside the media rooms was Kerry O'Keeffe, the former leggie who has become a commentary icon Down Under. As someone with his name might well be, he was interested to hear about the progress of Irish cricket. We chatted regularly during the game and, when the fix was officially exposed months later, he wrote in his newspaper column 'Paddy had spotted it straightaway'.

Paddy? Bloody Paddy? Fortunately our budding friendship survived that blip.

Christchurch – 11 January

By this stage of the journey there were still four Test nations I'd not visited; two of them were Sri Lanka and New Zealand. So, of course, when the senior team were scheduled to play an InterContinental Cup match against Afghanistan in Dambulla, it was inevitable that it would clash with the Under-19 World Cup on the south island.

Either destination was easily accessible from Thailand where I was now spending my winters, but I'd heard Queenstown was special, and that swayed my thinking. It was.

The first stop was Christchurch, though, a laid-back, minding-its-own-business country town that would be cruelly struck by an earthquake only 13 months later. The Ireland squad had a couple of practice matches and should have beaten West Indies.

I made my way out to Lincoln for the final warm-up on one of those days that starts off fine but then gets squally and cold. Very cold. I'd left my hoodie back at the hotel, so when a shower stopped play I went to take cover in the pavilion of what was basically a club ground.

'Pass, please?'

'Press. I'm with the Ireland team.'

'Accreditation Pass?'

'It's only a practice match, mate. It's back at the hotel.'

'Sorry, you can't come in then.' Bastard meant it too.

As I stood trying to shelter by the side of the building, the groundsman returned from putting on the covers. 'You look cold, son.'

Son? 'Yes, I am mate.'

'Get in the truck.'

Top man. We sat in his pick-up and introduced ourselves.

'My lad spent a couple of seasons in Ireland. Played for a club up north: Carrickfergus.'

'He'd know one of the Ireland coaches then.'

'Really?'

A while later Ryan Eagleson wandered out of the pavilion, and I called him over.

'Eagy, would you know a bloke by the name of Anthony Timpson?'

'Know him? He used to eat Sunday lunch at my mum's house every week.'

'This is his dad …'

Fate, eh? If it hadn't rained, or if I'd been allowed in the pavilion, the two of them would have walked past each other none the wiser.

The saying 'small world' came to mind, but then a couple of days later I got to Queenstown and realised that the world isn't small at all; it's big and it's awesome. What a stunning place. *Lord of the Rings* country. Mountains, lakes and the most amazing scenery. Spiritual too, even to someone who isn't spiritual. To paraphrase Oscar Wilde, it's not only worth seeing, but worth going to see.

Queenstown – 15 January

Alcohol was consumed with coach Matt Dwyer and assistant Eagy after the first match of the campaign, a five-wicket loss to South Africa. Andy Balbirnie, the skipper, had gone early and Stirling hadn't hung around too long either. Half-centuries from Ben Ackland and Lee Nelson, whose dad played in the 1994 ICC Trophy, followed by a blustery, red-cheeked cameo from Stuart Poynter had got Ireland to 216/6, but it wasn't nearly enough.

'So, how do we beat these Aussies?' Matt asked. Thoughtful sips of beer all round. There seemed little to no hope of upsetting a powerful, well-drilled side, captained by Mitch Marsh and containing Josh Hazlewood and Kane Richardson.

'Stirlo needs to bat 30 overs for us to have any chance,' Eagy said.

More beer. My turn. 'Don't expose him to the new ball. That's where the Aussies are strongest, and where the wickets are falling.'

Stirlo had batted at No.3 against South Africa, but what was important was when he came in, not where in the order. Matt toyed with the idea. 'Hold him back you mean?'

'Yes. Bat through the first 15 overs, then let Stirlo loose. He needs to bat 30 overs, but it doesn't have to be the first 30 overs.'

More beer. 'Yeah, that might be worth a try.'

A couple of days later, Stirlo came in at No.3 again, in the second over, and played on first ball to Richardson as Ireland were shot out for 65, losing by 209 runs.

'What happened to the plan to hold Stirlo back?'

'It was vetoed?'

'Why?'

'Because "Other teams don't do that",' Matt said, making no attempt to hide his contempt for the orthodoxy of his English boss, Mark Garaway. The Operations Manager was having none of this doing-things-differently lark.

Stirlo scored a century in the final Group B game to help Ireland chase down 217 to beat the US by five wickets. I decided against following the team to Napier, where, after beating Zimbabwe and losing heavily to Bangladesh in the Plate final, they finished tenth of 16 teams. Not a bad effort, but perhaps the minimum expected of a team containing George Dockrell, Craig Young and Stuart Thompson, as well as Balbirnie, Stirlo and Poynter.

I got back to Thailand just in time to discover Ireland had been skittled by Afghanistan in their second innings in Dambulla and had lost an IC Cup match for the first time since 2004. The champions would likely have to win in Harare later in the year to stay in the hunt for a fourth consecutive title.

Meanwhile, Matt resigned as Under-19 coach. His experience and especially his passion would be missed; he loves Irish cricket. Increasingly, though, Cricket Ireland was being run by people who were paid to love Irish cricket.

Dubai and Abu Dhabi – 9–13 February

While one left-arm spinner rode off into the sunset, another made his way to the UAE to join up with the senior squad for the first time. Dockrell had performed well in New Zealand, with his calm head as much as any ability to spin the ball, and was thrown in at the deep end, with Westie having undergone shoulder surgery which would end his 38-cap career. Simmo sensed divine intervention in the arrival of one leftie to replace the other. 'God's been good to me,' he said, after the 17-year-old had made a nerveless entrance onto the main stage.

God was also good to the coach in providing Cusie, as a long-term Mr Dependable all-rounder replacement for Botha. Different in styles, both men seemed to have bodies held together with chewing gum and string, particularly towards the end of their careers. Bits were falling off Boatsie when he pitched up for the 2011 World Cup and after contracting an illness he ended the tournament convalescing in a nursing facility, or what Big Roy described as an old folks' home, when he went to collect him. Cusie wasn't in much better shape after the 2015 edition.

It took me a while to warm to the Queenslander on the field, and I couldn't say I ever knew him off it. He didn't have the brashness of countrymen TJ or Brayso, or the cuddly charm of Lanky. Shy? Possibly. Reserved and understated, certainly. When interviewed about his early career playing grade cricket in Brisbane, he was asked if his contemporaries included any top players. He shrugged. 'I dunno. Mitchell Johnson?' His contribution during the Simmo era was immense; Ireland were never beaten if Cusie still had to bat or bowl, and nowhere was that better seen than in the 2010 World T20 qualifiers where he was named player of the tournament after Ireland had lost the final to Afghanistan.

Cusie returned 3/19 in a 22-run victory over the UAE and then made 65 from 44 balls against the Netherlands, in the two key games. Nobby might have had a gripe that the award didn't go to him for top-scoring in the tournament with 188 runs, and Simmo did have a moan about Ireland having to play the final only minutes after finishing their semi. Both finalists had already booked their tickets to the main event in the Caribbean, though.

Georgetown – 4 May

A quick trip to the World T20 was tempting, even if the Group D games were in one of the less alluring destinations. At the very least there would have been the chance to check out 'Love Deeply', but the dates didn't work and Guyana is not the easiest or cheapest place to get to, so I stayed at home. Probably just as well, given Ireland were bowled out for 68 by West Indies in the first of their two games before rain brought an abandonment against England, when replying to a modest 120/8.

Who top-scored for England? Do you really need to ask? Not content with denying Ireland victory at Stormont with his fielding, this time Eoin made 45 when the rest of his new colleagues were struggling. After batting for a total of 20.1 overs across the two games, Ireland headed home having given the eventual champions their toughest test.

Clontarf – 17 June

Could have won; should have won. At 80/0 and a little later 137/3 chasing an Australian total of 231/9, the home side were favourites, but then James Hopes bowled a tight line and got his dobbers to stick in the Castle Avenue pitch. 'You can't afford to lose wickets in bunches against teams like this because they will crush you,' Porty lamented, after the medium-pacer had taken 5/14 from nine overs to leave Ireland 39 runs short. The chance of a first ODI home win over one of the big boys had gone begging again, but a packed crowd enjoyed themselves and mid-afternoon a group of schoolkids were heard singing 'We deserve a Test match'.

The evening before the game an informal Cricket Writers get-together at the Railway Union ground had granted temporary membership to a mate of mine from Down Under who had never been near a typewriter, laptop or microphone. 'Where are you from?' Barry asked. The next day he gained entry as 'Kevin Stevens – Illawarra Times'. Accreditation was a lot less formal in those days, even if it had already moved on from the original piece of string around the wrist.

The Australians, led by Ricky Ponting, were popular visitors, staying on the island for several days of fundraising events and dinners, and were happy to mix in and meet people, unlike the England team who always wanted to be in and out as quickly as possible. Their big guns Ponting, Michael Clarke, Mike Hussey and Shane Watson all played too, ahead of an Ashes series. The difference in approach to the ECB's was marked, and appreciated.

Rotterdam, The Hague and Amsterdam – 1–10 July

Simmo rated winning the World League as one of his top achievements as coach because Ireland marched through the ten-day tournament, not only unbeaten but also untroubled, without Porty, Nobby and the rest of the county-contracted players. Victories over Kenya, Afghanistan, Scotland, Canada and the Netherlands, followed by a second slaying of the Scots in the final, by six wickets, owed much to an experienced core of Whitey, O'Brien the younger, Johnboy, TJ and Cusie; but Stirlo was now starting to score important runs, Under-19 skipper Balbirnie took his senior bow and Andy Poynter contributed an important half-century against the Afghans. A larger pool of talent was emerging.

Belfast – 15 July

A couple of ODIs against Bangladesh, who had beaten England the previous weekend, meant a chance to return to the Ardshane Country House, sadly for the final time. Valerie was retiring; absolutely, definitely this time. We would miss her. The thing with Valerie was she understood hospitality, and delivered the right amount to each guest, without ever fawning; it was just the best place to stay.

Understanding hospitality could not be levelled at Stormont. The press lunches still consisted of a plastic-packed sandwich, a bag of crisps, a small chocolate bar and a piece of fruit, in a brown paper carrier bag. Tea or coffee. The Ardmore Express had tried to improve this, by getting us something hot to eat, but to no avail. There was a sense of 'they're lucky to get anything for free, and should be grateful'.

Even this was an improvement on a few years previously when Scotty had told me, quite seriously, that as I was there to make money, I should not only pay for my own lunch, but make a contribution to the ICU costs of staging the match. He had no understanding of publicity.

After the toss, won by Ireland, a meaty Ulsterwoman arrived in the press tent with an enormous kettle-like container and plonked it down next to the cups and spoons.

'Here's your tea, boys!'

It was said like she was doing us an enormous favour. There were mumblings of thanks from the four or five media men present. We're a polite lot, generally.

Looking up, I said, 'No biscuits?'

'Biscuits!?' A tone of incredulity in her voice. I shrugged and stuck my head back in the old laptop.

A few minutes later, she returned triumphantly with a plate of digestives and Rich Teas.

'Here's your biscuits!'

I glanced over. 'No chocolate ones?'

To be fair, she laughed as much as everyone else.

The toss proved decisive. TJ and Big Boyd made early inroads and a Bangladesh total of 234/9 was overhauled with seven wickets and a full five overs to spare as Porty became the first batsman to score eight centuries for Ireland. Given the clear advantage of bowling first, it was strange that the skipper decided to bat in the second game, especially with rain around. Was it a repeat of the Kenya game in South Africa the previous year? Deliberately setting a harder challenge than was necessary? Ireland lost by six wickets and the series was shared.

Rathmines – 11–13 August

The holders needed to win their remaining three InterContinental Cup matches and began well with an innings victory over the Netherlands at the home of Leinster CC. The Dutch were poor, didn't look interested and lost in barely two-and-a-half days, which is never good news for a freelancer.

Although, having given up most of my gigs, I was now looking on such matches more as subsidised jaunts and there was a cracking little burger joint where alcohol was consumed on a couple of evenings with Barry, Emmet and Ger.

If only the game had been as enjoyable. The Netherlands were bowled out for 188 before tea on the first day, with Dockers taking four wickets. After a patchy start to the reply, a sixth-wicket partnership of 221 between White and Mooney ensured the first innings points; Whitey scored another IC Cup hundred and Johnboy made 107, his one international century.

The star performer in the Dutch second dig was Allan Eastwood, an opening bowler who became the first man from Roscrea, in Co Tipperary, to play for Ireland in more than a century. He had impressed Simmo in an A-team match against the MCC and continued to do so by taking four wickets as the visitors were bundled out for 136 in 40 overs.

It's not unusual for parents to watch on with pride as their offspring wins his or her first cap but there was something extra special about the Eastwoods' delight as their 'boy' had already turned 30. It was a late call to national duty – could he fashion a career for four or five years? He had the physique and action but, for whatever reason, only played another two first-class games and was not used in the two ODIs that followed at Clontarf. Ireland won both easily.

Harare – 20–23 September

Four-in-a-row remained a possibility after a brief hop over to Toronto where, again without the county players, Ireland won their penultimate IC Cup game by six wickets. A two-match ODI series followed. Canada sneaked the first match, via a D/L calculation, when bad light intervened with the outcome on a knife edge, then Stirling powered to 177 from 134 balls in the second.

The youngster, who had celebrated his 20th birthday four days earlier, belted five sixes in making the highest individual score by an Ireland player in an ODI. There were more than five overs of the innings remaining when he got out, so Stirlo would have had the time to go past Sachin Tendulkar's then record of 200 not out, set earlier in the year. Ireland won by 92 runs. Series shared.

The county players were back for the final match in Harare, except Rankin who was injured. Officially they were only playing a Zimbabwe XI, because the ICC Full Members – even though they were suspended at the time – could not be seen to be putting out their best team against an Associate, and only deigned to play in the IC Cup on the condition that everyone knew it wasn't their best team.

At the Harare Sports Club, Whitey and Johnboy again prospered with the bat – the former scoring his fourth IC Cup century in a total of 465 – but the bowlers could not produce on the flattest of pitches and it was mathematically impossible for Ireland to qualify for the final once Zimbabwe had secured first-innings points. The home side batted on into the final day and a third new ball was required to finish them off for 590, an unwanted record for the most overs bowled and runs conceded by Ireland in any innings.

After the formalities of a draw were completed, the Zimbabwe board withdrew their XI from the tournament, gifting a place in the final to Scotland, who comfortably lost to Afghanistan in Dubai. It should be emphasised, of course, that Zimbabwe's decision to withdraw and not contest the final at a neutral venue had nothing to do with Afghanistan looking stronger by the day, having already had the best of another drawn group game in Harare the previous year.

Koh Samed – 9 November

The best news of the year was announced while Barry, myself and a third mate were enjoying an island break, a couple of hours' drive south and east of Bangkok. Plus a ferry ride, obviously. The ICC, in a rare act of common sense, had given Ed special dispensation to play for Ireland in the World Cup, lopping a few weeks off the four years he was expected to serve from the last time he turned out for England. At the same time, a similar request by Hamish Marshall was turned down, as he was not deemed to have the same traditional ties to Ireland. Probably because he was a New Zealander.

Although on holiday, the Ardmore Express was still on call to write press releases for Cricket Ireland and I needed to file a few pars for the *Indo*. The internet in our hotel was not the best so we found ourselves, pina coladas at hand, tapping away on laptops at a beach bar.

Ed, at 32, was in his prime as a batsman, scoring runs by the bucketload. After moving from Middlesex to Sussex the year before, he had given up his ambition to play Test cricket with England and would fill the hole left in the Ireland batting by Eoin moving the other way. Unlike Ed, the little ginger fella would get his chance to play Tests and made a couple of centuries, but not many either side of the water would rate the Fingal man as a better bat in the longer form.

To me it was a cricketing crime that Ed didn't play 50 Tests or more. Maybe if he had appeared more committed to playing *for* England, rather than simply wanting to play Test cricket, it would have better served his cause. But he was never going to pretend he wasn't Irish. Sure, wasn't it enough that he was always England in the back garden in Bray as a kid, scoring runs off the West Indian attack of brother Dom? Apparently not. Ah well, England's loss was Ireland's gain; the maestro was coming home.

The Samed trip was memorable for other reasons, too. Left to their own devices that evening, our trio of lovely friends managed to lose two of the three pairs of shoes they had brought to the island, and Barry ended up marrying the one who held onto hers – but not before we had set out to buy a bar and ended up running a small hotel by Samed's main pier.

TREBLES ALL ROUND
2011–2014

2011

Koh Samed – January

A World Cup on the subcontinent is a splendid thing. I was at the first in 1987 working for a London evening paper that closed during the tournament. India was a different place then; it was still possible to cycle from city to city on relatively quiet roads for example, as Rupert Rumney and his mate had done a couple of years earlier. In Jaipur, during the World Cup, a front-page news story boasted that the local government had installed a third international telephone line, to deal with the extra demand expected. It was hideously expensive to use. We sent copy back to London via telex. Less than a quarter of a century later: busy motorways, unlimited cheap phone calls and data transfers via the internet.

Not much advance in the bureaucracy, mind. In Thailand, I was told I could only apply for a visa to visit India from my home country. I'm an Australian passport holder, living in London, I told them. Which wasn't entirely untrue. Some poor clerk somewhere is probably still tasked with framing a reply to that one. As I was returning to

London before the tournament, I played their game and applied using my British passport via the embassy in Victoria. With Ireland's group games days apart and all over the place, economics and peace of mind dictated a choice between a week in Bangalore, for the games against England and the hosts, or a trip to Kolkata for final group games against South Africa and the Netherlands. I chose the latter.

Why not a week in Bangalore and a second trip for the Kolkata games, you're thinking? Fly in and out from Thailand? So apply for a multi-entry visa, you mean? Life is too short …

Mirpur – 25 February

The format of the World Cup had been changed to ensure more guaranteed games for India after the financial disaster of crashing out after three matches in 2007. So, two groups of seven; the top four in each to contest quarter-finals. Ireland's first game against Bangladesh was likely to determine which of the two would have a chance of nudging out one of the established quartet of India, South Africa, England and West Indies, for a place in the last eight. And so it proved.

Bangladesh got off to a flyer after winning the toss, but were clawed back by Botha and Dockrell in the middle overs, and in hindsight the left-armer's 2/23 from ten should have been a warning that the hosts' modest 205 all out was better than it looked, given their spin-heavy attack. Ireland never got a grip on the chase, wickets fell regularly and, despite the O'Briens scoring 38 and 37, the game was lost by 27 runs.

Callender wrote: 'Ireland will now probably have to beat both England and the West Indies to have any chance of reaching the quarter-finals.' And, my word, they nearly did.

Bangalore – 2 March

The World Cup was being shown wall-to-wall in Thailand, so after viewing Ireland's victory over Pakistan four years ago in somewhat dodgy surroundings, this time I was able to sit back in comfort, with waitress service, and watch the show in the comfort of a sports bar. Not that we imagined an upset was on the cards as half-centuries from Kevin Pietersen, Jonathan Trott and Ian Bell took England towards 300 and counting. Johnboy claimed four late wickets, but a total of 327/8 meant Ireland would have to score more than any previous team had successfully chased to win a World Cup match.

The task didn't get any easier when the skipper was bowled first ball of the reply and despite getting starts, Stirlo, Ed and Nobby all failed to kick on. Graeme Swann struck three times and Ireland were 111/5 when Cusie walked out to join O'Brien the younger in the 25th over.

Down in the bowels of the stadium, Nobby and Ed were cursing themselves for getting out. 'We could have got those on that pitch,' Ed said. Nobby nodded. As they sat there in the dressing room, a roar went up, and a few minutes later another. The two men looked at each other. The crowd went crazy for a third time.

'Better get up there and see what's happening,' Nobby said.

Out in the middle, his brother was finding his range and teeing off. Two sixes in three balls off Swann, two more off both Jimmy Anderson and Tim Bresman. Momentum. Solid support came from Cusack. The five-over powerplay, when only three fielders could be outside the ring, was taken early and yielded 62 runs.

The chat was getting a bit tasty too. When O'Brien nodded his approval to one of the rare balls he failed to score off, Anderson snapped: 'How would you know if it was a fecking good ball?'

'Well, it was better than that one I just hit into the stands.'

Bad enough to be on the end of a slap down like that, but coming from a man with bright pink hair – the result of a charity 'Shave or Dye' challenge – must have made it even harder to take. The squad had all either coloured up or applied the razor the year before when they won in the UAE and Simmo thought it might bring them luck again. The coach led the way by shaving his head and sporting a blue beard. The team's efforts contributed to the Irish Cancer Society raising over a million euros.

It was also getting combative on the viewing platform, where the players sat a few feet apart. Pietersen, off the field injured, was still giving Andrew Strauss plenty of advice on bowling changes and fielding positions.

'If you know so much, why don't you get out there and give them some help?' Nobby wondered.

In an instant, the old adversaries were off their seats and squaring up, players and officials from both sides piled in, including Big Roy and Ashley Giles.

O'Brien the younger completed his century off 50 balls – beautiful symmetry. It was the fastest in World Cup history, and remained so after two more tournaments. What was almost as impressive, was the way he reined himself in after breaking the back of the task. Not risk free, of course, but more measured; just the one boundary from his last 21 balls. I'd have loved to have been there, yet hated it at the same time. The tension was bad enough 1,500 miles away. I did the only thing I could think of that might help the Irish cause and ordered a double Baileys.

Cusie was run out for 47 to end a sixth-wicket stand of 162 but Mooney maintained the momentum. Annoyingly for England, Johnboy struck three of his six boundaries off the final balls of previously tidy overs. Ireland still needed 11 to win from 11 balls when O'Brien was run out for 113. Fantastic effort. The stadium rose and cheered him back to the members.

TJ stood up to his full height, took a deep breath and said: 'Right, let's get this done.'

Dockers and Big Boyd behind him, the last two in, would have had trouble pulling on their gloves, such was the tension.

Johnston struck his first ball, a low full toss, past extra cover for four. That was the game there. Three needed off the last over. Anderson to Mooney. Beautifully timed off his legs past midwicket. No chance of the boundary fielder stopping it. Johnboy, the proudest Irishman you'll ever meet, celebrated as if he had beaten Cromwell himself, hugged TJ and ran off screaming 'Best fecking day of my life!'

The party went on long into the night, as did my reporting for the *Indo*. Front page, back page, inside, player profiles. Amazing what you can get done with coffee and adrenaline. It was 4.45am in Thailand when my head hit the pillow.

Bangalore – 3 March

If I was busy, it was nothing compared to the one-man Cricket Ireland media department. Pity the poor old

Ardmore Express; anyone and everyone wanted a piece of O'Brien the younger. On the night of the game, Barry got to sleep 'some time between three and five'. Hard to pin down exactly as alcohol had been consumed. He was woken three or four hours later by a ring tone that he didn't quite recognise because it was all three of his phones going at once. His UK number and local phones for India and Bangladesh supplied by the ICC. And they kept ringing for three days.

RSA, the Ireland sponsors, hired a room. Interviewers could ask the man of the match three questions. First came the radio stations and newspapers from New Zealand, then Australia. A short break and it was the turn of the Indian subcontinent to get busy, the Middle East and then the UK and Ireland were awake. Ger was hired to assist Barry and a rota was drawn up for the other players. A brief lull. Was that it? No. The Caribbean radio stations wanted a piece of the action too, and the win even made news in the USA. No sooner than the west coast of the States were finished for the day than New Zealand woke up. And so on.

One particularly persistent Indian journalist wanted to interview TJ, and wouldn't give up. Barry persuaded the weary old soldier to grant him a few minutes and the three of them convened in the hotel lobby. 'What do you think of MS Dhoni as a batsman, please?' TJ frowned, but gave a considered reply. 'And what do you think about Dhoni as a keeper?'

When the third question was also about the Indian skipper, TJ fumed: 'Mate, I'm here to talk about Ireland.'

Did he have any questions that were not Dhoni-related? Barry asked, helpfully. The writer thought for a minute. 'What is your favourite colour, please?'

After three days, Simmo said: 'Mr Chambers, I need to have a word. No more interviews. That's it now, we have a match to prepare for.'

It was the best thing he heard all trip.

Mohali – 11 March

The giant-killers suffered a routine five-wicket loss as India easily chased 207 all out at the same stadium, and then had to decamp to the hills of Chandigarh for the match that would decide their fate. An odd game, as it turned out. A couple of big individual scores on both sides, but little else. Opener Devon Smith scored a century for West Indies, but with only a 142/3 on the board after 35 overs, Ireland were looking good.

Kieron Pollard then cut loose, smashing 94 from 55 balls to give his side a decent, but by no means unbeatable, total of 275. Ireland's reply started slowly, before Joyce and Wilson picked up the pace, adding 91 for the fourth wicket.

Ed was bowled for 84, O'Brien the younger went cheaply, but the ask was still a realistic 77 from 50 balls, with five wickets in hand, when Darren Sammy went up for an lbw appeal against Willo and it was given by umpire Asoka de Silva.

The batsman, on 61, immediately reviewed and the replay showed that the ball had struck him outside the line. Ashocka, as he is known, stuck with his original decision, on the basis there was no shot attempted. The Belfast man refused to leave the middle. Ulster says No! How would he not be playing a shot in the final ten overs of a run chase? More confusion. Eventually, almost in tears, Willo had to depart. Seen as a 'finisher' at Surrey, this could have been his career-defining moment. It probably still is, just not in the way he would have wished.

Cusie was stumped without further addition and the chase fell 44 short. The sense of injustice was burning in the dressing room and Barry was sure to remind the skipper to be careful with his words in the post-match presser. The first question was inevitably about the lbw. Porty played a straight bat: big fan of DRS, but not sure it got that one right.

The Ardmore Express spotted Simmo at the back of the room, waving his arms frantically. 'Sorry guys, can we just hold it there for a minute. I need to speak to the coach.'

Was Simmo worried that his skipper was going to say too much and risk a ban? Quite the opposite. 'Tell Porty to say what he thinks – don't hold back,' said livid Phil.

Barry whispered the message into the ear of the incredulous skipper, who said: 'Really?'

With a far cooler head than his coach, Porterfield smiled at the assembled press. 'Bet you'd love to know what that was all about? Well, I'm not going to tell you!' He remained diplomatic, but still received an ICC reprimand for his observations.

While what-could-have-been continued to rankle, Ireland were probably apportioning too much blame in Ashocka's direction for their almost certain elimination. What about all those half-trackers that Pollard got stuck into? Slower ball bouncers. Yes, very trendy at the time, but also very hittable if spotted early. And why wasn't Dockers given more than three overs? Everyone knew that Pollard was susceptible to spin. Look there for the reasons behind the defeat, or perhaps Ed being bowled on 84. That shouldn't happen to a batsman of his class, either.

Kolkata – 13 March

Bags packed, ready to go. I've always loved India – except when I'm actually there. I find the frustrations and irritations of the place to be claustrophobic. Incredible India, my arse. Why doesn't anything work like it should? Why isn't this or that available? Why do things so differently to everywhere else in the world?

Foreign exchange, for example. I flew into Kolkata without a rupee in my pocket. Bound to be a cash machine at an international airport. Nope. Not one single ATM. Fly into Harare, where they don't have the greatest recent history with currency, and your Visa card works. At Kolkata international, in 2011: not one ATM. There is a money-changer, of course.

And there is an ATM at the domestic terminal about 600m away, I'm told. A sweaty ten-minute trek with both bags later, I find it. Unplugged, in a dusty room. So, a sweaty trek back to the international terminal to change the one £20 note in my wallet.

'Can you fill in this form, please? And this form?'

'I only want to change £20!'

Infuriatingly the second form demands all my passport details, which I supply, and then hand over my passport, which is photocopied.

'You English taught us bureaucracy.'

We also taught the Sri Lankans, but you can change money at Colombo international with a calculator and no paperwork in about 30 seconds.

Kolkata was different again to anywhere else I'd been in India. Busy, but poor. Loads of repair shops and small businesses. Lots and lots of people, all going somewhere and nowhere at the same time. To ensure there were no hitches on the match day, I took a walk down to the stadium where I'd been told to collect my press accreditation.

'Sorry, you cannot come in without accreditation.'

'But I've come to collect my accreditation – and it's inside!'

The guard did the wobbly head thing. 'You can collect tomorrow.'

Eden Gardens – 15 March

To be fair, the system worked smoothly on the day and I collected my lanyards, with the minimum of fuss, from a Portakabin office outside the protected zone. A few minutes later I was inside Eden Gardens for the first time. It's massive. It wasn't hard to imagine those crowds of over 100,000 squeezing in to watch a Test match against Pakistan in the late 1990s, or similar attendances for ODIs.

A gigantic open theatre, its size exaggerated by the gentle slope of the banks of seating, but like its surrounds a little tired, maybe. The press box could certainly have done with a clean and tidy. The old ground was rebuilt in 1993. I'd have loved to have seen its predecessor; the Eden Gardens where Tony Greig had captained England, and Tony Lewis and his eyebrows before him. And the World Cup Final in 1987, of course. I'd missed that when the *Evening News* closed.

After covering the rest of that tournament, I was back in London when another England captain attempted to reverse sweep his opposite number and in doing so handed the trophy to Australia.

Or not. Poor old Gatt still maintains that the shot was necessary because his side were behind in their chase. Right or wrong, it is an iconic moment in the history of the World Cup.

Would the famous old ground witness another one as Ireland battled to reach the quarter-finals for the first time? Alas, no. Never in contention in a game they needed to win to retain hope of reaching the last eight. JP Duminy missed out on a century by one run in a South African total of 272/7 and Morne Morkel looked frighteningly quick as the Boys in Green were shot out for 141 in reply.

Kolkata – 16 March

The visiting media and members of the Ireland team were invited to a reception, of some kind, at a community centre. Dignitaries, speeches and, more importantly, free food and drink. The O'Briens were both there. I watched Nobby working the room and wondered what his family's new-found fame must be like for him. Since they were kids he was always the main man who would look out for his not-so-little brother. Now, overnight, he had become the supporting act.

It must have been a bit hard to take but he was showing no signs of it, as he did what Nobby does: glad-handing, making contacts, swapping business cards, and even charming the locals with a few words of their dialect. A chance like this was also too good to pass up.

'Nobby, I know you're really busy, but there are some kids outside looking for an autograph,' I said. 'Is there any chance … you could have a word with Kev?'

Eden Gardens – 18 March

The campaign deserved to end on a high note, and Stirlo didn't let us down, scoring a century, as Ireland again chased north of 300 to beat the Netherlands in a cracking game. Ryan ten Doeschate also made three figures, Stirlo took a couple of wickets with his off spin and in a bizarre ending to the Dutch innings, the last four balls each produced a run out.

Unlike the chase in Bangalore, Ireland were always in control. Stirlo and the skipper added 177 for the first wicket in 27 overs. The Belfast boy struck two sixes in his 101, made from just 72 balls. It was a masterclass, albeit a sweaty masterclass in the heat, and he was out on his feet by the end of it. There is a lot about Stirlo that reminds me of Gatt; similar physique, of course, and mannerisms, but also powerful forearms punching shots through the off side and strong wrists. Plays the reverse sweep, too. As he tried to rehydrate, flat on his back in the dressing room, the O'Briens took their side past the winning post with six wickets and 14 balls to spare.

At some early hour the following morning I was off to the airport, leaving Emmet gently snoring on his side of the room. I checked I had my passport before I left. What I didn't check was whether I had the big man's as well. Stopping off in Dubai several hours later, my phone and email were queued with messages all along the lines of 'Have you walked off with my passport?' I hadn't. Ridiculous suggestion. It was definitely my passport that had got me through immigration, which was now in my top pocket. It was. So whose was this in my wallet?

There are times in life when you simply can't apologise enough. In my defence, I was sure that Republic of Ireland passports were blue, so I must have put his burgundy-coloured one in my wallet for safekeeping, assuming it was mine. Ultimately, the EU was to blame.

Ardmore – 4 April

The back-slapping and congratulations for yet again punching above their weight on the global stage had barely subsided when news came through that, in the wake of India lifting the trophy in Mumbai, the ICC had decided that the next World Cup would be restricted to ten teams.

It would be a round robin featuring the Full Members, and would guarantee India nine televised games. No Ireland, though, despite their wonderful victories over Pakistan, Bangladesh and England; no Scotland, Kenya, Canada or the Netherlands; and no chance for emerging nations like Afghanistan to participate either.

It was a blow to the solar plexus and one that in the early days of Twitter was not going to pass without comment. Several players let their feelings be known and when Nobby asked what all the fuss was about, Barry responded: 'Read your emails, we've been shafted.'

He awoke the following day to a double-page spread in one of the Irish red tops, headlined 'SHAFTED!' above a report that led on his tweet. The sentiment was fortunately in tune with the feelings of the Cricket Ireland hierarchy, otherwise their media manager's excuse that he didn't realise his message could be read publicly may not have saved him.

Weight of opinion fell in behind the Associates' cause, forcing the ICC to revert to the 14-team format for the 2015 World Cup. A senior ECB official sneered: 'You may have won the battle, but you won't win the war.'

If only cricket were a sport and not a business, eh?

Ask most fans, and their ideal structure for the 50-overs tournament is 16 teams, four groups of four, with the top two in each group qualifying for quarter-finals. The whole event would be over in three weeks. Sweet. If we have to ensure India play a minimum number of games, then the 14-team set-up is probably the best of the rest. Beyond 'huge' it's hard to quantify the effect that Ireland's performances in 2007 and 2011 had on the consciousness back home. Before that win against Pakistan, it wasn't unusual for Dublin taxi drivers to ask: 'Do we play cricket?' Not any more.

So let's not deny those others who dare to dream their day in the sun too.

Belfast – 30 May

It took a while for people to accept that Stirlo was the real deal and it was probably his 109 against Pakistan at Stormont, his first ODI century against a Full Member, that convinced the remaining waverers as to the genuine quality of the local lad.

Waqar Younis, the coach of Pakistan, was in no doubt, after his side had completed a 2-0 series win. The visitors had dismissed Ireland for 96 in the first game and chased down 238/8 to win with five wickets and eight balls to spare, two days later.

'Stirling's was one of the best knocks I've seen for a while,' Waqar said. 'He plays proper cricketing shots and you enjoy it as a spectator. He can hit the ball far, he has got good footwork and he's young. Stirling has plenty of time and he's not scared of playing shots against any bowler which is brilliant.'

You won't read a better summary.

After Namibia had been beaten in the first two World League 50-overs matches, at the start of qualifying for the 2015 World Cup, Stirlo hit his third ODI century of the year in a losing cause against Scotland in Edinburgh. Ireland would have thought 320/8 enough but Richie Berrington hit a match-winning 56 off 23 balls. A match against Sri Lanka in the tri-series was rained off.

Derry – 5 August

Ireland hosted the ten-team Under-19 World Cup qualifiers, and what should have been a formality to finish in the top six of a ten-team round robin that included Vanuatu, was anything but. The Boys in Green only just squeezed past the USA by one wicket, following that with another arse-nipper, holding off Afghanistan by four runs and, after losing to Scotland, only had two wickets and three balls to spare against Kenya.

After those four matches in Leinster, the remainder of the tournament was staged in the north-west and Barry treated a group of us to a night out in Derry; scorers, journos, and a couple of CricketEurope stringers. At some point the conversation touched on the InterContinental Cup and *that* declaration in Namibia.

The lad to my immediate left, in a perfect Dougal from *Father Ted*, which was his normal voice, said: 'Declaring behind – who would have thought of that?'

I looked across to the Ardmore Express, who was laughing. He still swears it wasn't a set-up.

A pub crawl followed near to Shipquay Street, which is the steepest in Europe, apparently. In one of the bars, a local took exception to Michael Taylor's red sweater, with its Ballymena CC badge. 'I know we've got a peace process now, but that's taking the piss!'

A man who helped win *University Challenge* and had been a finalist on *Mastermind* should possibly have known better than to be advertising the Rev. Paisley's hometown on his chest in these parts.

What sort of eejit would do a thing like that, Ted?

We wandered into another city pub hosting a quiz night. The competition was fierce. Earnest consultation in whispers, a sly text or two. Big prize on offer, we assumed. A shame we hadn't arrived in time to take part with the Ballymena Brainbox on board.

A little while later, the winning table was presented with a bag of crisps. The prize, I kid you not, was a jumbo-sized packet of cheese and onion. Odd lot in Derry.

Coleraine – 8 August

Ireland secured their place at the Under-19 World Cup with a well-judged six-wicket victory over Namibia. Dockers led his side to victory with 83 not out, while Shane Getkate was unbeaten on 59 as the hosts passed a testing 245/9 with three overs to spare. A month and a half earlier, one half of the partnership had been lying in a coma in Solihull hospital after suffering a heart attack. Getkate was found to have Wolff-Parkinson-White syndrome, an extra pathway in the heart in simple terms, and needed three whacks of CPR to start him up again after collapsing near the boundary while playing for Warwickshire Seconds.

Doctors cleared him to resume training three weeks after the incident, with only a one per cent chance of suffering a similar episode, and he top-scored in wins over Kenya and Canada, albeit the latter a mere ten not out after the Canucks were skittled for 37 at Limavady.

The fun part of covering an underage tournament is looking for those with the potential to kick on and make the senior side. There were slim pickings among this lot, though. Dockers was already there, of course, and Getkate was preparing for his third Under-19 World Cup, so hardly new.

Who else? A young seamer Graeme McCarter had something about him, but not the pace to go with it, and Barry McCarthy, an all-rounder who played for Pembroke looked OK. Both were to play a few games of county cricket. The rest of the crop were mediocre and after qualifying in third place on home soil, they probably punched above their weight to finish 12th of 16 in the World Cup itself.

Clontarf – 25 August

England had the chance to extract a morsel of revenge for Bangalore and took it by 11 runs, in another rain-affected ODI at Castle Avenue. No grumpy Colly this time, but that other little ginger bloke made 59 for the visitors. The Ardmore Express, who has spent years, before and since, complaining about over-officious stewards ruining his camera angles, was this time indebted to a jobsworth for not allowing him to move positions as Stirling bowled to Morgan. The ensuing return catch was perfectly framed where he was, and Stirlo's dive made several papers the following day. Right place, right time.

O'Brien the younger threatened a repeat of his heroics with a couple of sixes, but while again competitive, Ireland were never ahead of the chase. The wait for that elusive first home victory over one of the big boys would have to wait at least another year.

Portrush – 3 November

After Ireland had begun their defence of the InterContinental Cup with solid wins over Namibia and

Canada, and two crushing World League victories over the Canadians, it was time for the annual Cricket Writers of Ireland dinner and awards.

It was held in the north-west for the first time, and gave us all a chance to stay at the Port Hotel, a seaside establishment I'd heard so much about over the years from Big Roy. A little like its owner's international career, though, the telling was more impressive than the actual, and expecting something between The Ritz and Mar-a-Lago, we found a friendly two-star hotel nestling in the centre of town.

Given a preferential deal – or off-season rates as they are known in the business – it was only right that we installed the big man in our Hall of Fame. The bare statistics of his 30-cap career, spanning 19 seasons, do not tell the full story of a glorious playing contribution to Irish cricket, but Roy will happily fill in the gaps. It is an education to hear how his fiery fast bowling took dozens of wickets for far lesser bowlers at the other end, not to mention his underrated batting. That average of 10.5 is massively misleading, apparently.

I once asked who he most resembled as a player. 'Well, you see young Ed Joyce? He reminds me a lot of myself at a similar age.' A pause for effect. 'But I could bowl as well, of course.'

The CWI do take the Hall of Fame seriously and, all joking aside, Roy's inauguration was more than justified by his further contributions as a selector, committee man and particularly in his team-manager role. He has been one of the big men of Ireland cricket in more ways than one.

Cape Town – 11 November

I'd always fancied watching a Test match at Newlands, and persuaded the Ardmore Express to join me. Again his reputation for being in the right place at the right time was enhanced when Australia collapsed to 21/9 in their second innings. No Test team has ever lost a ninth wicket so cheaply, but that wasn't even the weirdest thing of a game that only lasted two and a half days.

On the final morning, at one minute to 11, South Africa were 111/1. If you're thinking that must have happened loads of times, you haven't noted the date. Extraordinary. It reminded me of a show-stopping moment at Old Trafford, back in the day. Middlesex were on top when my co-commentator John Gwynne announced: 'Well, would you believe it? It's the eighth of the eighth, 1988, and Lancashire are 88/8!'

Fabulous spot, Newlands. Backdrop of Table Mountain and a triumph of town planning with a brewery next to the cricket ground. Does any of this have an Irish connection other than the presence of the Ardmore Express? Well, tenuously. Nathan Lyon made 14 as Australia were bowled out for 47. It was only the eighth time a last man had top-scored in a Test innings and not something I'd seen before. A once-in-a-lifetime experience? How wrong can you can be.

2012

Mombasa – 12–13 February

Simmo didn't make many mistakes but a standoff with Nobby over missing a trip to Kenya was one, and it continued for more than three years. An InterContinental

Cup game clashed with the Bangladesh Premier League, which was offering the wicketkeeper US$80,000 for a few weeks' work. His Cricket Ireland contract was worth €20,000 per annum and did not require him to play every first-class match. Accordingly, Nobby made himself available for the one-dayers that followed the IC Cup game, but that wasn't good enough for the all-or-nothing coach who handed the gloves to Wilson and did not return them.

It was a stubborn decision because if there was any doubt as to who was the better keeper, there was absolutely none as to Willo being a superior outfielder. Indeed, stunning at times. But, no, Simmo's face was set, albeit with a severed nose, and it was to cost Ireland at least one big win.

Nobby missed a cracking, low-scoring IC Cup match in Mombasa. After ceding their status as the top non-Test-playing side to Ireland and developing an inferiority complex, as reported by Antoinette in South Africa, the Kenyans decided their best shot at victory was to prepare a raging turner. If it suited left-arm spinner Hiren Varaiya, who took 6/22 as Ireland collapsed from 43/1 to 75 all out, it was also tailor-made for Dockers and Albert van der Merwe.

The new Irish Spin Twins reduced Kenya to 51/7 and threatened to claim the first-innings points before the hosts rallied to 109.

Ed led a counterattack and Ireland ended a day of 22 wickets – all caught – leading by 47. The maestro fell ill overnight and could not resume on the second morning, with Dockers also succumbing to food poisoning. The pair hoped they might be able to sleep it off, but both were required in the middle before lunch. Ed added three runs for a top score of 54 and his room-mate was last to go as another extraordinary collapse saw Ireland slip from 142/4 to 152 all out. Kenya needed 119 to win.

Somehow Dockers not only managed to bowl in the second innings, but took four wickets as the home side's batsmen came and went ridiculously quickly. At 36/8 it looked as though Ireland would win comfortably, but the new gloveman dropped a catch and missed a stumping, and the margin of victory was only ten runs when Van der Merwe took the final wicket. The tall bespectacled off-spinner, who looked far more school teacherly than either of the original 'Spin Twins' who both were, had match figures of 11/68. Dockers took the other nine for 87.

Kenya managed to win the first of the World League matches, by seven wickets, to ever so slightly dent Ireland's prospects of reaching the next World Cup. The Boys in Green levelled up, taking the second match by 117 runs, after Ed had scored 88, and then won all three T20s. Nobby hadn't been missed too much.

United Arab Emirates – 13–24 March

Nor was the Sandymount scrapper's absence noticed when Ireland hit peak form in the World T20 qualifiers, winning ten games in a row to imperiously take the title. Strangely enough, after losing their opener to Namibia, by four runs, the champions' toughest game was a two-wicket victory over Italy. It took an unbeaten 30 from Willo to avoid an embarrassing loss.

Stirlo got stronger and stronger as the tournament progressed, making 41, 35, 61 not out and 33 in the last four round-robin games. Could he carry it into finals day? Yes, he could: 59 not out as Ireland avenged their defeat by Namibia, chasing down 94/6 in only 10.1 overs, and then

79 in the final against Afghanistan. The opener reached his half-century from 17 balls, bettering his own Ireland record; only Yuvraj Singh, of India, had achieved the mark quicker at that time.

Max Sorensen, who had made his debut in Mombasa, also had a good double-header, bowling an unheard of two maidens in the semi-final and removing top-scorer Mohammad Shahzad as Ireland took the title with a five-wicket win. Simmo had plucked Sorensen out of Dublin club cricket, fancying the South African's big hitting and fast-medium seamers could be particularly useful in T20s.

He didn't make many mistakes.

At the start of the year, in partnership with the Ardmore Express, I'd bought a small hotel on the Thai island of Samed, so I had a legitimate excuse for missing Mombasa and the UAE: the business needed knocking into shape. The *Indo* still wanted copy, though, and it did seem about as cosmopolitan as you could get to be an Englishman watching a stream of a South African playing for Ireland against Afghanistan in the United Arab Emirates, while drinking German beer on a tropical island. Go back only 18 years to the start of this journey and tell me I'd be doing that one day, and I'd have laughed. I was smiling now, mind.

Belfast – 23 June

Tim Murtagh made his Ireland debut in an ODI against Australia, but didn't make it on to the field at Stormont, except to be awarded his cap. The Middlesex seamer, whose dad was born in Dublin, had been on the radar for a while. He was a member of the World T20 qualifying squad, without getting a game, and didn't manage to roll his arm over in anger on a very wet weekend in Belfast, either. Cricket Ireland had phoned sponsors the day before and advised against travelling any distance, as there was little chance of play.

It wasn't raining on the morning of the match, but very gloomy.

'I don't remember seeing that water feature last night, Barry?'

'That's the hotel car park, DT.'

A fully covered outfield and a Herculean effort by the groundstaff saw the match begin in front of a decent-sized crowd. Brett Lee clattered Porty's stumps first ball and repeated the trick two deliveries later to remove Ed. Nobby, back in the side, if not behind the stumps, was walking out to face the fourth ball of the match. Stirlo made a merry 24 before the heavens opened after 10.4 overs, and the game was quickly abandoned.

To the relief of Cricket Ireland the cut-off for refunds was ten overs. A fortune saved but could an island with such poor weather realistically be considered as contenders to play Test cricket? A semi-serious discussion took place in the press tent as to the viability of playing home games in the UAE? Or Spain, maybe? It was a thought, and one that reoccurred later in a soggy summer when South Africa cut short an A-tour and returned home in search of blue skies.

Clontarf – 5 July

Rain also claimed one of the two World League matches against Afghanistan, while the other was a low-scoring affair at Castle Avenue. Put in, Ireland battled their way to 163 all out in 47 overs on a cabbage patch of a pitch. A couple of radio stations had sent reporters. One of them launched into his live halfway piece, listing the wickets to fall as he had jotted them down. Only O'Brien the younger had come to terms with the surface, apparently, making 31 from 32 balls. The rest had struggled although Murtagh contributed a useful 15 towards the end.

A problem with ad-libbing updates from a scorecard, especially concentrating on wickets to fall, is that you can overlook performances; in this case a patient man of the match-winning 67 not out from Ed, who came in at No.3. Another problem is that in a press tent everyone else can hear. When the reporter handed back to the studio, Ger said: 'No mention of Joyce then?' There was an awkward silence that lasted well into Afghanistan's reply of 104 all out. Cusie took 3/17 on his home ground.

Rathmines – 9–12 July

The first two days of the following InterContinental Cup match were washed out too. Hopeless summer. When play got underway on the third afternoon a much-depleted Ireland side not only claimed the first-innings points, but nearly pulled off an unlikely win. O'Brien the younger, captaining in the absence of Porty, won an important toss. Sorensen took four wickets, TJ two in an almost unplayable opening spell and Cusie the others as Afghanistan were shot out for 84.

Ireland had the lead before stumps and rapidly progressed to 251/4 declared, Willo making a top score of 73. Could they take ten wickets again in the two remaining sessions? An opening stand of 106 seemed to have answered that but then debutant Stuart Thompson stepped up with three wickets in a lively first spell and the only team to beat Ireland in an IC Cup match since 2004 were relieved to shake hands on a draw, 41 ahead with only three wickets left.

Colombo – 19 September

After a tight T20 series in Belfast – won 3-0 by Bangladesh but with two of the games decided by one run and a couple of wickets – Ireland hit back to beat the Tigers by five runs in a warm-up for the World T20. Predictably they failed to get the better of Australia in the main event and, not able to escape the rain in Sri Lanka either, had their second and final group game against West Indies abandoned after making 129/6.

Porty fell first ball in both games. While some batsmen have golden summers, the skipper had a golden duck summer – appropriate, maybe, given the weather. Four times – in games against Afghanistan, Australia (twice) and West Indies – he faced the first ball of the innings but wasn't around for the second.

The Boys in Green flew home with a reputation firmly established: peerless among their non-Test-match-playing peers, competitive against the lower end of the top table and no longer to be taken lightly by the big boys.

2013

Sharjah – 10 March

The most successful year in the history of Irish cricket began with an InterContinental Cup match, away to the United Arab Emirates. It was staged in Sharjah and my first visit to the Emirate north of Dubai could have been a prolonged one. A very prolonged one.

I'd arranged to stay in an apartment hotel with Barry and Callender, who got there before me. Barry sent a message: 'Slip a bottle of JD in your bag – it's dry here.' I touched down after midnight and almost forgot, but a side step into the Dubai airport duty free saw me emerge with a box of Heinekens. Never been a whisky fan. After queuing for a cab outside, I loaded my two bags into the boot along with the beer. 'Sharjah, please,' I told the driver.

He looked at me warily, then looked towards the now closed boot: 'Ooh, alcohol …'

There used to be a clearly defined border between Dubai, where there are many bars, and Sharjah where there is one, the members-only Wanderers Club. Now one Emirate merges into the other. As we drove, I thought about Sharjah being dry. Surely it wouldn't be a massive problem.

We pulled up at the back of a thankfully quiet apartment building, and the driver gingerly helped me unload the contraband. The lobby was deserted except for a night porter, who took one look at the Heinekens and said: 'Ooh, alcohol.'

Upstairs, I was greeted if that's the right word by Barry. 'What the feck have you got there?!!'

'You said to get a bottle of JD, remember?'

'I said Jack Daniels – and hide it in your bag – this place is as strict as Saudi.'

An ICC official didn't improve our nerves next morning when she explained it was a serious crime to be caught in possession of the packaging and empty bottles, never mind the alcohol itself. Sharjah had been bailed out by Saudi Arabia a few years back and the money came with strings attached.

It used to be the most liberal of the Emirates and is my favourite: not as pretentious or flashy as Dubai, with a nice pace to it, excellent places to eat and more modest shopping malls. Some of the restaurants were spectacularly good, but how can a bloke order steak or seafood and then not have the option of a glass of wine to wash it down? A German beer, even.

'How was the lobster, sir? … and the Diet Coke?'

The following morning we bundled the cardboard wrappers into a holdall and took a taxi back to Dubai. Once over the border, we found a Metro station and quietly emptied the contents of our bag in a waste bin. Phew!

Sharjah – 12–15 March

There was no such drama or excitement over the next few days. The UAE produced a flatter surface than the Sheikh Zayed expressway and, after winning the toss, Porty and his top order went about filling their boots – and not with Heineken. Half-centuries for the skipper and Stirlo were followed by centuries from Ed and Nobby. The former, who had walked off 99 not out on the first day, would surely have recorded Ireland's highest individual score – passing Eoin's 209 – had he not been unluckily run out for 155 by a deflected drive at the non-striker's end.

Willo survived a close lbw call first ball and was disappointed to fall 16 short of what would have been his second century for Ireland, while O'Brien the younger and Johnboy had fun before the declaration. The home side were one down to Murtagh at the close, but the first half of the game had yielded only eight wickets.

Back at base, Barry and I were steadily working our way through the Heinekens, but what to do with the empties? Walking out of the apartment building with a clinking bag was too risky. (It probably wasn't, but that's how it felt.)

Lying in bed, a solution presented itself. The wardrobe in my room was about 8ft tall and topped with a deep pelmet that went all the way around. So after a wash to remove any beery odours, and a wipe to remove fingerprints, the offending containers were lain down one by one on top of it. Out of sight and mind. There was no chance that any of the 12 green bottles would accidentally fall and they may well still be there.

Ireland failed to take a wicket during the first two sessions of the third day and though it was unlikely that the UAE would better the visitors' 589/7, there seemed little way of forcing an outright victory. TJ broke a stand of 187 in his first over with the second new ball, George Dockrell finally tasted success and struck again next ball, while Johnboy showed his physical prowess by powering out two more going into the last hour, or so, of a scorching hot day.

'How do we win this from here?' Lewie's words from 2005 came back to me. I took a little walk around the boundary and saved TJ the effort of bending to pick up his water bottle. It wasn't an ODI, Doney.

'You can still win this, you know?'

He looked at me with that little half smile. 'This isn't Namibia, mate. That was ten years ago.' Less than eight, actually. I waited. 'Go on, then. How?'

I took a deep breath. 'Get them to declare overnight, forfeit your second innings and they chase what's left.'

This would ensure first-innings points for Ireland and the UAE were unlikely to have time to get the 300-odd to win. We both knew the older, somewhat rotund, chaps at the top of the UAE order would jump at another knock, as opposed to a couple of sessions in the field. It would also send yet another positive message to the ICC.

I'm told Operation Townsend Mk II was briefly discussed at that night's team meeting, without gaining much traction. The main focus of the trip was the far more important matter of the two World Cup qualifying matches to follow. No point risking injuries or heat exhaustion. I'd have gone for it. Then again, I've never fielded three sessions in 36 degrees of heat.

The final day played out much as expected. TJ added three wickets – including his 250th – to finish with 4/62 as the home side were bowled out for 360. Ireland collected the first-innings points, declined to enforce the follow-on, and Porty declared shortly after reaching his ninth international century. Match drawn. TJ claimed the pitch was one of the three flattest he had encountered: the other two being the Windhoek final in 2005 and Nairobi three years later.

Sharjah – 18 March

The two World League matches provided routine wins for a team on the top of its game. First Willo took the honours, making an unbeaten 72, as Ireland chased down the home side's 165 all out with five wickets and eight overs to spare. Two days later, the Surrey man was again the finisher, in a six-wicket victory, after Porty had broken the back of the chase with a solid 77. Mission accomplished, and Cricket Ireland president for the year, Robin Walsh, led an evening of celebration in the Wanderers. Alcohol was consumed. Legally.

In the taxi back to our apartment, Callender and the Ardmore Express were discussing the various merits of Sharjah and Dubai. Neither has a particularly strong accent to my ear but, with a quizzical look, our Bangladeshi driver turned to me and asked: 'What language are they speaking, please?'

When I told him, he said: 'Do they play cricket in Ireland?'

London – 8 April

Then Margaret Thatcher died. The passing of the former British PM at the age of 87 was not an occasion for universal mourning; indeed, communities in former coal-mining villages talked of throwing street parties and a recording of 'The Wicked Witch is Dead' shot to the top of the pop charts. In Dublin, avowed Republican John Mooney should have known better than to tweet: 'I hope it was slow and painful.' No mention of Thatcher but everyone knew. Uproar.

The *News Letter* in Belfast caught on to the story and demanded Mooney be sacked; Cricket Ireland ran around putting out fires. CEO Warren Deutrom was outstanding on Radio Ulster: composed and confident as he agreed the all-rounder was wrong and apologised during a live debate with a frothing reporter from the newspaper.

I'd sent Johnboy a text along the lines of: 'The woman caused enough damage and division alive, don't let her harm you and your family now she's dead'. By the time he read it, the tweet had been deleted, but it was too late to prevent a disciplinary hearing. He was reprimanded, warned about his future behaviour and banned for three matches: two for Leinster Lightning and the first one-day international against Pakistan.

Clontarf – 23 May

Emmet described it as a 'brutally cold day' as a crowd of around 2,000 who turned up for the first of two one-day

BOUNDARY BANTER: Eight years older, and a couple of stone heavier, the author proposes Operation Townsend Mk II to Trent Johnston in Sharjah. Photo: Barry Chambers

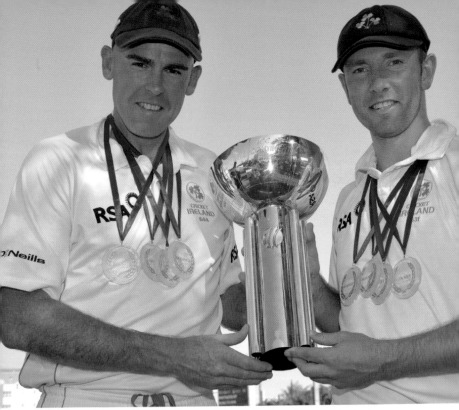

FORMIDABLE FEAT: Johnston, left, and White featured in the four InterContinental Cup Final victories over Kenya, Canada, Namibia and Afghanistan. Photo: Barry Chambers

PRESS GANG: The author, Ger Siggins, Emmet Riordan, John Kenny, Ian Callender and Odran Flynn make a book presentation to Robin Walsh at Stormont. Photo: Barry Chambers

DOUBLE TROUBLE: My favourite Joyce and her twin, Cecelia. I'm fairly sure it's Isobel on the right but they really should be made to wear name badges.
Photo: Barry Chambers

WINNERS ARE GRINNERS: Phil Simmons lifted 11 trophies during his eight years as Ireland coach, including three IC Cups and three World T20 qualifiers.
Photo: Barry Chambers

SITTING PRETTY: *An enthusiastic crowd enjoyed the sunshine as Ireland hosted their inaugural Test match against Pakistan at picturesque Malahide.*
Photo: Rowland White

TIM SPIRIT: *Murtagh is thrilled to bits with his first Test wicket against Pakistan – either that or he has finally registered on the TV speed gun.*
Photo: Rowland White

MOVING ON: *Long-time manager Roy Torrens no doubt imparting a few words of wisdom to skipper William Porterfield, left, and his eventual successor Andrew Balbirnie.*
Photo: Barry Chambers

Ireland v England
Lord's
24-27th July 2019
Test Match

PLAYER	POSITION
William Porterfield (Capt)	1
James McCollum	2
Andrew Balbirnie	3
Paul Stirling	4
Kevin O'Brien	5
Gary Wilson (wk)	6
Stuart Thompson	7
Mark Adair	8
Andrew McBrine	9
Tim Murtagh	10
Boyd Rankin	11
SUBSTITUTES	
Simi Singh	SUB
Lorcan Tucker	SUB
Craig Young	SUB

Signed: _____
Chris Siddell – Team Manager

ULTIMATE TEST:
Those who feared
Ireland would
struggle at the Home
of Cricket were left
speechless when
England were bowled
out for 85 on the first
morning.
Photos: Adrian
Raftery/Craig
Easdown

ENGLAND   **85 for 10**

BURNS	C WILSON B MURTAGH	6
ROY	C STIRLING B MURTAGH	5
DENLY	LBW B ADAIR	23
ROOT	LBW B ADAIR	2
BAIRSTOW	B MURTAGH	0
ALI	C WILSON B MURTAGH	0
WOAKES	LBW B MURTAGH	0
CURRAN	C MCCOLLUM B RANKIN	18
BROAD	C WILSON B RANKIN	3
STONE	B ADAIR	19
LEACH	NOT OUT	1

The Test Experts

BLARNEY ARMY: *From executive boxes to the party stand and from the Kalahari desert to Tasmania and on to Lord's, Ireland never lack for colourful travelling support. Photos: Adrian Raftery, Willie Dwyer, Alan Lewis, Craig Easdown*

LORD'S AND MASTER: A morning to remember for Murtagh '… and there, as Timothy makes his way up the pavilion steps, this journey ends'
Photo: www.mattbright.co.uk

internationals against Pakistan were not only rained on a few times, but hailed on too. Mohammad Hafeez made an unbeaten 122 for Pakistan in an innings of 266/5 that was interrupted four times, and reduced to 47 overs. Set a D/L target of 276 to win, Stirlo replied with 103 – his fifth ODI century included a six onto the clubhouse roof – and O'Brien the younger defied the increasingly bitter weather to keep Ireland in the hunt. Just about.

When brother Nobby fell to the first ball of the 44th over, Ireland still needed 36 to win. I couldn't help myself and tweeted, 'Just the moment you'd want to see Johnboy walking in' and tagged the *News Letter* reporter in the tweet. He replied along the lines of 'You're a supporter – I'm a journalist'.

There is an accusation in sports journalism, often aimed at the Australian media, of being 'fans with typewriters'. (For younger readers, a typewriter was an early mechanical version of a laptop that printed words directly onto paper.) The Aussies would respond by saying: 'We don't bag our players, like you. What good does that do?'

The *News Letter* man and I would be on different sides of the argument. My sympathies have always been with the players, of both sides. Dropped catches, for example. No honest player deliberately drops a catch, so in match reports why not simply say: 'Smith was dropped at mid-on'? Why is it necessary to tag on 'by Bloggs', or whoever? What does that add? Yes, if someone has dropped a succession of chances it is a story: 'Bloggs has now dropped four catches in three games at second slip.' Relevant. Why is Bloggs still fielding there? Otherwise, no. The bloke has suffered enough by dropping the catch, without me rubbing it in.

Back at Castle Avenue, TJ filled the Mooney role, giving O'Brien good support in the final overs, although not as much as some comedy fielding by the visitors. Ireland needed 15 off the last bowled by Saeed Ajmal, who could barely hold the ball in the cold; 13 off the last three. O'Brien struck a six and a two. The off-spinner fired a loose one down leg, O'Brien got across swung it away for four. Match tied.

As the batsmen embraced, TJ said: 'If you'd missed that, it would have been a wide – and I don't think the keeper was getting across.'

Ah, well …

Clontarf – 26 May

The second game was another cracker – and a tad warmer. A tad. Ireland should have won. Ed arrived at the crease to face the last ball of the first over and batted through the innings for 116 not out, from 132 balls. It was a career-best at the time, matched Eoin's feat of scoring an ODI century for different countries, and led his side to a useful 229/9.

A slow, seaming pitch, not dissimilar to the one for the Australia game in 2010, was perfect for Johnston and Murtagh, who reduced Pakistan to 17/4. It should have been better. TJ saw two catches dropped behind the wicket, before either Misbah-ul-Haq or Shoaib Malik had scored. One made 24, the other 43. Wilson was the culprit, of course, and a furious TJ approached Simmo after the game, insisting Nobby be handed back the gloves. The coach was not for turning.

Despite those misses, when Cusie took his second, Pakistan were 133/7. Enter Wahab Riaz. Better known for his speed with the ball, Riaz proceeded to smash four sixes and as many fours, while Kamran Akmal added a couple of maximums on his way to a top score of 81. Ireland dug in and were still just about favourites with 32 needed from the last four, but then an over disappeared for 24 and the game was up.

Six years later, Ireland were still looking for a first home ODI win over one of the 'traditional' big teams, never mind a series victory. They have never come closer than that chilly week.

Deventer – 1–3 July

When Ireland won the World Cricket League in 2010, with what was effectively an A team, Simmo knew that the Netherlands had been conquered. A superior side, in every way, through the 1990s and still a threat for most of the following decade, the Dutch were now beaten on home soil again in a one-sided InterContinental Cup tie. Ireland were missing four county regulars, plus Boyd Rankin, who was presumably injured, yet still dismissed the home side for fewer than 150 in both innings.

Ireland's win by 279 runs featured the one century of John Anderson, a well-organised right-hander and purveyor of occasional leg-spin. The South African was captain of Dublin club side Merrion, and despite coming late to international cricket at the age of 29, his technique and temperament should have seen him feature in at least a couple of Tests. Instead, he surprisingly announced his retirement from international cricket in 2018, a year after marrying Isobel Joyce. Not the worst compensation, to be fair.

The only Dutch player to reach 50 was Tom Cooper, who delighted fans of old comedians when he strayed out of his crease and was stumped by Stuart Poynter – just like that! Dockrell dismissed him in both innings as he returned match figures of 9/71. Ireland had qualified for a fourth IC Cup final with a game to spare.

Amstelveen – 7 July

A wedding took me back to London on the Saturday and there I'd intended to stay, only to get a message from Brian Murgatroyd, an old media mate, asking whether I'd be interested in flying down to Windhoek to commentate on the World League games between Namibia and Afghanistan? If so, I should get back to Amsterdam and meet the producer, Azhar Habib, who was streaming the matches between the Netherlands and Ireland as part of the same ICC deal, with Murgers on the mic.

A hastily arranged flight got me to the ground in Amstelveen a few overs before Ireland were bowled out for 236. I found Murgers between innings. 'Come and say hello to Azhar.' We walked over to the production truck where a tall Indian was having a smoke.

'This is David Townsend, who I was talking to you about,' Murgers said.

Azhar smiled, held out his hand and said: 'Pleased to meet you.'

And that was it! No interview, no 'Can you do a few overs in the second innings so we can assess you?' Nothing.

So, I watched O'Brien the younger take 4/13 as the Dutch stuttered to 148 all out in reply, congratulated Ginger again on his siring record, and went off for tea with Ruud Onstein. After a couple of beers and a delicious shared plate of *bitterballen* with the old fella before we left the clubhouse, it was a surprise to learn from his lovely wife

Kea that the two of them had become vegans, for health reasons. Mostly Ruud's health, which hadn't been exactly rude in recent times.

After dinner we drove the couple of miles from their home to the seafront, bought ice creams and took a stroll along the promenade on a gorgeous summer evening. Not for the first time I found myself just a little jealous of the life Ruud lived.

Ireland needed one point from the second game to qualify for the World Cup – and got exactly that. Ed top-scored with 96 not out in a total of 268/5, having missed the chance of a century when TJ turned down a second run from the penultimate ball of the innings. The visitors didn't bowl well and the last over arrived with the home side needing 13 to win. The first three balls went into Ruud's scoring book as dots, but Johnboy kept banging in his half-track slower ball bouncers and, getting used to them, Michael Rippon hit a two and a four, then smashed the final delivery over long-on to tie the scores.

Malahide – 3 September

For most of the summer – it seemed like forever – I'd been inundated with emails and social media messages from Andrew Leonard, the marketing man at Cricket Ireland, imploring me to buy tickets for the visit of England. The campaign was relentless, but boy did it pay off. A crowd in excess of 10,000 at a cricket match in Dublin? Yep. Never got half that number before, or since. And the sun shone.

The little ginger fella, who was captaining his adopted side for the first time on the ground where he had played club cricket as a teenager, enlivened the pre-match press conference insisting that Stirlo should follow his lead and play for England. 'Paul knows my thoughts.' It wasn't the most diplomatic thing to say, but it was pure Eoin.

I arrived on the eve of the match and was soon helping Barry with the final touches to the media centre. The WiFi would be working, the engineer promised. Just give him a bit more time. The Ardmore Express was ready for a pint, but there was no way he was leaving the ground until he was satisfied that one half of the media's food and WiFi requirement was fulfilled.

Pleased with himself, the engineer said: 'Right, all we need now is a password?'

Those of us milling around came up with several variations on 'Where's KP' as the great man had declined his invitation to play. Then I hit on an idea. 'How about Bangalore2011?'

Chuckles. Perfect.

An hour before play the following morning, Mike Atherton popped his head around the door. 'Anyone know the WiFi password, please?'

'Bangalore2011'

'You are kidding?'

'No.'

'That's brilliant!' The former England captain left laughing.

Eoin put Ireland into bat and opened the bowling with a familiar figure. So he hadn't been injured all summer, Big Boyd had swapped flags too. He bowled beautifully, having Stirlo caught and forcing Ed so far back in his crease that he dislodged a bail with his foot. Porty held the innings together, hitting 14 fours and a six in his sixth ODI century before he too fell to his fellow north-wester for 112. Rankin added Johnboy on his way to figures of 4/46 before Max

Sorensen cleared the ropes twice in a cheery little cameo at the end.

Ireland posted 269/7 and the enormous gathering was hopeful at half-time. Among them was Hendo, who had been flown over for the occasion by Cricket Ireland. He was close to a tear. Had someone mentioned that Viv lbw again?

'You know, I would never have thought this possible,' he said, sweeping his arm around the pop-up stadium. 'It makes me very proud to think I played a small part in it.'

Hendo wasn't the only one impressed. A senior ICC figure looked around the capacity crowd and purred: 'This is becoming a serious cricketing economy.'

Johnston opened the bowling for Ireland. 'Trent reckons he's only got 100 overs left in him,' Hendo confided. 'I told him "Then make them good ones!"' TJ claimed the first and then Murtagh came to the party with three wickets.

When James Taylor was bowled, the visitors were 48/4 and most of the 10,000 were ready to celebrate another famous win. The England captain, or 'the wee bollix', depending on your viewpoint, had different ideas and took the game away from Ireland with an unbeaten 124. Ravi Bopara also made a century and England won by six wickets, easing up.

What a mixed-up match. The best England bowler grew up on a farm in Co. Tyrone, the best Ireland bowler was born and bred in south London and an Irishman won man of the match after leading England to victory.

Belfast – 6 September

Three days later, Ireland played the first of two World League ODIs against Scotland in Belfast. The home side had already qualified for the World Cup; the visitors needed one win to join them and avoid the last-chance saloon of a qualifying tournament in New Zealand. Never give a sucker an even break, they say, but chasing a victory target of 224, it looked as though Ireland had done just that when they collapsed to 146/7 after the openers had added 95 in only 17 overs.

Johnston and Sorensen halted the decline, Murtagh continued the recovery, yet when Maxi was stumped in the penultimate over, the Boys in Green were still long odds against.

The prospect of beating the auld enemy for the first time on their own patch since 2005 had several Cricket Scotland aficionados all but dancing a jig on the pavilion balcony. Alcohol had been consumed and they were singing aloud, as each ball took their side closer. 'Twelve from six,' rang out as the final over began. A couple of balls later 'ten from four' then an even more triumphant 'nine from three!'

They had not reckoned with the Lambeth Lara, as Murtagh was ironically known to Middlesex fans. A nickname that owed more to his birthplace, left-handedness and alliteration, than to any similarity with Brian Charles. Except ... Bang! The fourth ball sailed back over the head of the bowler and crashed into the sightscreen. A much quieter and less confident 'three from two.' No sooner had the refrain left the balcony than Wallop! Murtagh square cut the fifth ball past point for four.

'It was all under control, we had a ball to spare,' Timothy said, straight-faced.

Funny how things stick in the back of the mind, and reappear decades later. At a house party in the 1980s, Keith Fuller, a very good Surrey league cricketer, was nearing the punchline of a bawdy story about an old girlfriend, when he suddenly blurted out, 'Then he hit a six and a four, and the game was over!' Initially confused, we realised his missus had walked into the kitchen behind us. It became a catchphrase that season, and then forgotten. Well almost …

Ireland won the second game comfortably, dismissing the deflated Scots for 165 before a Nobby half-century took them to victory with 17 overs to spare. It was just about the complete performance which was surely going to test Callender who, to the amusement of his colleagues, began every presser – without fail – by highlighting a deficiency of some sort. How would he start this time, we wondered, as the skipper made his way over to the tent.

Scoop didn't let us down. 'Well, William, that's another toss you've lost!'

Scotland were then steamrollered by an innings and 44 runs at Clontarf in the InterContinental Cup. That defeat was probably their nadir results-wise but, in terms of stolen victories and emotional devastation, the Murtagh miracle was worse. Indeed, it was on a par with Gregor Maiden's mayhem at East Grinstead all those years ago.

Strabane – 21 September

My time with the Ireland team has taught me plenty, including that it's possible to be standing on a platform at London Bridge at 11am and still catch a flight to Belfast an hour later. I've also learned that after dashing from the Gatwick train station to the North Terminal, with a bag, it takes a bloke in his mid-fifties about 20 minutes to properly get his breath back.

The occasion was the Cricket Writers' dinner, held in the north-west again. We had invited Ruud as an overseas guest, and Simmo attended, along with players from Leinster Lightning and the North-West Warriors who had just completed their first season of the new Inter-Provincial competition that afternoon.

I hosted a question-and-answer session before we sat down to eat. It was interesting to hear Ruud talk about his international career that made Roy Torrens's 30 caps in 18 years seem prolific. The Dutch bank manager never played a first-class game. Inevitably there were questions about Test-match status, and in response, Simmo said, 'We expect to be playing Test cricket in 2018.'

He was very specific about the year. Ireland were, of course, banging hard on the ICC door at the time, but there was no certainty of it opening, and definitely no timeline – 2018? – what did Simmo know then?

Ruud had a wonderful time and kept thanking us for the invitation. He may also have told his story about beating Australia in 1964 – but only if asked. A modest man, he never promotes his achievement as some might, and only ever scores the winning runs, in his telling.

What he has not mentioned to me, even once, is that his feat was somewhere between Murtagh and Odoyo's in the pantheon of stunning finishes – three of the last four balls he faced from Bob Cowper going for 6, 4 and 6.

… and the game was over.

Dubai – 19 November

The World T20 qualifiers were a triumph for Ireland, who sailed through the tournament winning eight of their nine matches, plus a warm-up against the Netherlands. It would have been a clean sweep but for the game against Italy being abandoned without a ball bowled. TJ, in his final few weeks with the team, tweeted 'Game rained off in the desert – playing CV now complete!'

I'd done enough for Azhar in Windhoek to be offered a few more TV commentary shifts, along with a very nice suite for the two weeks in Al Barsha, and found myself sitting next to one of the best in the business, Debayan Sen, an Indian commentator who not only knew what he was looking at, but also came prepared with volumes of notes and stats. He put my hastily scribbled efforts to shame. With such a pro on board, it was easy to sit back and provide the analysis, and a little bit of humour.

The latter got me into bother at the ICC Academy. Scotland had lost their opening game to Bermuda, and while they were collapsing from 85/4 to 91 all out against Kenya, I chuckled: 'I've just had a text from someone in the Irish camp, saying "Is this Denmark in disguise?"'

The Danes were getting hammered in every game and we were encouraged to interact with the audience. It was also funny but TJ wasn't amused. Furious, in fact.

'Disrespectful, mate. You made that up!'

Nope. It did come from someone in the Ireland camp – but not from a player. I should have made that clear.

Abu Dhabi – 30 November

The final of the qualifiers against Afghanistan was TJ's penultimate game and one of his finest. Promoted to No.4 after a combination of Stirlo, Porty and O'Brien the younger had smashed 82 from the six powerplay overs, TJ proceeded to add 64 with Stirlo from barely five overs. The Belfast boy fell for 76, but TJ charged on, matching the opener's four sixes as he reached his first T20 half-century. His 62 from 32 balls also contained five fours and drew prolonged applause from the Afghan team and supporters as he departed in the 19th over. The Pashto equivalent of 'We'll not see his like again' was no doubt muttered.

The big man wasn't finished there, though. In a game where Ireland scored their highest T20 total of 225/7 – a record that was still standing six years later – he bowled a maiden, and took three wickets. Man of the match? Yep, the judges got that one right.

Two down, one to go. After clinching the T20 World qualifiers to add to their 50-over World League success, the treble was very much on.

Dubai – 10–13 December

The fourth InterContinental Cup final I'd seen was scheduled over five days at the ICC Academy, between the best two Associate teams. It was effectively a Test match between two sides who would be playing the real thing within five years. The game was again streamed and I got to commentate, in the absence of Murgatroyd who was off covering veterans' beach soccer on ice, or whatever. Loves a niche TV event does Murgers.

Ireland lost the toss, batted, and not very well. The top four, all county players, plus Andy White, were removing their pads before lunch. Afghanistan had already won on Twitter. Anderson gave the score some respectability with a solid half-century, Mooney cleared the ropes for the only six of the innings in a muscular 33 but a total of 187 was well below par. Was the team thrown by the last-minute withdrawal of Murtagh and Wilson, perhaps? The first having flown home to be with his wife at a difficult time, and the latter taken ill overnight.

Johnboy gave Ireland a foothold in the match with three wickets in the final session of the first day after a superb opening spell from Johnston that did everything but deliver a wicket. TJ did pick up a couple on the second day, Mooney completed his first five-fer and Nobby made the most of his reinstatement behind the stumps with three catches and a pair of stumpings off Dockers. Against all logic, Ireland had a first-innings lead of five. That was the game there.

The old firm of Ed and Nobby took it further away from Afghanistan with a third-wicket partnership of 110. Nobby was 13 short of what would have been a third century in as many finals when he was sixth out; his brother made a valuable 47 and after an hour-long final innings TJ was last to go for 31.

Afghanistan needed 345 to win and their fans weren't happy. The TV twitter feed had gone into meltdown during the afternoon when I was joined in the commentary box by Shafiq Stanikzai, their team manager, who I had met in Windhoek. Great guy. Brave too. One tweeter asked whether 'the problem' with the team wasn't down to the Afghan board being corrupt?

I said, 'Thanks for that tweet, Nadran, but you don't really expect me to read it out, do you?'

Shafiq leant over, and looked at it. 'No problem, David. I'll answer that.'

I frowned at him and mouthed 'Are you sure?' And answer it he did – absolutely no corruption, of course.

TJ took his 273rd and final wicket with the fifth ball of the Afghan pursuit, but hobbled off seven deliveries later – a disappointing way to end a magnificent career. If indeed it was.

We quietly wondered if the old showman would reappear the following morning but instead he joined me in the box for an hour or so of reminiscing about his ten years on the international stage. It was a vintage performance in more ways than one – I'd brought the commemorative bottle of red wine that we had all been given in Namibia in 2005.

'Still got mine, too,' TJ said.

While we talked, a sixth-wicket stand of 114 looked as though it might just deny TJ a fourth title. The second new ball proved decisive, though. There was never anything subtle about Johnboy's bowling. Whereas most bowlers try to beat the bat, you felt Mooney wanted to muscle his way through it. Yes, he did a bit off the pitch, but without any great pace he seemed able to take wickets with his sheer physical presence. And a glare or two.

Whatever it was, the Afghanistan tail had no answer to it once Maxi had removed Nabi. Mooney collected his second Michelle and match figures of 10/81 as Ireland won by 122 runs. Again the man-of-the-match judges had an easy task.

Celebrations began in the early afternoon. TJ and Whitey had their photo taken together; the two who had played in all the finals.

'You were there for all four too, DT!'

Didn't play, though. Leave me out.

Plenty of back-slapping. Robin Walsh was in his element. What a year for the old BBC News producer to be President of Cricket Ireland! Trebles all round, as they used to cry in the bars near Broadcasting House.

2014

Sydney – 3 January

The year again started at the best cricket ground in the world, the SCG. First visited in 1982, when it still had its raucous grass hill of Yabba fame at the Randwick End, the venue has been almost completely rebuilt, with only the Pavilion, Ladies' Pavilion, Brewongle and Churchill stands remaining from that Ashes tour led by Bob Willis. Loved it then, love it now. There is nothing quite like walking down from Paddington on a fresh summer day, with the scent of Jacaranda in the air. The buzz, the chatter, the anticipation of another battle between the old rivals.

This time, it wasn't Willis but another tall Warwickshire fast bowler who was about to walk out in an England shirt. Ignored for the first four Tests, Boyd Rankin was thrown in for his debut, along with Gary Ballance and Scott Borthwick, by a visiting side 4-0 down and in disarray.

Was he fit, we wondered? His first over was a loosener, his second saw a couple whizz past the nose. 'Where have they been hiding this fella?' the Aussie to my left wondered. It didn't last; he left the field injured, midway through an over. A spasm, apparently.

Big Boyd's first meaningful action was to save the follow-on with a glorious drive. He claimed a wicket in the second innings, the last, and was the final wicket to fall himself second time around as England lost by the little matter of 281 runs. It's a fair assumption this wasn't the Ashes debut he would have dreamed of as a kid, but it was a Test cap all the same, and what Ed would have given for one of those. Or any of his Irish mates.

How would TJ have responded if Australia had come calling at the end of the 2009/2010 series? I wondered. Nothing to stop him being picked at that time and, on form, he would not have been a bad choice because the Aussies were in a right old mess. An Ashes Test on his home ground weighed against an uncertain future with

Ireland? Easy in hindsight, perhaps. But then again? Don't underestimate the pull of the Baggy Green.

Port of Spain – 3 February

An invitation to take part in the West Indies' domestic 50-over competition was accepted by Ireland, a year away from their third World Cup and still hungry for competitive fixtures. After losing to Guyana, the team bus was about to set off for the second match against Jamaica when a head-count revealed someone missing. Had anyone seen him at breakfast? No.

A search party found Johnboy in a bad way, curled up in bed under bunched sheets. He was suffering from what Cricket Ireland described as a 'stress-related issue'. Whether or not it was a full-blown nervous breakdown is one for the specialists, but Mooney was in no state to continue on tour and was flown back to Dublin that night.

When he opened up publicly about what had happened, about his problems with drink and depression, and how he had not only contemplated suicide, but planned how he would carry it out, his story made the front pages as well as the back. For such a proud, passionate and physically strong man, talking about his vulnerabilities, his counselling and how he had never got over the trauma of seeing his father collapse and die in front of him as an 11-year-old took as much courage as he had ever needed in the middle.

Kingston – 19 February

After missing the domestic games, Ed was available for the three internationals that followed and steered Ireland to victory with a well-paced 40 not out, as the visitors chased down 116/8, in the first of two T20s against West Indies in Jamaica. Ireland should have won the second game too after restricting the home side to 96/9 but fell 11 runs short on a pitch that was dying with all the subtlety of a silent-movie star. What had happened to the lightning-fast, gleaming Sabina Park pitches that pacemen queued up to bowl on in the 1980s?

Aside from the corpse it was played on, the second game was also memorable for its TV commentary. To say that the local broadcasters were not familiar with the Ireland team would be presumptive because they never mentioned them at all. As one-eyed as a cyclops meeting a cat walking backwards, the local experts at first bemoaned West Indies' 'loss', and then, when the chase foundered, heaped praise on their men for defending such a small total.

The lack of research and knowledge among big-name commentators is a regular bugbear for fans of the non-Test-playing teams. Former star players parachuted in to call ICC qualifier events are generally not the best informed, with the odd notable exception. There is no excuse for it with so much data literally at their fingertips. Earn your money, guys.

Sylhet – 21 March

The first tournament of the post-Johnston era, in Bangladesh, did not end well. In the opening round of the World T20, Ireland looked on course to progress after squeezing past Zimbabwe off the last ball with three wickets to spare, and then comfortably seeing off the UAE. Not comfortably enough, though. With the Emiratis losing all their games, and Zimbabwe beating the Netherlands – the final group game began with three teams still in the hunt for top spot. Ireland, with an inferior run-rate, could not afford to lose; the Dutch had to win big.

Stirlo went early, but the skipper rattled to 47, Andy Poynter smashed a half-century and O'Brien the younger brutally bashed 42 from 16 balls. Surely 189/4 would be enough? Especially as to qualify on run-rate, the Netherlands would have to reach their target in a maximum of 14.2 overs, and were bound to lose wickets trying to go nearly 50 per cent quicker than Ireland. A slower victory sent Zimbabwe through.

Up stepped Stephan Myburgh to hammer 24 from the second over. Twenty. Four. The runs flowed, gushed, torrented. The Dutch, who had only beaten Ireland once during TJ's international career – and then when he was absent ill – reached their target with three balls to spare. Yep, home and hosed in 13.5 overs with six wickets in hand.

Clontarf – 6 May

Six weeks later, Sri Lanka limped to 219/8 in more than three times as many overs in the first of two ODIs at Castle Avenue, and Ireland had every hope of ending their home drought against one of the traditional Test teams, albeit one of the more recent arrivals at the top table.

'We gave up playing them when they were still Ceylon because they weren't considered good enough,' Scotty once told me. I've been unable to find any correlation for his claim, or indeed any evidence that Ireland ever played Ceylon. But Scotty was never wrong. Sri Lanka were certainly too good for Ireland on this occasion, dismissing the home side for 140. Nobby was fluent, but no one else; the skipper took 87 balls to make a top score of 37.

Dublin – 7 May

An evening game between the Cricket Writers and an Independent Newspapers team had been arranged for the rest day, at College Park in the city centre. The Australians had played Ireland there in 1938, without Bradman, though. Now the iconic Dublin University ground was to host another collection of ne'er do wells.

'You'll play, DT?'

'No, I'll watch.'

I'd not officially retired, but I'd not set foot on a cricket field since the afternoon Gazza crocked himself in the 1991 FA Cup Final. Barry morphed into Mrs Doyle.

'Ah, g'wan, g'wan, g'wan!' And I did go on, in a pair of almost white chinos and a Middlesex sweater borrowed from Ger.

Barry had also persuaded an international cricket captain to bowl a few overs for us. Very impressive overs, too. Left-arm around the wicket. Shades of Derek Underwood, but far more attractive (not that Deadly wasn't, mind). It was Isobel Joyce; skipper of the Ireland women's team, sister of Ed and future wife of lucky so-and-so John Anderson.

Now, an admission here; I wasn't the biggest fan of female cricket at the time. In subsequent years I've watched a couple of thrilling qualifiers, followed the rapid improvements at the top level and learned to appreciate it for what it is, rather than forever making comparisons with the men's game. I'm now a fan. Back then I would have been, let's say, dismissive. Watching Izzy bowl that evening was probably the start of my conversion: good rhythm, good line and length, and at a decent pace. I was impressed. She was a proper cricketer.

The rest of us looked like a pub team, if that particular pub had a third XI. Barry was the best of a very poor bunch. The Ardmore Express of yore claimed a couple of wickets, and then another. Everyone had to bowl two overs. My first couple of slow-medium trundles were aimed into the corridor but inexplicably strayed down the leg side. Barry helpfully suggested that I might be a little thicker around the middle than in my prime, and I should realign my belly in my delivery stride. It worked. Fourth ball was driven to cover where Izzy fumbled but held on.

It was the dismissal the world had been waiting for: caught Joyce, bowled Townsend. I teased her later about employing both knees in taking the catch. Izzy replied that she always found it better to go with two knees rather than just the one.

By contrast, one of the best catches College Park has witnessed in its long history was to end the innings. Billy Siggins from the pavilion end, whippy medium pace, fine edge wide of slip's left hand, past him, but no! Amazing reactions for an old bloke. One-handed, left-handed. I walked off, possibly for the last time, being slapped on the back, feigning modesty like Ryan Watson. I still haven't officially retired, but that's probably the last thing I'll do on a cricket pitch.

The Cricket Writers chased down a smallish target. Alcohol was consumed. I may have re-enacted my catch a couple of times.

Clontarf – 8 May

Overnight rain and the covers were on. Not an unusual sight in Ireland. Sunshine forecast for the afternoon so the possibility of a shortened match, but word reached us that water had seeped onto the pitch. If I'd still had a *Betfair* account, I'd have had a few quid on the game not being played – and piled on when a fresh rumour circulated that one of the match officials had re-booked on an earlier flight. After lunch there was another inspection. Lots of discussion. The captains shook hands. We know what that means. The market on a completed game was open for another three minutes, or so. This is why bookmakers pay for information from the ground, and the ICC try to identify and eject spectators with laptops who are looking to gain a few seconds' advantage, or in this case minutes.

Betting is a problem in cricket. Match fixing? It doesn't happen much; most players would not deliberately lose a game. Spot fixing? That's different. A wide here, a no-ball there. Specialist markets and in-play betting are open to abuse. In-play particularly. One example: a team are cruising to victory, 20 needed off six overs, say, with seven wickets in hand. Unbackable. The opposition, meanwhile, are north of 50/1. A long way north. Then a couple of wickets fall, a maiden over, another tight over, another wicket. Batsmen look to be panicking. Suddenly the bowling side are 3/1. The arbitrage between those two positions is huge.

The batting team find the runs they need and win comfortably enough. Was the result fixed? No. Were the odds manipulated? Quite possibly.

Malahide – 8–12 September

After a summer of rehabilitation, Johnboy returned for the three-match one-day international series against Scotland in good health and fine form. Ireland needed his experience as the county-contracted pros were unavailable. Scotland were near to full strength; Ireland won the series 2-1. Johnboy bowled a couple of maidens in the first match and struck a lusty 96 from 77 balls in the last. He was out in the final over, looking for a third six to take him to what would have been a second century for Ireland. Never mind, the Fingal man was back in the middle and looking forward to his third World Cup.

TESTING TIMES
2015–2019

2015

Dubai – 7 January

Oh dear, 'Ireland bowler injured and out of the World Cup'. No, not Rankin, he was still with England. It was Murtagh who fractured a bone in his foot during a pre-tournament training camp. Given the grind of county cricket, he had a very good fitness record but, Sod's Law, there was no chance of recovering in time for what would have been his only World Cup. I'd watched him develop and mature with both Middlesex and Ireland, fine-tuning his seam-bowling skills as well as toning down his cheeky-chappie antics, and really felt for the bloke.

In his first years at Lord's, he could be a pain. Too much the joker, you felt; a bit forced at times. But Middlesex have always indulged a bit of larrikin malarkey, if on-field performances warranted it. And he was never going to be in the Phil Tufnell league of bad-boy behaviour, no matter how hard he tried.

It was Ed who suggested that his then Middlesex team-mate might want to declare for the country of his father's birth and by Murtagh's admission he should probably have applied for an Irish passport a few years earlier than he did. Maybe then he would have squeezed into the 2011 squad. Or maybe not, because he was still improving and that was a very strong Ireland team. As years passed, he had become better and better as an opening bowler, and was now a grand master of his trade: no pace, but immaculate length with a bit of wobble and nibble both ways.

The big ones only come around every four years, so as far as World Cups go, he would have to settle for those Under-19 appearances with England in Sri Lanka at the turn of the century. What none of us could have guessed, when the depressing news broke, is that Timothy's best international days were still ahead of him.

Nelson – 16 February

The third World Cup campaign got underway against West Indies in a small New Zealand town at the top of the south island. Ireland had requested a match or two in Sydney, Melbourne and Perth, where their diaspora would have guaranteed big crowds and support, if only for the novelty value. The ICC gave them games everywhere but.

Why? Was there still resistance to letting people see that the Boys in Green could draw a crowd? Imagine India versus Ireland at the SCG. The attendance would have been enormous, colourful and noisy. But, no, those two teams were scheduled to meet in Hamilton, another Kiwi backwater.

West Indies were one of six opponents in Group B, and one of four Ireland realistically had in their sights. India and South Africa would be tough, Zimbabwe and the UAE they expected to beat, and Pakistan, in their final game, could blow hot or cold. Especially if they had already qualified for the quarter-finals.

Ireland had prepared well with warm-up matches in Dubai and Sydney and were focused, whereas their opponents were perhaps less ready, with an unsettled camp plus strong and persistent rumours of Phil Simmons having been approached to take over as coach after the tournament. Ireland started tightly.

Andy McBrine came on for the seventh over and sent down a 'tell-the-grandkids-about-that-one' maiden to the mighty Chris Gayle, wickets tumbled and at halfway the Test-match side were 93/5. Lendl Simmons and Darren Sammy then started to find their range and the former did his best to spoil Uncle Phil's day, reaching a century in the final over. Andre Russell tucked in too as 43 runs came from the last 18 balls and from being in control suddenly a total of 304/7 looked formidable.

Well, formidable to an onlooker, maybe, but not at all daunting to the Ireland top four who didn't give West Indies even a sniff of winning. Porty made 23, Stirlo hit 92 off 84 balls and was man of the match, Ed stroked 84 and Nobby was 79 not out when Johnboy again struck the winning boundary. OK, from 273/2 just before Joyce got out in the 40th over, Ireland should have won by more than four wickets – and quicker. Would the late stumble prove expensive later in the tournament, should net run-rate come into play? The cynics among us suspected that West Indies might come good against one of the other cartel teams.

But that was for another day (five days later against Pakistan as it turned out), now was for celebrating another stunning win and becoming the first World Cup team to successfully chase more than 300 on three occasions. The Boys in Green were not so much hammering on the door of ICC Full Membership as running at it with a battering ram. I decided it was time to underline the point in the *Indo* and wrote the following intro:

> 'Perhaps it needs Bob Geldof to storm into the ICC offices in Dubai, slam his fist on the table and demand: "Give us your f***ing Test status!" Or better still, that self-proclaimed cricket nut Martin McGuinness. Because it's hard to see what more Ireland can do – on or off the field – to budge the global custodians of the game from clinging desperately to their ever more untenable status quo.'

Brisbane – 25 February

I've been to the Queensland capital a few times and never really enjoyed the place. Too hot and sticky for my liking. On my first visit in 1982 I stayed at a Temperance hotel which boasted 'Australia's largest non-alcohol bar', which was a very small shelf of drinks. The city has changed much since then and is now far removed from that backward country town of dodgy politicians, where nearly everything closed by 8.30 in the evening and breakfast in another hotel was served between 5.30 and 7.

I'm still not won over. If anything, Brisbane is less appealing without its quirkiness. Take the Woolloongabba, to give the ground its full name, where I sat in the sun on concrete steps next to an 82-year-old pineapple farmer during the Gatting tour.

'Are you not tempted to treat yourself to a proper seat at your age, Joe?'

'Ah, we're bred tough out here, mate.'

It's all proper seats now. A massive, modern, multi-coloured stadium where it is impossible to tell where the lovely old Cricketers' Club had been, and which end Joe and I had sat waiting for the shade to arrive mid-afternoon.

It is impressive, though. Kevin Howells, the BBC reporter, chuckles about interviewing Andy McBrine before Ireland training one morning. Luckily, it wasn't live.

'What about this for a ground, Andrew?'

The Donemana man looked around in awe. 'Fecking amazing, isn't it?'

The same could not be said for the weather. A cyclone had caused the abandonment of the Australia against Bangladesh game and there were doubts whether Ireland would get on against the United Arab Emirates. This would have been a calamity, as it was seen as a banker.

The rain did clear, though, and a cracking match ensued. One reason put forward by the ICC for reducing the number of teams in the World Cup was that it would cut down on the one-sided games, yet the closest fought matches in 2015 nearly all featured a smaller nation or two. This was one of them.

Stirlo was employed for a full quota of ten overs and took 2/27 as the UAE were held to 278/9. Ireland stuttered in pursuit with Porty, Ed and Balbirnie all getting out in the 30s. A blistering 50 off 25 balls from O'Brien the younger seemed to have settled the issue, but when Wilson, who had anchored the innings with 80, was eighth out, a dozen runs were still needed. Cusack and Dockrell got the job done with two wickets and four balls to spare. It says something of the strength of the batting that Maxi was the unused last man.

If that match was much closer than expected, the next game wasn't. South Africa ran riot, smashing 411/4 in Canberra and Ireland barely got halfway in reply. The damage to their net run-rate was severe and the way things were panning out it looked as though two more wins would be needed to reach the quarter-finals.

Hobart – 7 March

The climate in southern Tasmania being more Belfast than Bulawayo should have suited Ireland but another high-scoring match ensued with little respite, never mind encouragement, for the bowlers. Big scores were a feature of the tournament by now, with 400 passed three times and 300 reached in nearly half the group matches. No individual claimed O'Brien's 50-ball century record, though, despite a couple of near misses, and it still stood after the 2019 edition.

Asked to bat, Ireland lost Stirlo early, but Ed and Balbo not only laid the foundations of another massive total but built the walls and put in the roof joists. Ed stroked 112 in that beautifully controlled 'I've-got-this' way of his, hitting three sixes in the process, while Balbo fell three short of his century, having cleared the ropes four times. The roof was finished off with a rapid 25 from Wilson; surely 331/8 would be enough?

It certainly looked that way as Zimbabwe lost four wickets for 74, but then Brendan Taylor and Sean Williams did an Ed and Balbo, the former hitting 121 and the latter caught on the boundary by Mooney for 96. Or was he? Just how close was Johnboy's boot to the rope when he held the catch at full pelt? Seemingly endless TV replays from various angles were all inconclusive as the third umpire wrestled with a decision that with 32 still needed would decide the result.

Williams took it out of his hands by accepting Johnboy's word and despite a late wobble, the victory was Ireland's by five runs when the skipper held a catch from the third ball of the final over. The look of relief, release and ecstasy stretched across Porty's face when he triumphantly threw the ball in the air showed just how much it meant. Pure gurn.

Remarkably, on the other side of the world, Gerry Adams's keynote speech at *Ard Fheis*, the annual party conference of Sinn Fein, had to be delayed because delegates were watching the cricket finish, and the hall was empty.

The Johnboy 'did he, didn't he?' debate was reignited when a Zimbabwe journalist wrote a match report disgracefully headlined 'Alcoholic dumps Zim out of WC'. The reporter, who will not be name-checked here, questioned the integrity of a self-confessed alcoholic when asked if his boot had touched the rope.

It was a vile piece written by someone who had, three years previously, been banned by the Zimbabwean FA for match fixing. But, horrible as his words were, the reporter should not take all the blame. The newspaper production process would have meant his article passing under several pairs of eyes before production, and headlines are written by sub-editors, not the author.

We can all be guilty of letting emotions influence our scribblings, particularly with the blood still pumping after a thrilling finish, and a cool-headed sub has probably saved me on the odd occasion. What went wrong that time I have no idea. The Zimbabwe team, through skipper Taylor, were quick to publicly apologise, but there was still a bad taste in the mouth when the team arrived back in New Zealand for their penultimate group game against India.

A neutral might look at the 2015 World Cup schedule and wonder why Ireland were asked to travel from Hobart to Hamilton, an exhausting 4,000km trek, involving two flights and a long bus journey, and check into their hotel at 1am on the eve of the India match? A cynic might provide the answer, although there was little likelihood of a fresh team troubling the defending champions, never mind the tired outfit who were bowled out for 259 and lost by eight wickets.

Adelaide – 15 March

Late to a third World Cup in a row, I pitched up in my second-favourite Australian city to find the Ireland team and press in good form and looking forward to what was effectively a last 16 match against Pakistan, with the winners guaranteed to go through to the quarter-finals.

The first players I ran into were Johnboy and Peter Chase, coming out of the team hotel. A bit of how's-it-going chat. Chaser was struggling for fitness and hadn't played a game.

'I'd have thought you'd have had this bloke's place by now?' I said.

'He'll have to fight me for it,' Johnboy scowled. He didn't appear to be joking.

On the eve of the game there was a reception thrown by the team's kit sponsors. Big Roy, in his element, made an off-the-cuff speech. This would be his last game as manager and he was going to go out in style. The kit, he told us, was tailored for each player and the backroom staff, and Roy confided how he got the manufacturers to sew an XXXXXL label into Simmo's shirt, and only an XXL into his own.

'Bejaysus coach, you're going to have to do something about that weight you're carrying around. Hard to believe you're three sizes bigger than me.'

He would be missed; they both would if the rumours about Simmons and West Indies were true. After a difficult start, the two big men – both XXXL, if truth be told – had formed a powerful axis that worked well for the team, and had become firm friends. Both Alpha males, they would continue to lock horns on a number of subjects, as well as on the golf course. Mention of Roy's handicap was guaranteed to send the coach's blood pressure soaring.

Which of them would be hardest to replace? No contest, because as good as Simmo was, Roy was irreplaceable, at least in terms of bluff and bluster, as well as getting things done. Organisation wasn't his strong point, but if you wanted a couple of cases of lager in a dry state, a decent exchange rate, extra baggage or anything else then the big man would fix it.

His unique style was seen in action for the final time the next day when a dispute arose between Pete Johnston, the video analyst, and his opposite number. Johnston had set up his equipment in what the Pakistanis thought was their room. A standoff ensued and both team managers were called. Roy arrived, took a look at the situation, and said: 'Now we don't want this to become a big issue, do we?'

The other manager, dwarfed in height, if not in girth, smiled: 'No, Roy, of course not.'

'Thank you so much for your understanding' Torrens said. He extended his hand and was gone before the other man realised what he had shaken on.

By then I was feasting my eyes on the new Adelaide Oval for the first time, after a redevelopment that had cost upwards of 450m local dollars, raising the capacity to 53,500.

Compared to what it replaced, it was monstrous, but in no way a monstrosity. A state-of-the-art stadium with massive stands forming a horseshoe, but with a nod to tradition by keeping one end open with its grass banks, the glorious old manual scoreboard retained and a view from the Don Bradman pavilion to St Peter's Cathedral beyond. If I had a criticism, it was that the playing area was more spherical than before; no more all-run fives to the straight boundaries.

My first experience of the ground, back in 1982, had been magical when, after an overnight bus ride from Melbourne, I had crossed the River Torrens ('Bejaysus we get everywhere!') and turned left across the park. The Richardson Gates loomed into view; a spine-tingling moment for any visitor with a sense of the history. The click of an ancient turnstile heralded another glorious vision: the red tin of the roof on the Members area, a sweep of grass and bench seating around two-thirds of an absurdly long and narrow arena.

Even then it was nearly 50 years since that most controversial of Ashes Tests. We've all seen the grainy black and white footage of Larwood felling Oldfield at the height – or perhaps the nadir – of the Bodyline series. This was where it happened. If it hadn't changed much by the early 1980s, it most certainly had now.

Would history be made again? Could Ireland upset Pakistan a second time? Sadly, no. Not from the moment Porty chose to bat and Stirlo was late on a straight one in the fourth over were the underdogs ever in with a chance. Sure, the skipper scored 107, but the support acts all fluffed their lines and 237 was well shy of competitive. There was also a sense that Pakistan had another couple of gears, if necessary, and they eased home with seven wickets to spare. The dream that had shimmered so seductively in Nelson, and teased again in Hobart, was finally gone as Ireland were eliminated on run-rate. It would be the last World Cup for Ed, Nobby, Cusie and Johnboy, and probably Porty, O'Brien the younger, Wilson and Big Boyd too.

The post-tournament party was long and loud. Part-wake, part farewell to Roy and Simmo, who was by now all but admitting his Irish race was run. Alcohol was consumed. I thanked Roy for all his help over the years; told him that he had played an important part in getting the team this far. The English press and broadcasters were there in numbers.

'How much longer do this lot have to wait before they play Test cricket?' I demanded of Jonathan Agnew, the BBC's main man.

'It's not that simple, is it?' he smiled, sweetly. Yes it bloody well is, Aggers, if only you'd take off your blinkers, I didn't say.

Barry and I decamped to Sydney where Sri Lanka were thrashed by South Africa in the first quarter-final. Ireland would have made a better game of it, or at least fought harder. With a couple of days to kill, I introduced the Ardmore Express to the stunning cliff walk from Coogee around to Bondi. About halfway, an excited group of Chinese tourists were pointing down below where a school of dolphins had joined the surfers off

Bronte beach. What a spectacle as they dived in and out of the kids, showing off their superior aqua skills before swimming away bored.

'Does that happen often?' Barry asked. I'd done the walk more than 50 times and never once seen anything remotely like it. Right time; right place.

Two days later, word flew around the Etihad lounge that Business Class was overbooked for the first leg back to Ireland. Barry was not amused; he was not going to fly 14 hours to Abu Dhabi in economy without a fuss. A big north-west sort of a fuss. Sure enough, as his boarding pass was presented at the gate, the computer bleeped.

'Mr Chambers, I have to inform you that our Business Class section is full …' The Ardmore Express took a deep breath and prepared to start in off his long run. '… so we've upgraded you to First Class.'

Some people, eh?

Leeds – 29 April

There is always a down after the high of a big tournament, but mine lasted longer than usual. Was I starting to lose interest, was I falling out of love with Irish cricket? The future did not look rosy, or inspire confidence, never mind excitement. Cusie was on the brink of retirement, his body had had enough, Ed and Nobby were in their twilight years, none of the new intake of players were stirring my interest on the field, never mind in the bar after, and the appointment of John Bracewell, as coach, didn't exactly get the juices flowing.

It was the safe choice. The veteran New Zealander was a steady hand at the wheel for a couple of years as Ireland pushed for a fifth InterContinental Cup and with it a shot at Test status. The logic was fine, but wouldn't a younger, more energetic bloke like Dale Benkenstein, who was also mooted, have been the way to go. Fresh ideas, something to prove?

Malahide – 8 May

The biennial ODI against England the following week did little to lift the mood. Murtagh was injured and we didn't get to see how the Ireland attack would cope without him because there was only time for the home side to limp to 56/4 before rain arrived. A damp miserable affair was called off three hours later. It was as far removed from the 2013 sell-out as was imaginable.

As the rain fell, a few of us in the media area again discussed playing home matches in Dubai or Abu Dhabi. The 2017 England game was apparently being proposed for the end of April. What was the point? At least at the end of August or early September there was a chance of warmth and some sunshine. April? In Dublin, or worse still Belfast? Dearie me.

Malahide – 2–5 June

If there were a couple of batsman who could always be relied on to lift the heart it would be Stirling and Joyce, and the two of them turned it on against the UAE, adding 231 at the start of a new InterContinental Cup campaign. A very important campaign, with the ICC promising the winners a crack at joining the top table of Full Members, which meant playing Test matches, of course. How this would come about wasn't clear, though. The first day saw 420 runs scored. In their contrasting styles, Stirlo powered his way to 146, an effort that was dwarfed by that of Ed who sailed on serenely to 231, the highest individual score for Ireland.

An evening or three spent in the village of Malahide was a joy, too, with its upmarket bars and restaurants. It's the perfect location for Ireland to play international cricket, with a nearby train station linking into central Dublin and a ground surrounded by mature trees and overlooked by a castle. Fingal Council invested heavily to move earth, build banks for seating and turn the square. Then various interests started pulling in different directions. Local residents were not keen on the installation of floodlights, Malahide wanted first dibs on the square for club games, and Cricket Ireland plans to build a pavilion complex similar to Chester-le-Street foundered. If only the different factions could pull together it could become one of the world's very best venues. If only Wee John were still around.

Hopefully the UAE enjoyed their stay in the village because there was little to cheer them in the middle as they were bowled out twice and lost by an innings and 26 runs, even if the teams had to show up on the final day with Ireland only a wicket from victory, a task that required four balls. No one likes that – except the freelancers.

If my mood had been lifted somewhat by both the weather, the nights out and a successful first step on the road to another IC Cup title, the rain and gloom returned soon after in Bready, when two warm-up games ahead of the World T20 qualifiers were washed out and the other two were won by Scotland.

Belfast – 15 July

If there was a tournament which confirmed the end of Ireland's dominance at Associate level, it was the World

T20 qualifiers. The hosts had started brightly enough with victories over Namibia and the United States, and then bowled out Nepal for 53.

All going to plan; another triumphant march to the tournament proper was well underway when Porty chose to bat against Papua New Guinea at Stormont and his side were unable to defend 123/9. It wasn't so much that the Pacific Islanders had got home with two wickets and seven balls to spare, but that they had the belief to do so.

A couple of years previously, Ireland had laid waste to all bar Afghanistan at this tournament and were expected to do the same on home soil. For half a dozen years, at least, the aura surrounding the Boys in Green had protected them from defeats such as this; teams had got close but simply did not had the *cojones* to finish the job. That invincibility disappeared on a mad afternoon in Sylhet and, if the Netherlands could beat the mighty Irish, so could others. First PNG and then Hong Kong in the next Group A game at Malahide. Both genuine shocks.

Ireland still topped the group and qualified without the anxiety of play-offs, but then lost to the Dutch again in the semi-finals. No trophy, and no final appearance for the first time in five qualifiers. As the push towards ICC Full Membership continued apace, you began to wonder whether the moment had passed? It had for Cusie, who finally listened to his body and retired.

Dublin – 20 July

After a long illness, Derek Scott passed away in a nursing home at the age of 85. He had lived to see his beloved Ireland compete in three World Cups, although it's unlikely he knew much about the last one. That great brain of his, with its vast knowledge of the history and stats of Irish cricket, wasn't in the best shape in his final years. Much information would have died with him, but for his expansive library and research, including his logging of records and scorecards back to 1855; an invaluable labour of love.

Scotty never made so much as a half-century in senior cricket but he was, nevertheless, a great of the game on the island. After taking over as ICU Secretary in 1974, he charted a course through some of the worst years of the Troubles. 'There is no border in Irish cricket and never will be,' he said more than once. As Hon. Sec., he was also prominent in lobbying for Associate membership of the ICC. Stubborn, dogmatic and, of course, never wrong, it wasn't easy to like the old so-and-so, but I grew to, as well as appreciating his enormous contribution.

Belfast – 27 August

A disappointing domestic season both results and weather-wise concluded at Stormont with a rain-affected ODI against Australia, who had just lost an Ashes series across the water. A match that started late and was shortened four times by the weather finally saw Ireland chasing a D/L target of 181 from 24 overs. After both openers had fallen in the first ten balls, the old firm of Ed and Nobby made a fist of it, rewarding the patient crowd by adding 86 in 12 overs before wickets began to fall again and the home side were dismissed for 157.

The trip over was made by a couple of nights' stay in a 'hotel' off the Dundonald Road, which was actually just a big family house with a spare bedroom. The proprietor, Conor, was most accommodating. A nearby pub? Yes, just down to the main road and turn right.

'It's not hard to find but I'd better come with you in case you get lost.'

There was no breakfast, but a wonderful late supper of freshly caught and grilled trout was waiting for us when we returned a couple of hours later. The place was 'a find' but I've not been able to stay since as it's always booked for some reason.

Harare – 17–20 October

It was always my intention to return to Windhoek for the IC Cup match, so why not tack on a week in Zimbabwe for the four-day game that preceded it? Why not indeed. It would be the eighth of the ten Test-playing countries visited, only leaving Sri Lanka and Bangladesh. I did once touch down in Colombo, on the way to somewhere else, but didn't get off the tarmac so that couldn't be counted.

We would have happily touched down anywhere on the flight from Johannesburg to Harare, mind, as long as we could do so safely. The plane was the smallest I'd flown in, with a single row of seats on one side and two on the other. Then we were hit by a thunderstorm. The little tube with the jet engine at the back was buffeted and thrown everywhere. I'm not religious; I don't pray. Dear God, get us out of this alive, please. Never has terra firma been more welcome.

Odd to find a cash machine at the airport – I was expecting a rip-off money-changer – and odder still to see US dollars spewing out. My taxi driver was an optimistic sort: the country had improved since its darkest days, he insisted. Yes, Mugabe was still in charge but he wouldn't live forever. The country hoped to reintroduce the Zim dollar soon. He offered to sell me an old trillion dollar note, as a souvenir.

The tales of hyper-inflation had always bemused me. How does that work? How do you close a shop every couple of hours to reprice? Apart from the financial horrors, exactly how do the logistics apply to charging ten times more for a pint of milk in the evening than you did in the morning? The other thing you can't escape with the currency is how filthy bank notes become if you don't replace them. Every purchase was rounded up to the nearest dollar and change came in limp, black carriers of the plague. Disgusting things.

At the team hotel I encountered Big Roy's replacement for the first time: Chris Siddell, an energetic young bloke from the north-east of England. 'Manage', as he was already known, liked to go running, had completed a marathon or two and looked as fit as half the team. He was also a great organiser; about as far removed from his predecessor as it was possible to be.

Could he find the right chocolate bars for Stirlo, though, and keep Nobby in order on a wet night in Skerries? Apparently, he could. And Johnboy was a fan, which was enough for me. 'Roy was Roy, this fella is top drawer.'

The Harare Sports Club was a hospitable place to watch a few days' bat-dominated cricket. It hadn't changed a lot since it was the Salisbury Sports Club, would be my guess. Very colonial feel, still. Good bars, good facilities. I found Davy Houghton helping out at nets. It seemed like another lifetime when the Zimbabwean was batting consultant in at that first ICC Trophy.

The home side had beaten Ireland 2-1 in the preceding ODI series, and showed their greater strength in depth as

Malcolm Waller, who was only on the fringes of the first team, made a century in both innings of a genteel draw. It was a useful exercise ahead of the important part of the tour.

Windhoek – 24–27 October

By some strange coincidence, the IC Cup match took place on the tenth anniversary of Operation Townsend. Only Nobby remained of the players from 2005, and he and I were the two survivors from the original Namibia 30. Wee John and Scotty had shuffled off, John Caldwell would follow within months. Adi was assistant coach of South Africa, Knoxy had joined the family business, Fitzy was working for International Rugby. Arthur Vincent was still around and had enjoyed a second short term as President when Jimmy Joyce decided he couldn't see out his year. David O'Connor was yet to assume the role. As to the rest of the North County Four, who knew? A lot changes in ten years.

The Wanderers' pitch was still a batting paradise, though, and Namibia should have made a lot more than 251 after winning the toss. Ireland did. Specifically Ed, who scored his second double century in as many IC Cup matches. He dominated the second day, and when he was out for 205, Nobby came and went for a golden duck. How the local farmers guffawed.

The skipper, who had supported Ed in a record second-wicket stand of 326, went to bed on 153 and added a further 33 the following morning. O'Brien the younger and Mooney piled on the agony as the home side wilted. Johnboy was 53 not out, when Porty declared on 570/6. It was his second unbeaten half-century of the trip and was to be his last innings for Ireland.

Murtagh took three wickets in a probing opening spell to raise hopes of a three-day win but Namibia held on, seven down. Not much chance of rain saving them in the Kalahari. Ireland mopped up well before lunch, banked the maximum 20 points, and in two minibuses we all went to Joe's to celebrate that evening. All, that is, apart from Johnboy.

'He's fine, just wants to be on his own,' Nobby said.

Contemplating his future, maybe? Later that year, after 182 matches that brought him 2,605 runs and 144 wickets, the great Irish warrior retired.

I'd miss him more than any of them.

Bangkok – 29 November

Where else would Barry and I finally happen upon an Irish leg-spinner who could land six perfect deliveries an over than next to a cock-fighting stadium in Thailand? A blonde leggie wearing the No.23 shirt, at that. Bowling, Shane! Two overs and I was a fan. A couple of problems, though: a bit on the old side at 36 and a bit on the female side, too.

Which was probably just as well given Ciara Metcalfe was mesmerising opposition batters as well as myself in the women's World T20 qualifiers. Two of her four overs were maidens as Ireland beat China by 28 runs on their way to winning Group B.

Was it a stretch to say she was the best leg-spinner of either sex in Ireland, as I may have done in the *Indo*? Not as good as Greg Thompson in his mid-teens, that's for sure, and possibly still second to Conor Hoey, who was continuing to take wickets by the bucketload in Leinster two decades after winning his last cap. But other than that …?

The final, on the same ground, saw Ciara take 3/14 as Bangladesh made 105/3 and after a stuttering chase Ireland needed two from the final ball or a single to force the game into a Super Over. And then … a Mankad! What about that? The Bangladesh women leapt around celebrating their 'win'; fury from the Ireland bench. The Ardmore Express and I may have let our feelings be known too.

After consulting with the umpires and realising that the final ball would still have to be bowled, common sense prevailed, the appeal was withdrawn, and Lucy O'Reilly hit the winning runs over midwicket. Ireland captain Izzy Joyce was still visibly incensed when she spoke to us 15 minutes later. It had been a feisty confrontation. Fierce, even. I vowed never to use the term 'handbags' again.

Bready – 21 December

The big man was back. After 11 appearances for England, including that one Test in Sydney, Boyd Rankin declared for Ireland again and was welcomed with open arms. At his best he had that awkward length and steep bounce that the very best batsmen find difficult, never mind those poor little Italy amateurs he terrorised all those years ago. A yard slower now, maybe, but fitter than he had been for years, there was half of an opening attack with Murtagh that would serve Ireland well for a couple of years, hopefully more.

2016

Townsville – 31 January

A week in what Aussies call the Top End to watch the next InterContinental Cup match against Papua New Guinea sounded like an idea, but there was no way to get there from Thailand. At least none that made any sense financially or time-wise. In mainland UK, and to a lesser extent Ireland, we've got used to flying almost anywhere quickly and cheaply. Try getting from Bangkok to Townsville. I looked at all sorts of options, including going through Indonesia. Nothing worked.

So I missed a workmanlike performance that again earned maximum points at the Tony Ireland Stadium. Another step on the ladder to a crack at earning Test status. The ICC still hadn't quite finalised what hoops the winners of the IC Cup would have to jump through to gain Full Membership, but there was talk about home and away matches against the lowest-ranked big boy – which probably meant Zimbabwe. How many of these games would they have to win? Would they need to win home and away? No one knew, so all Ireland could do was get their heads down, win a fifth title and take it from there.

The defending champions faced stiffer opposition than they had encountered in their first two games and were made to toil for a modest 289 all out, Nobby top-scoring with 63. Murtagh made sure of the first-innings points, though, taking four wickets to secure a lead of 101. With rain around, Porty had a tricky declaration to make, but got it spot on. PNG were asked to make 346 in an hour plus a day. The weather held, Big Boyd took three wickets and a 145-run win was in the bag before tea.

Dharamsala – 9–13 March

It was a barometer of my enthusiasm for both the shortest form and another trip to India that it never occurred to me to go to the World T20. A picturesque setting in the foothills of the Himalayas was appealing, but dealing with another mountain of paperwork was not. As it turned out, wading through the visa process would probably have taken longer than Ireland's participation.

Again ICC weeded out most of the pesky little teams by introducing a 'first round' that didn't include the top eight sides. Ireland found themselves in a group with Bangladesh, the Netherlands and Oman. Get past the first two to qualify, you'd have thought. Think again because the opening match against Oman did not go to plan. Ireland would have been happy enough with 154/5 and seemed to have control of the match when the Omanis lost their fifth wicket on 90, with six overs left. No one, though, had reckoned with Amir Ali, a chubby all-rounder with thick-lensed glasses. Certainly not Barry.

'If this is all they've got left …' he muttered.

As Amir started to locate the middle of his equally chubby bat, Porty got in a right mess with his bowling and Rankin could only send down three of his permitted quota of four overs. Big Boyd's excellent final over, the 19th, only leaked four runs, leaving 14 required off the last. The skipper could have asked one of the spinners to bowl, or Murtagh even. Instead he threw the ball to Max Sorensen.

Feeling under the weather, I was following the game in bed. I remember leaping up and shouting 'Not bloody Max!' to an empty apartment.

Now Maxi had many virtues; he was a fine white-ball exponent, particularly T20s, big hitter, bit of pace and carry at times. But bowling the final over in a pressure situation would not figure prominently on his CV and the game was all but over when his first delivery, a no-ball, went for four. He did have Amir caught behind for a match-winning 32 off 17 balls, but it was too late and Oman were home by two wickets with two balls to spare.

Porty attempted to explain that Max had been finding his yorker lengths better than anyone in the nets. *In the nets!* In those situations you have to go with your gut and turn to the bloke who is most likely to perform. That one decision was symptomatic of how far Ireland had strayed from winning cricket matches to following pathways and manuals. Even Porty. Know your players. In the absence of a TJ or Cusie, you would look to Stirlo or Andy 'Scra' McBrine for the necessary ice in the veins. Not bloody Max.

Ireland were out two days later when their must-win clash with Bangladesh was rained off, although not before the group favourites had charged to 94/2 off eight overs. A wet, miserable campaign ended with defeat by the Netherlands in a six-overs slog. The grim news didn't end there: Andy Balbirnie, who had been playing in pain for months, needed a hip operation and would be out of action for months. There had been several times during this journey that I'd regretted missing tournaments, or parts of them. This wasn't one.

Malahide – 16–18 June

A two-match ODI series against Sri Lanka brought two more heavy defeats. The first game was a contest, with Sri Lanka posting 303/7 and Ireland keeping in touch to the point of needing 145 off the final 20 – not impossible, with seven wickets in hand. Porty then fell for 73 and the innings collapsed in a heap either side of 200. The less said about the second, the better: Sri Lanka made 377/8, a record on Irish soil, and the home side would have lost by far more than 136 but for Scra bashing an improbable ODI best of 79.

Go back a decade or so and it's impossible to imagine a score of 377 in 50 overs on any pitch in Ireland. OK, ODI batting has changed, but the biggest difference was the surface. Cricket Ireland had hired former Somerset groundsman Philip Frost to prepare pitches and the man previously responsible for batting paradises at Taunton had started rolling out roads at The Village.

Our players have to learn how to bat and bowl on good pitches, was the official line. Why? I know why, because that's what it said in their How to Develop an International Cricket Team manual; the one that was being used for all these daft decisions, like Maxi bowling the last over in Dharamsala.

Do Bangladesh prepare green seamers because their batsmen need to learn how to play on them? No. Do Australia prepare slow, low featherbeds to improve the repertoire of their quicks? No. So why on earth weren't Ireland playing to their strengths? Because there was nothing about that in the manual, obviously. Matt Dwyer and I had a right old moan to each other.

Belfast – 17 July

Ireland hosted Afghanistan for a series of five ODIs at Stormont that started with a win apiece, and a game rained off, then erupted into controversy when Mohammad Nabi claimed a run out against Ed in the fourth match. To suggest Ed was in a bit of nick would be an understatement. He had stroked 62 in the first game, an unbeaten century as Ireland levelled the series two days later, and was confidently eyeing Afghanistan's total of 229/7 when he struck what looked like a boundary to the Newtownards Road boundary.

Nabi gave chase, knocked the ball back well after it had crossed the rope and, with the batsmen stopping for a midwicket chat, Ed was 'run out' for 12. Surely the umpires had seen that it was a four? No. Ed had to go. One man who did see what had happened, and had taken several photos that left no one in any doubt, was the Ardmore Express. Right time; right place. Barry had followed Nabi with his lens and clicked a few shots that were online within minutes. Even quicker, the abuse started. No way was Nabi a cheat. The great man wouldn't do something like that. Those shots must be Photoshopped. Not just from the odd one-eyed Afghanistan fan, of which there are a few, but dozens of them.

Ed responded in the manner of a cricketing gentleman: refusing to discuss the issue after Ireland had lost by 79 runs, and then making his highest one-day score, carrying his bat in the final game. A stunningly determined 160 not out helped his side to 265/5, which was 12 runs too good for Afghanistan, and the series was drawn.

Nabi later owned up and was reprimanded by the ICC, who buried his confession on their website, much to the annoyance of the slighted Ardmore Express.

Malahide – 18 August

Another belter of a track at The Village and another belting for Ireland, as they were bowled out by Pakistan for 82 and lost by a whopping 255 runs. Occasionally you will run into an opponent in irresistible form and there is not a lot you can do about it. Sharjeel Khan plundered 152 off 86 balls, including nine sixes, before he became Barry

McCarthy's third wicket. I liked the look of the Pembroke seamer. Bit about him. Lively fast medium and a habit of taking wickets. It was easy to see why he was already on Durham's books. His 4/62 gave him a tally of 18 wickets from his first seven games, all of them ODIs.

There was nothing else to get excited about. The temporary stands were again half full. Why? Not enough publicity, particularly among the Pakistani community in Dublin? Local fans not wanting to see their side hammered on flat pitches? Or just over-optimistic expectations?

Each of those temporary seats costs money to install, so why not restrict the capacity to a number you are going fill, say 1,200 or 1,500? Some people may not be able to get a ticket. So what? Pack out a smaller ground, create a demand as well as an atmosphere.

'Are you going to the cricket?'

'No, couldn't get a ticket.'

That has to make sense. And while you're at it, how about building a couple of permanent toilet blocks either side of the ground? How hard can that be? Those green portable things are not only expensive to hire every year, but also scary. Click your heels a couple of times on a windy day and you could be blown halfway to Kansas – or so it always seems to me.

Belfast – 30 August–2 September

I wasn't alone in becoming downhearted and disillusioned. It was during this summer that the Ardmore Express decided his race was run as media manager, although he limped along a while longer. 'Too many hammerings. I was able to start writing match reports 30 minutes into our innings.'

There was still the comfort blanket of the IC Cup, though, and Ireland collected a maximum 20 points for a fourth time with a 70-run victory over Hong Kong, at Stormont. The match followed a similar pattern to the one earlier in the year with the defending champions reaching 316, thanks to Porty making 88 and his best mate Willo falling five short of what would have been his second century for Ireland.

Hong Kong grafted for more than 100 overs, but three wickets each to Dockrell and Chase pegged them to 237. Again the weather was the biggest threat to an outright win, but four wickets from Murtagh and Ireland were able to scramble over the line in the final session.

It had been hard work. The home side had needed every ounce of their experience, of which there was plenty. Only four players were the lively side of 30 and two of those – Stirlo and Dockers – had been around forever. The other two were the seamers Craig Young and Chaser who only played because Rankin was injured. Where were the new faces? What exactly were those pathways and the Academy producing?

'The Manual says …'

Still, steady as she goes for now. Bracewell was doing what he had been hired for. Ireland sat atop the IC Cup ladder, 19 points clear of Afghanistan who were next up, on their 'home' ground near Delhi.

Lord's – 23 September

Tactics, results, pitch preparation, player development, temporary stands, frightening toilet facilities … I was getting far too gloomy and needed something to lift the spirits. It came in the shape of Middlesex's first County Championship title for 23 years, clinched on an extraordinary final afternoon of the season against defending champions Yorkshire, and sealed by a Toby Roland-Jones hat-trick in front of a huge crowd. It couldn't have been much better – unless it was a Murtagh hat-trick.

Middlesex had been my county since the days of Peter Parfitt and Fred Titmus, and they are also Ireland's county, given the many players who have represented both the Shamrock and the Seaxes down the years. Stirlo, still not a regular against the red ball, missed the victory as he was already in Benoni for a couple of random ODIs, but spare a thought for poor Timothy. No sooner had he collected his medal and gulped down a glass of champagne than he was on his way to Heathrow for an overnight flight to join the squad. Cricket Ireland, who had got so many things wrong in 2016, at least had the good sense to allow their best bowler to complete his county season, even if he was denied the evening's celebrations.

A day after touching down in Johannesburg, Murtagh was Ireland's most economical bowler in a 206-run defeat by South Africa, and two days later took the only wicket as Australia romped to another one-sided win. Quite what was gained by playing those two games I have no idea. Fortunately, nothing much was lost.

2017

Sydney – 8 January

One of the joys of visiting Sydney is taking the 380 bus out to Bondi beach and having lunch at the RSL club at the north end. The food is simple, but there are few better views back along the iconic expanse of sand on a sunny day. Take your passport for temporary membership and try to get a table outside. That's where I met Andy Balbirnie for a couple of plates of John Dory and a catch-up. He was recovering well after his hip operation. Everything was going to plan: a few runs in local cricket and the time and facilities to work on his fitness. Balbo admitted it had been a mistake to try to play in the World T20 and doing so had probably cost him his Middlesex contract.

We talked about the future. Who were the new players coming through to look out for? How much longer could Ed and Nobby go on? And how tough would it be without them? I told him that, good as he was, I'd love to see him step up to that next level and become one of those one or two key batsmen every team has; the ones who supporters hate to see get out. He wasn't quite there yet, but he was definitely on the way back.

Colombo – 16 February

As months go, February was right up there. It started with the ICC proposing that Ireland and Afghanistan join their exclusive band of Full Members – which sounded like a done deal but would not be ratified until the next Board meeting in June – and continued with my first trip to Colombo. The purpose was to commentate on the Women's World Cup qualifiers, with Ireland hoping to join the main tournament in England later in the summer.

What a great place Sri Lanka is; like India without the less agreeable bits. The TV crew were billeted at the Colombo Court, a mile or two away from a clutch of five-star hotels where the teams stayed. Fabulous spot. Large suites, four-poster beds, waterfall showers (which was at odds with the hotel's claim to being the most environmentally friendly in the city, as was its air-con cooling of outdoor areas, but never mind), cooked-to-order breakfasts, a roof-top bar with live music, and mango and arrack cocktails.

And what great company in the commentary box: Ebony Rainford-Brent, of *Test Match Special* fame, and Anjum Chopra, the former India captain. Ebony dived into the local culture, dancing with the pitch-side band, and befriending an ancient, toothy cab driver who took us to Galle on a day off, while Anjum was wonderfully old school, scolding a waiter for bringing two eggs when she had only ordered one and refusing point-blank to ride in a tuk-tuk until she absolutely had to – and then loving it. 'I've not been in one of those things for 15 years!'

The work itself was a challenge. I'd never commentated on a women's game and there are a few pitfalls. We were told to refer to 'batters', although Ebony and Anjum were the main culprits for using 'batsmen' and were quite happy with it as a term. It's not easy to change long-formed habits. Third man is problematical too. Third person? Best to just go with 'third'. The biggest trap to avoid is constantly comparing and contrasting with the men's game. Enjoy it for what it is: nowhere near as fast or powerful, but skilful and competitive all the same.

I had dinner with Isobel, her twin Cecelia and a couple of the other players after they had lost to Bangladesh, and were on the brink of elimination. Not for the first time I was taken by the dedication of the Ireland team, who were still two years away from any sort of professional central contracts. It was back to 1995, and Uel Graham in that Italian restaurant; what this lot needed was a wad of cash behind them.

A couple of good feeds were also had in the Colombo Cricket Café, which has a themed menu offering such delights as Knott's Nachos, Murali's Mulligatawny, Sanga's Seafood and Thommo's Thai. Players from around the world featured, although none from Ireland; 'Thommo' being Jeff Thomson. With Test cricket on the horizon, perhaps it was time to add a couple of steaks: a Stirloin and a Portyhouse, maybe?

Ireland finished bottom of the Super Six; India played South Africa in the final. Good match; great finish. Eight to win off two balls, last pair at the crease and Harmanpreet Kaur launched a mighty blow over midwicket. A six and a two … and the game was over.

It was the second women's final I'd seen and the second one to go to the death. Over three million had watched our live stream of the final overs.

Greater Noida – 28–30 March

If the ICC were to confirm Ireland and Afghanistan as Full Members in June, as expected, then winning the InterContinental Cup held less significance. No longer would doing so offer the chance to beat Zimbabwe an unspecified number of times, home and away, to gain Test status. Or whatever. It was still the IC Cup, though, and effectively a final with both teams neck and neck at the top of the table, so not to be missed. Even if it did involve another trip to India, where Afghanistan had found a new temporary home, south of Delhi.

I'd sat down in plenty of time to see what new hurdles had been added to the process of obtaining a visa since the World Cup. Glory be! It could now be done online. No catches. Relatively straightforward and, at least for me, it seemed to work. A comfortable taxi ride from Indira Gandhi International to Greater Noida too, a decent four-star hotel with a few familiar faces to say 'Hello' to on arrival, including Big Roy.

So far, so good. OK, Greater Noida isn't on the tourist trail. To be kind, it's the Croydon of New Delhi. Bland but harmless. Or so I thought.

Midway through the second day of an innings loss, I started to feel a little dizzy and needed a rapid visit to the bathroom. A bad case of south-of-Delhi belly. Horrible affliction. Easy to make jokes about Ireland needing the runs more than me as they were bowled out for 261 in reply to a suffocating 537/8 declared. But seriously, not funny. I got through the next day and a bit somehow, which is more than could be said for the Ireland batting that appeared to give up the fight and only lasted 40 overs following on.

Nabi opened the bowling and took six wickets second time around, but he was up to his old tricks claiming a slip catch that he dived for, dropped and then picked up off the grass. We were able to show this despicable act clearly on the stream. No one could claim otherwise, this time.

By contrast, Nobby had held a stunning low catch only to have it ruled out because the umpires couldn't be sure it had carried. It had. That's to take nothing away from Afghanistan who were clearly the better side and went top of the IC Cup table, having also beaten Ireland 3-0 in the preceding T20 series and 3-2 in the ODIs.

'They've gone past us, haven't they?' Nobby said. 'We've got some catching up to do.' He wasn't referring to the table.

Lord's – 7 May

If the sight of ticket touts at work and supporters queuing to get into the ground at Bristol two days previously wasn't enough, the sea of green helping to pack out Lord's for the second ODI against England was extraordinary. Two decades ago, Ireland used to play the MCC here in front of 200 people, half of them ICU committee men in their egg-stained blazers.

Callender, Ger and myself were now guests of the English press, who were out in force. A full TMS crew had been assembled and the Sky cameras were there too. As good as the temporary media facilities are at Malahide, this was proper. Ireland had been rumbled by Adil Rashid in Bristol, losing by seven wickets in barely half a day, and I was a little nervous that this first clash with England at Headquarters would go the same way. Either that or I still wasn't over whatever it was I'd caught in Greater Noida.

Rankin was injured but otherwise Ireland were at full strength and our fears of a second drubbing were confounded, despite England making 328/6. The visitors replied with spirit: a lively 48 from Stirlo at the top and Porty walloping his way to 82 at first drop. There was never any prospect of a repeat of Bangalore, although the target was almost the same, but an 85-run loss was just about respectable.

The one worry was Ed, who had retired from county cricket at the end of the previous season and looked scratchy making 16 from 43 balls. He would be waiting, more keenly than most, for the outcome of the ICC Council meeting at The Oval. How quickly after that could Ireland arrange an inaugural Test? Just the one cap would be something. Keep going old fella …

Dublin – 14 May

A tri-series against Bangladesh and New Zealand at Malahide helped fill the time waiting. Bangladesh had kicked on in recent years and now had no fear of such encounters, even in alien conditions, and New Zealand were one of the five Test sides that Ireland had never beaten. Never come close to beating, either. Although at opposite ends of the earth, there are similarities, not least in size of populations. The Kiwis have the better weather, of course, as well as a much longer tradition of competing at the highest level, but you would like to think – as has happened with rugby union – Ireland will close the gap in the years ahead.

The Boys in Green had a sniff of winning the first of their two encounters, needing 102 from 15 overs, with Nobby and Willo well set. The latter was then fifth out in the next over for 30 and, although the keeper went on to complete his eighth and last international century, he found little help from a long tail. What Nobby claimed later that year to be his best innings for Ireland – surprisingly pipping the famous 72 against Pakistan – ended when he was stumped for 109, straining for a sixth six, as the required run-rate nudged ten an over. The home side lost by 51 runs, and were beaten again a week later by 190.

The Oval – 22 June

So, here it was: the big day; the culmination of all those performances on the field plus the tireless efforts of Wee John and Warren Deutrom in the corridors of power. Yet when it was officially announced that Ireland, along with Afghanistan, had become a Full Member of the ICC and would be playing Test matches in the near future, I found myself underwhelmed.

Why? Partly because it had been expected, of course, partly because I had copy to write for the *Indo*, but mostly because I was no longer sure it was merited. Were this bunch good enough to play Test cricket?

Fair play to the ICC development department, and Richard Done in particular, who had pushed and pushed to get the two their elevated status. No one would argue that Afghanistan were not worthy recipients, but I'd have found it hard to make a case that the other newbies were any better on current performances than that lot across the Irish Sea and up a bit. Yes, Cricket Ireland was now an impressive organisation, with good corporate governance, no doubt, but first and foremost shouldn't it be about the quality of their cricketers and the cricket played?

And why should ICC Full Member status be something that is bestowed forever?

When a golden generation raises the standard for a nation, as the likes of McCallan, Botha, Johnston, *et al*, did for Ireland, why should it be years later that their less talented successors reap the rewards? Surely the ICC needs to be looking for a system that enables talent from anywhere in the world to rise to the top quickly, as it theoretically can in one-day cricket.

What if a couple of wildly talented families were to emerge in, say, Jersey; dominate locally at Associate level; have the beating of Zimbabwe and other lower-level Full Members; even reach the last four of a World Cup. How does that team get to play a Test match? It doesn't. We know that Jersey will never have the 'serious cricket economy' necessary for Full Membership and we expect that in a decade or two their titans will be succeeded by a very average bunch.

That is essentially what happened in Nairobi in the 1990s. The Tikolos and Odoyos were good enough to play

Test cricket, a generation later Kenya are languishing in World League Division Three.

Equally, Ed and the O'Briens deserved to play at the top level in their prime and it is a crime that Kyle, TJ and Johnboy will never be able to show their grandkids a Test cap.

Ah, if only cricket were a sport and not a business …

St Helier – 31 July

One of the joys of being a single bloke – and there are a few – is that you can spoil yourself occasionally. I get down to Australia most Christmases and New Years to watch a bit of cricket, for example, and at least one four-day match at Scarborough is another fixture in the annual calendar. The downside is that when you get home after such a treat, life can seem a bit flat.

I can't remember where I'd been, but I was in just such a mood when the Ardmore Express called to update me on the first few games of the Under-19 World Cup qualifier in Jersey.

'Get yourself over here then,' he said. 'Could be a cracking decider against Scotland.'

Nah, impulse trips like that are always super-expensive, aren't they? Nothing available at the last minute. Worth a look, though. I'd never been to the Channel Islands. Well worth a look, as it turned out. Very reasonable return flight, and a lovely little hotel with a late-room cancellation. Why not? Half an hour later it was booked.

Barry was right about the decider. Ireland had crept past Scotland by two wickets in the first of their two encounters, with Neil Rock and Josh Little conjuring an unlikely seventh-wicket stand of 63 from 34 balls to rescue a desperate situation, but the Scots had a superior run-rate and would qualify if they won the final game.

There are probably flat-screen TVs bigger than Jersey, but I still managed to get lost on my way to Grainville for the showdown. As I approached the ground, Heatley was coming the other way, cigarette on, shaking his head. 'Not good.' Not good at all – Ireland were 27/5 and had lost 'Pebbles' Rock too before I'd located a coffee.

Captain Harry Tector was standing defiant but no one wanted to stay with him. Even Little got out in a daft way. Heatley's lad battled on until it was just him and last man Varun Chopra. The pitch wasn't easy. If Ireland could scrape past a 100 … on 94, Harry lobbed a soft catch to a fielder inside the ring. It was a Geoffrey's granny of a catch, and it was dropped. The skipper completed his half-century and was last out for 55, from 139 balls with just the one four. Extras was second-highest scorer with 18, no one else managed double figures in a total of 108.

With the advantage of knowing how many they needed, Scotland saw off Little and the pacy Aaron Cawley. Scotland reached 94 for the loss of five wickets. Yes, 94. Then panic set in. One brings two, they say. On this occasion it brought four, the right side of 100.

Last pair at the crease, 11 to win. Seven when Little started his last over. A single, exposing the No.11. Block lad. Don't go for glory. Was it the temptation or the tension that was too much. A wild swing and Rock was solid under the chance. Ireland had won by five runs and were going to the World Cup finals.

Lovely spot, St Helier. Clean, friendly and affluent, of course, with a decent mix of bars and restaurants. I'd happily go back any time, but there is no chance of Jersey ever becoming a Test nation – golden generation or not – until they sort out those sluggish pitches. One of them is called Farmer's Field. Enough said.

Dublin – 12 October

The hierarchy of Cricket Ireland put plenty of thought into choosing the right opponents for the first Test match. It had to be one of the more traditional countries, ruling out Afghanistan, Zimbabwe and Bangladesh, but also a team that could possibly be beaten, ruling out Australia and India, and probably England, South Africa and New Zealand. Perhaps for sentimental reasons, looking back to Afridi and Saqlain, and the 2007 World Cup, and possibly because they had been supportive of Ireland as they sought a higher status, the invite went to Pakistan.

Two weeks later it was announced that the game would start on 11 May the following season, and not at the end of April, as had been feared. Cricket Ireland stressed that the venue had yet to be settled, which I passed on to readers of the *Indo*, with the confident addendum 'but it will be staged at Malahide'.

Within hours of the paper hitting doormats, I received a stroppy message from a senior Malahide member demanding a retraction as 'the committee have not yet agreed to that'.

So the club hierarchy were in some doubt as to whether they would deign to host Ireland's first Test match, were they? Dearie me. Even the other MCC would not have been pompous enough to debate that one.

Sharjah – 5 December

For a team who had won the title four times, and in some ways considered it *their* tournament, the last two rounds of the InterContinental Cup were a disappointment. Balbo had become the third batsman to score a double century for Ireland, making 205 not out against the Netherlands in August, but an unresponsive pitch at Malahide had delivered a draw and all but ended any chance of finishing above Afghanistan on the ladder.

The final round of matches were played simultaneously in the UAE. Ireland needed to beat Scotland, which they did by 203 runs, and hope Afghanistan slipped up against the hosts in Abu Dhabi, a game I again commentated on for Azhar.

Asghar Afghan lost the toss, but then told our TV interviewer, 'It makes no difference, we'll win anyway!' And they did, by ten wickets, to top the table with 121 points, 12 ahead of Ireland with the Dutch a distant third. It was a shame there was no final.

In all, Ireland played 39 IC Cup matches, losing only three: twice to Afghanistan and once to the Clontarf groundsman. The Afghans, who were not on the radar when the first tournament was played in 2004, competed in three editions, winning two and only losing one match: the 2013 final.

The year's fixtures ended with yet another ODI series against Afghanistan; this time three matches in Sharjah. The first game witnessed the debut of a new mystery spinner, Mujeeb Ur Rahman; the mystery being as much his real age as to whether Ireland could spot his carrom ball. It was claimed he was 16; he was clearly much older. Why should this matter? Well, for the most part it doesn't, of course, except Mujeeb lays claim to being the first ODI player born in the 21st century, and that honour truly belongs to someone else.

Whether a teenager or not, it was an impressive debut. Mujeeb ran through the Ireland top order, taking 4/24 from his ten overs, although the skipper hung around long enough to work out a few of his secrets. Afghanistan seized a 1-0 lead by a massive 138 runs, but Ireland recovered well, winning the next two games with equal conviction to take the series and give departing coach John Bracewell a victorious send-off.

His successor Graham Ford, the South African, was already with the squad to ensure a smooth transition and by now bowling coach Rob Cassell had his feet firmly under the table and was doing a good job fine-tuning the seamers, if the purposeful performances of Murtagh and particularly Rankin were any guide.

During the second game, the US journalist Peter Della Penna, Callender and myself were invited to dine in the VIP area. Dearie me. It was like wandering on to the set of a *Mad Max* movie. Sharjah has a reputation for attracting an 'interesting' character or two, but some of these guys were genuinely scary just to look at. Which we tried not to.

Most of them seemed to be missing something: an eye here, a hand or arm there. Callender at a free buffet was never going to notice, but Peter and I exchanged a couple of wary glances.

Who were they and where had this rogues' gallery all come from? You could have probably made a whole new bloke from the missing parts. It would have been amusing to see them invited for drinks with the MCC committee at Lord's. Or, better still, Malahide.

2018

Harare – 4 March

An important year started well with a clean sweep of four ODIs, in a tri-series against Scotland and the UAE, in Dubai. The victories over a resurgent Scotland, especially, were a morale boost ahead of the World Cup qualifying campaign where Ireland were fourth favourites for one of the two available places. The squad was much as expected, but there was a familiar figure missing from the press box. Call me old-fashioned, but there was no way I was going to go grovelling for a media pass to some government department. Never have done, never will.

I'm sure the Zimbabwean Ministry for Propaganda would have rubber-stamped me – mere mention of my Anti-Apartheid Orange Boycott would have been enough – but it wasn't going to happen. Navigating the ICC's online accreditation application is a tough task in itself without adding another hurdle. What is a pixel – and why don't I ever have enough?

The more complicated these procedures get from year to year, the more you wonder what was wrong with Barry's patented piece-of-string-tied-around-the-wrist system?

So with a ticket supplied by a squad member, I found myself in the crowd at midwicket for the opening match against the Netherlands. It was great fun. A bit of chat with the locals, including a ten-year-old off-spinner who had recently taken his first five-fer in a school match and, at the other end of the scale, Russell Tiffin. I'd not seen the retired Test umpire since Nairobi a decade before. The match was being played at his club, the Old Hararians. Food and beer was available. I'd have to do this more often.

Ireland batted competently. Balbo top-scored with 68 and took man of the match which probably should have gone to Nobby for a breezy 49 off 35 balls, including two sixes. It rained at lunchtime and if 268/7 wasn't a daunting enough total on a slow pitch, the Netherlands were asked to get 243 off a reduced 41 overs. Murtagh bowled Max O'Dowd first ball and the wickets were shared between the seamers. My new ten-year-old mate, who wasn't impressed by the Dutch spinners, was even less taken with the wicketless Dockrell. Ireland won by 93 runs, a useful margin if net run-rate came into play.

Harare – 6 March

The second match was at the Harare Sports Club, where I managed to watch from the Members Pavilion and latched onto the remains of an enormous tray of apparently free barbecued steaks after Ireland had seen off Papua New Guinea by four wickets. The victory would have been much wider, but for a magnificent 151 from PNG opener Tony Ura that set all sorts of individual records. Porty replied with his 11th ODI century, yet the outcome remained in doubt until the first ball of the final over.

The following evening was spent in the team hotel, enjoying a couple of beers with the O'Briens and their parents, Ginger and Camilla. Nobby reckoned Ireland would have to beat two of West Indies, Zimbabwe and Afghanistan to qualify, although the Afghans had made a shaky start without their skipper, who was recovering from an appendectomy. He also didn't think we'd see too many scores in excess of 300; a total that had become the norm in so many 50-overs games. The pitches were far too slow.

Talking with Nobby and a couple of other players was enlightening. There was no discord in the squad but there didn't seem to be the same togetherness that had been a feature of other campaigns. The players did their training, attended the team meetings and performed their best – but something was missing. The unity of purpose was there, but perhaps the intensity of old was missing. I got the impression they were all very keen to qualify – but not desperate – and at no point was I confident they would.

Port Elizabeth – 10 March

Another reason I hadn't bothered with accreditation is that the qualifiers clashed with Australia playing a Test match at St George's Park. A decade after the IC Cup final win over Namibia, I kept my promise to return and while Ireland were losing a key game to West Indies, I was watching a former Carrickfergus star putting an increasingly out-of-control Aussie side to the sword a week before Sandpapergate. A fine century by AB de Villiers was watched by a crowd in the very low thousands. It was an especially poor turn out as good seats were less than a tenner. The brass band alone was worth the admission, and the two flights it took to get there.

Back at the hotel, I found highlights of the Ireland game. Murtagh had bagged four wickets from the top and tail of the innings, but 101 from Rovman Powell powered West Indies to 257/8. It was a target that was always just out of reach, despite Ed and O'Brien the younger setting up an eight-an-over bash down the back end. Both fell in the 37th over, though, and Ireland were bowled out for 205.

In the final group game, Porterfield and Stirling put on exactly that many for the first wicket against the UAE at Old Hararians. Stirlo made 126 while the skipper fell eight short of his century. A mammoth 313/6 proved 226 too many as Big Boyd claimed four wickets and Simi Singh three. Ireland were into the Super Sixes.

Harare – 23 March

A whole chapter could probably be written about the shenanigans that went on in the last week of the qualifiers: Ireland lost lamely to Zimbabwe by 107 runs on a pitch that died under their batting boots, had disagreements over selection, Ed withdrew from the last two games with 'a niggle', they beat Scotland and, despite having only two Super Sixes wins, were still in with a shout going into the final game against Afghanistan who, after scraping into the second stage, were picking up momentum.

Elsewhere, Scotland were robbed of a victory, that would have seen them qualify at the expense of West Indies, by an umpiring decision that was so bad I almost felt sorry for them. Almost. It came on the back of an lbw that wasn't given in the Ireland game, allowing Balbo to make a match-winning century. Hard luck, lads. It was almost 20 years since that World Cup night in Glasgow, but still not long enough. I did feel for Zimbabwe, mind. The hosts only had to beat the winless UAE to reach the World Cup and somehow contrived to lose by three runs. My ten-year-old mate would have been in tears.

So the final World Cup place would go to Ireland or Afghanistan, who met in the last game, with Simmo coaching the opposition. Ireland won the toss. Stirling battled to 55 from 87 balls before running himself out, the O'Briens both contributed at nearly a run a ball, but the innings was crying out for an Ed special. A niggle? You don't miss an important game like that with a niggle. It had to be something more. What a boost to the Afghans to see the man who had dominated them, less than two years previously, sitting out the crunch match.

Without Joyce, Ireland limped to 209/7. Any hopes it would be enough were ended by a rapid Mohammad Shahzad half-century. Although Simi clawed it back a little with 3/30, Asghar appeared like an heroic Pashtun warrior, blood still oozing from his appendix surgery, no doubt, to stroke 39 not out from 29 balls and win the game with five wickets and as many balls to spare.

So no hop across the Irish Sea next year. No chance to tweak the bigger boys' noses again and send the pubs in Dublin cricket crazy for a couple of weeks. It felt like the end of an era. The last of the golden generation would be gone by 2023 when the big one came around again. Eight years is a long time between tournaments, and no guarantee it wouldn't be longer. Just how damaging this would be in the long run was anyone's guess.

Dublin – 1 May

While Stirling and Murtagh could prepare for the historic first Test match by playing for Middlesex, the remainder of the squad had a 12-a-side warm-up against Somerset in Taunton and one competitive InterPro match at Sydney Parade to get into some sort of nick for the biggest day of their cricketing lives.

Eight of the other nine who would start at Malahide featured in the three-day game at the home of Pembroke, the odd man out being Willo. It was particularly cold and far from perfect preparation, but Nobby enjoyed himself, hitting 165, and Stuart Thompson probably secured his

Test place with another century. The North West Warriors made 509/9 and, despite Balbirnie replying with 114 not out, Leinster Lightning had to follow on before the match dwindled to a draw.

The decision by the ECB to ban Ireland players from county sides, once existing contracts expired, will have a negative effect on the progress and improvement of their near neighbours. A more forward-thinking organisation would have found a way to continue a relationship that had benefitted both parties. Ed, Nobby, Big Boyd, Porty and Stirlo all learned and gained immeasurable experience from their time across the water, something the InterPros will not be able to replicate for a long while, if ever. The standard is improving, though. When the three teams were created in 2013, the Northern Knights being the other, the three-day games were usually over in two. Fast forward five years and, now officially first-class, most were going the distance. It was still nowhere near the quality of the County Championship, of course, but then neither are the set-ups in Zimbabwe or Afghanistan.

Malahide – 10–15 May

Barry collected me from the airport on the eve of the Test match and we settled into a couple of pints and a chat at the White Sands Hotel. Not an evening for double Jack Daniels, please. Big day tomorrow. Cricket Ireland had invited various dignitaries, including President Michael D. Higgins, plus all current and former internationals of both sexes, to mark and celebrate the occasion; we invited a car parts salesman from Belfast. Iain Knox had given up full-time physiotherapy to move into the family business, but he was the same old Knoxy, bubbling with mischief and tall tales.

The morning dawned on a wild and wet day. The Irish Sea was browny, grey; big and ugly. Lots of overnight rain, and more forecast. Was the big fella upstairs having his say on the idea of Ireland playing Test cricket? It was horrible.

'We should try playing these games in spring or summer,' the gateman said.

Nobby popped into the press tent to explain that rain wasn't the only problem, the wind was so strong it would have been dangerous to remove the tarpaulins covering the square, never mind put them back on again. The umpires had little choice. After waiting 141 years to play Test cricket, Ireland would have to wait a further day.

Gibney's, the Malahide pub, was buzzing that evening: the Dwyers, of course, Lewie and Heatley, David O'Connor, Greg Molins, ex-players, even a couple from the squad who weren't playing, and Isobel who gave me a hug. Alcohol was consumed. Lots of it. The extended Irish cricket family, proving an old mate's belief that the game exists primarily to provide the focus for an afternoon in the park. Or in this case, a day-long piss-up.

As Paddy O'Hara once told us, if the first day is rained off then the second day becomes the first day, and what a glorious one it was too. The gateman was whistling 'What a difference a day makes'. Caps were awarded. A wonderful occasion for everyone, but particularly for Ed. At last. A nice moment too for Stella Downes, scoring in a Test match after so many years as deputy to the immaculate Murray Power.

The Ireland team gathered for their official team photo. Tyrone Kane was the one surprise pick, getting the fourth seam-bowling berth ahead of Barry McCarthy. Kane provide Guerilla Cricket, the off-beat commentary team from England, with their best jingle – an adaptation of the Prince classic *Purple Rain*. How Cricket Ireland came to grant the official radio rights to their inaugural Test to a sweary bunch of posh lads from the Home Counties is anyone's guess, mind.

Porty won the toss and bowled. I walked around the ground to watch the first ball from beside the sightscreen. Murtagh was given the honour and a mad attempt to run a single saw Imam-ul-Haq flattened in a sandwich of fielders. If Brian O'Driscoll was among the crowd of 4,500 he would have approved. It was some start. The bespectacled opener got to his feet, rearranging his glasses like Captain Mainwaring, and continued to call and run as one might expect from a nephew of Inzamam.

The home side were on the board when Rankin claimed his second Test wicket and Ireland's first, and Timothy followed up next ball by removing Imam. Thompson joined in with another. Murtagh, bowling with guile, claimed a second after lunch and, when the north-west pair of Big Boyd and Thommo also doubled up, Pakistan were 159/6 and in a spot of bother. An unbroken 109 for the seventh wicket steered the visitors to calmer waters and we went home, most of us via Gibney's, knowing we had seen a day of proper Test cricket.

On the third day, more sun greeted another large crowd, including the President and past Presidents of Cricket Ireland and the Irish Cricket Union, a real President, Michael D. Higgins, dozens of former Ireland internationals, and Mick Jagger, who turned up for the final session.

Murtagh struck early, as he does, and had the best figures of 4/45 when Pakistan declared on 310/9, giving

Ireland's top order a twitchy little half an hour before lunch. Hoping for a wicket, maybe two, the visitors took three. Ed, after scoring Ireland's first Test run, was debatably lbw for four, Balbirnie plumb and Porty lost his off stump.

When Nobby was a third lbw victim, Ireland were 7/4 and the all-time Test low of 26 was in greater danger than the follow-on target of 161. There were a good few 'in my days' coming from the direction of the hospitality tents.

O'Brien the younger prospered, though, looking in his element before slapping to cover on 40, and Wilson, improvising bravely with a suspected cracked bone in his elbow, made 33 not out. All out 130 and asked to follow on. It was the first time Pakistan had enforced since 2002 when, after making 643, they dismissed New Zealand for 73. Now that was a lead.

Joyce walked out again to open, possibly seeing the amusing side of waiting decades for a Test innings only for two to come along on the same day. Buses. With Jagger looking on, Ireland closed on 64/0. Unbeaten overnight on his age of 39, Ed might well have considered that the 74-year-old Rolling Stone wasn't the power he once was, but had no immediate retirement plans. Two other septuagenarians had no plans of retiring early that evening either. Big Roy and Robin Walsh joined us for drinks in the White Sands. Great company, as ever, but I managed to slip upstairs before Barry's inevitable round of double JDs arrived.

The gateman thought it would be all over on the fourth day, which was actually the third. He would have been looking smug when Ed ran himself out, not quite beating a direct hit. 'I should have dived.' Steady now, old fella. Balbo recorded Ireland's first pair and Nobby lost two stumps on

18. Stirling again reached double figures, but not 20. He was 'the greatest living Irishman' according to the comedy radio crew, who had someone with a faux Cork accent doing the Belfast lad's jingle. But what's a bit of cultural ignorance among friends, eh?

The writing was on the wall when Wilson was sixth out for 12, but O'Brien the younger had other ideas and set about constructing Ireland's first Test century. It took him 136 balls more than the 50 needed for that epic knock against England in 2011, and included 12 fours. As the Boys in Green (trimmings) moved firmly into credit, romantics dreamed of Headingley 1981 and wondered, could this be the fourth time a Test team grabbed victory after following on?

The cynics among us scratched our heads over some of Pakistan's field positions, especially taking the second new ball with two slips and no gully. Thommo scored 53 and gave great support in a seventh-wicket stand of 114, and Kane dug in for eight not out from 67 balls. The home side led by 139 overnight, with three wickets in hand, and the centurion joked about being first on the 'imaginary honours board'.

That night in Gibney's we discussed where the younger O'Brien fitted in the pantheon, and whether he was, as Micky McCrum would have it, the greatest Irish cricketer of all time? The GOAT. Not as stylish as Ed, of course, or as successful as Eoin, as relentless as Monty or perhaps not making the same impact as TJ, but what a breadth of work: in the middle at the end in Kingston, the main man four years later in Bangalore, two of the most punishing centuries I've seen against Kenya, telling spells of medium pace, most caps and a couple of years away from becoming only the 14th batsman to score an international century in all three formats.

'Stellar, flamboyant, solid and oh so Irish,' according to Micky. I'd add understated too, which is probably why he doesn't immediately spring to mind as the GOAT, but it's hard to argue with his achievements and longevity.

Sadly, our hero didn't add to his overnight 118 and the innings folded on 339. Pakistan, needing 160 to win, quickly lost three for 14. With the romantics now convinced a Miracle of Malahide was in the offing, I was fearing another Sickness of Sydney. The home side pressed but dropped what could have been a crucial catch with 100 still needed, and the visitors ran out winners by five wickets.

'I'm extremely proud of how we went about it, all five days. I can't fault anyone,' Porty said. 'Most of our batters, myself included, would have wanted to have their first innings again but everything else was fine.'

There would be tougher Tests ahead, especially on overseas featherbeds, but Ireland left Malahide knowing that they had competed with one of the established powers. The 11th team to play at the highest level had put on a decent show, at the perfect location. For me, it only started to sink in on the flight home: Ireland had played a Test match – a bloody Test match!

Dublin – 24 May

A couple of weeks after winning that long-coveted cap, Ed announced his retirement from all cricket. I had seen the first ball he faced in an Ireland shirt and the last, and wished I'd seen more in between. Promise me a Joyce century, especially early in his career, and I'd have driven a couple of hours to be there. Fluency, grace, timing; a joy to watch. His stance became more crouched and ugly later on, but the style of strokes remained. That one Test appearance will be cherished, but he should have played so many more.

In the 2006/07 Ashes tour party, he sat in the England dressing room and watched as Paul Collingwood's inadequacies were exposed everywhere except on a flat track in Adelaide, and carried the drinks for a final Test team that featured Monty Panesar batting at No.7. What a waste. But England's loss was Middlesex and Sussex's gain, and the gain of those who regularly watched county cricket. Ireland, too, had some very good years out of the finest batsman the island has produced.

Malahide – 27–29 June

The hordes of India fans who made the pilgrimage to The Village to worship His Kohliness may have gained a glimpse of the great man, but they would have needed to be quick to get a photo of him with bat in hand. India bettered 200 in two T20 internationals against Ireland, winning both easily, but Virat Kohli failed to reach double figures in either game.

Was it his way of paying tribute to Brian Lara, who always struggled against the Boys in Green? Probably not. Whereas Lara's Achilles had been Irish spin, the great Indian was twice undone by lanky seam. Peter Chase claimed the holy trinity of MS Dhoni, Rohit Sharma and Kohli in the space of four balls in the first game, and when Kohli delighted the majority of a near 9,000 crowd by opening in the second game, Chaser bagged him again for nine.

Belfast – 27–31 August

Another ODI series against Afghanistan, and another close one. The production line of unorthodox Afghanis had now given us Hazratullah Zazai, an opening batsman of frightening power, if limited technique.

You do wonder, in the age of T20s, if the more developed cricketing powers aren't missing a trick when they put talented youngsters onto 'pathways' at a young age and coach all the quirks and instinct out of them. There was nothing coached about Zazai and if he had been on a pathway it was well off the beaten track. Yet the blacksmith of an opener hammered 74 off 33 balls to win a T20I at Bready and followed up with 82 off 54 as a 2-0 series win extended Afghanistan's run of victories in the shortest format.

Zazai could not repeat his carnage over the longer distance at Stormont, though. He was out cheaply in the first game which his side won by 29 runs, and fell to Murtagh for a single in the second as Timothy followed up four wickets in the first match with an even better 4/30. His day wasn't finished. Balbirnie guided Ireland towards the visitors' 182/9, with a composed 60, but the chase faltered and Murtagh needed to pick up his bat and see Ireland over the line by three wickets.

Porty then made one of his daft bat-first decisions in the third match and his side were bowled out for 124, with only Wilson reaching 20. Afghanistan lost two wickets as they cantered home in 23.5 overs. Rashid Khan, who took eight wickets across the three games, was man of the series; Murtagh had taken nine.

I was in the radio commentary box for BBC Northern Ireland with, among others, Peter Gillespie. A fine man for a chat and a yarn, and someone who had been around in various capacities for most of my time following the team.

'It'll be 25 years next year, I told him.'

'You should write a book, DT.' It was a thought.

Lord's – 25 September

I bumped into Nobby in the Tavern towards the end of the English season and, without saying as much, it was clear he was just about done in the middle. After retiring from county cricket in 2016, he had expanded his players' agent role and was developing a career in TV commentary boxes, where he was a chirpy natural. In addition to those pressures on his time, he had just become a dad.

I tried to persuade him that this was the place to bow out next summer, when Ireland played their first Test at Headquarters. If a fourth World Cup campaign had been on offer he would probably have stayed on, but a couple of weeks later he announced he was following Ed into the retirement meadow. He scored 6,097 runs for Ireland and his record 225 catches and 38 stumpings will take some beating.

I'd always had a soft spot for the penultimate O'Brien and we had become even better buddies after I chose him as My Favourite Player for a feature in *The Cricketer*. He probably wasn't my absolute favourite; Parfitt, Titmus, Gatt, Ed and Stirlo would all pip him, but I wanted to tell the little green bike story. He also deserved it for once loudly announcing my arrival at Uxbridge, during a county game against Northants. I've been acknowledged many times by a boundary fielder but to hear a booming 'David Townsend!' when spotted by the keeper in the middle was a bit special, even if it bemused other spectators.

Georgetown – 17 November

While Nobby joined the golden generation of men who had departed in dribs and drabs, the four veterans in the women's team all retired together, after Ireland had lost their final World T20 group game.

Ciara Metcalfe, Clare Shillington and the Joyce twins, a quartet known affectionately as the 'grannies' by their young team-mates, had ploughed on through the barren years of women's cricket, using up annual holiday allowances and making many other sacrifices to play for their country. Time had run out for them with the promise of central contracts on the horizon and team-mates Kim Garth and Gaby Lewis set for lucrative careers in the burgeoning T20 leagues around the world. Garth had already starred for the Sydney Sixers in two Big Bash finals.

Shillington, the first Irish woman to make 100 appearances, could hit a long ball, Cecelia Joyce was a fine opener, especially in the longer game, and when Metcalfe landed her leggies, she was a joy to watch. I would miss Isobel the most, though. Of all her achievements during a career that spanned two decades, starting me towards appreciating the women's game would have to be right up there. Along with winning a Test cap 16 years before brother Ed.

Sydney – 4 December

It's not often that I've been asked out for a drink by an 18-year-old, and never by a Randy Pete, but that's exactly what happened one afternoon when I went to check on the progress of Harry Tector, who was scoring a few runs for Sydney grade side Randwick Petersham. I'd not spoken to Heatley's lad since he had captained the Under-19s at the previous year's qualifiers in Jersey.

'Where are you staying, David?'

'Just up the road in Randwick.'

'Me too. Do you fancy a beer one evening?'

What an impressive young man. Bought his round, too. Easy to see why he had been installed as captain of the Ireland Wolves for their tour of Sri Lanka in January, despite his tender years.

The trip would not go well for Harry in terms of runs, and the Wolves didn't record a win, but don't measure the success of such ventures purely in those terms. Without the fallback of county cricket to gain playing time and experience, the Wolves programme was now a key to the success of the senior team – the nursery of future Test and ODI stars, and the Sri Lanka trip produced a couple.

James McCollum showed why he was in pole position to take one of the batting positions vacated by Ed and Nobby, while James Cameron-Dow spun himself into contention. The month away also gave Mark Adair the chance to start making headway again after an underwhelming spell with Warwickshire.

Harry would have to bide his time before he followed McCollum off the rank, and Balbo was ahead of him to replace the skipper when Porty's long reign eventually ended, but I had no doubts after a couple of schooners in the Coach and Horses that I'd been drinking with a future Ireland captain.

2019

Koh Samed – 8 March

Another trip to India loomed for Ireland's first away Test match, where Afghanistan would be the 'home side'. The reluctance to play matches in Kabul, or any other centre of that cricket-mad country is understandable, given the security situation. Although it comes as much from the Afghan players, as from visiting teams, after the abduction of Nabi's father in 2013.

So Dehradun, at the foot of the Himalayas, is where it would be staged and again the online visa application worked perfectly. Also I made an effort to stay vegetarian for the trip, and didn't suffer the dreaded runs. There was bound to be a hitch somewhere along the line, though; this was India, after all, and this time it was provided by Jet Airways going out of business in instalments.

A few days before I was due to leave Thailand, I was informed by email that the first leg of my return flight, from Dehradun to Delhi, had been cancelled. No alternative offered or details of any compensation. A phone call saw me rerouted via Mumbai. The airline ceased trading altogether a few weeks later. OK, it wasn't exactly the last chopper out of Saigon, but with India and me there is always something.

Dehradun – 14 March

John Mooney, now employed as fielding coach by Afghanistan, reckoned I'd love this part of north-west India, but I didn't see too much to like in the taxi from the airport, and nothing changed during a week there. Perhaps I'd missed the sarcasm in our Messenger exchange. Dehradun is poor, really poor; but it's also uncared for. Heaps of rubbish here, building materials there, and nothing tidy, except one better-off area we drove through on the way to the Rajiv Gandhi stadium. I'm guessing when every day is a struggle to provide for yourself and your family then a good clean-up isn't top of the list but, dearie me, it was depressing.

Not without the odd light moment, though. One of the younger Irish supporters, a musician, who had made the long trip from London, liked to walk everywhere and ignored local advice to get a tuk-tuk home after a heavy rainstorm one evening, only to disappear up to his midriff in an open drain, on an ill-lit road. The tuk-tuk would have cost 50p, including tip.

Callender had been there since the start of the nine-match series and had seen Afghanistan again wipe the floor with Ireland in the three T20s, but the ODI series shared 2-2, with a game rained off. He had the restaurant staff well trained to his needs: nothing at all spicy and the right order of toast, eggs, fruit and goodness knows what else for breakfast. A local taxi was also at his beck and call, and took us out to the ground to watch training on the eve of the game.

I sat down with Balbo for a preview piece – he was in fine form after two big centuries in the ODI series – and grabbed a word or two with Johnboy about the mood in the Afghanistan camp.

'I imagine the pitch is going to turn square from the first ball?'

'I'm not sure I'm supposed to discuss stuff like that, am I?'

Bloody ACU – but fair play to them, they were obviously getting the message over. At least to the support staff.

Dehradun – 15 March
The 50th anniversary of the greatest afternoon in any sport produced another day to remember. Porty won the toss

and understandably chose to bat, only to find the surface a mite sticky and at its most difficult in the first session. One or two balls gripped, but none with any great alarm and certainly nothing that could be blamed for the tumble of seven wickets for 25 runs after the skipper and Stirlo had added 37.

It was a sorry procession. Balbo did at least get his first runs in Test cricket via a streaky edge through the cordon – but no more. Not many Test match No.3s can boast a runs tally exclusively in boundaries after their first three knocks. Nor an average of 1.33, for that matter.

Andy McBrine and James Cameron-Dow, two of the five debutants in the side, stuck around for a while with another, Dockers, but a woeful 85/9 was on the board when Murtagh walked out to bat soon after lunch. The Lambeth Lara had done little in an Ireland shirt to live up to his moniker since that final over blitz against Scotland almost six years ago and if the groundsman hadn't started the motor roller, he did have the key in the ignition.

Oh ye of little faith. Murtagh batted beautifully, as he often does before he gets bored and starts clearing the front leg. Runs started to flow and it wasn't long before Timothy was the owner of the first six stuck in a Test match by an Ireland batsman – a lofted drive back over the head of Nabi, a shot he repeated for the same result, off the same bowler, an over later. The front leg was starting to misbehave itself when he crunched a four over mid-on to bring up the 50 partnership, but his luck held for another seven overs.

What fun! Except for the increasingly frustrated Afghans. Murtagh's half-century came up off 72 balls, his 11th in first-class matches, and the last pair had added 87, more than doubling the score to 172 all out when Dockrell nicked off for 39. For the second time I'd seen a No.11 top score in a Test innings, and the Lambeth Lara was in his element when he spoke to the press after play.

'I've never scored a century and feel I was robbed of one there today when Dockers got out.'

Maintaining a straight face, he added that he had told the Ireland batsmen that his hotel bedroom door would be open if any of them wanted advice.

Dehradun – 17 March

Ireland stuck to their task well on a hot second day, with not much in the pitch. Murtagh removed Rahmat Shah, two short of what would have been Afghanistan's first Test century (he claimed the honour later in the year against Bangladesh), but the hosts returned a more than useful first-innings lead of 142 and had removed the skipper a second time before stumps.

St Paddy's Day dawned and a fightback of sorts was mounted after the early loss of Stirlo, who became the first of three Ireland batsmen to rue the absence of a review system, having nearly middled the ball that claimed him lbw.

Slowly but surely, Balbo found his Test feet, and at the other end young McCollum looked every bit the future, as the two of them added 104 for the third wicket. Ireland only trailed by five when Balbo edged behind on 82; McCollum quickly followed for 39.

Again the middle order came and went but O'Brien the younger and Dockers put together 63 for the seventh wicket, allowing the visitors to dream of a lead in excess of 200, only for both to be sawn off by lbw decisions when, at very best, the ball would have been kissing leg stump. O'Brien's 56 was his third 40+ score in four Test innings.

A three-day finish loomed, but Murtagh was having none of it. The Lambeth Lara again found batting comfortable as he made 27, to add to his 54 not out in the first innings, and briefly, before he holed out, his Test batting average touched 91. Ireland were only the third team to manage two 50+ partnerships for the tenth wicket in the same Test, and no last man had twice bettered 25 before. The hotel bedroom door would remain open.

Dehradun – 18 March

Ireland needed nine wickets to pull off an unlikely win, but any hope of inducing a panic in the Afghan ranks went begging when a straightforward chance was spilled early on at short extra off Dockrell. The hosts were within a boundary of victory when their second wicket fell to a stumping and, having caught Mohammad Shahzad the evening before, Stuart Poynter, in what would be his only Test, completed the keeper's treble by running out Nabi.

'If we'd batted first time remotely like we did in the second innings, then it could have been a completely different game,' the skipper said, after Afghanistan had won by seven wickets. Yes, and if your auntie had testicles she'd be gender-confused, as the (updated) old saying goes.

An end-of-tour party was convened at the team hotel, offering the chance to catch up with Timothy and a few of the others I'd missed before the game. Alcohol was consumed. Poor old Manage was already dreading the check-in of three tonnes of cricket equipment at an Indian airport. 'Two forms filled out for each piece, please, Mr Sid.'

Malahide – 3 May

The ECB were still insisting on playing the biennial ODI in the middle of winter, and resting players like Ben Stokes and Jos Buttler. Before Ireland became a Full Member, the discussions about a date went something like this: Ring, ring … 'Hello, Cricket Ireland?'

'ECB here. We'll play you on the 28th of April. Goodbye.'

I doubt it has changed much since.

With the Island View not available, I decided to give Airbnb a go and found a lovely house, about a mile from the ground. Double bedroom, share with owners, breakfast, 50 euros a night. What wasn't to like? The Irish have a well-earned reputation for hospitality, too, of course. Maybe I'd strike lucky and find another Conor.

I touched down early evening and made my way to the digs. Rang the bell. No reply. Rang it again. Nothing. Bugger! What do I do now? Luckily, as I was searching for a WiFi signal, the door opened. Small man, big smile.

'You must be David?'

'That's me.'

'Sorry, I was just out the front watching the football.'

'What's the score?'

'Arsenal leading 2-1 at half-time.'

'Great! Arsenal are my team.'

'Mine too.'

'Is there anywhere I could perhaps watch the second half?' Hint, hint.

'There's a pub about half a mile down the road, I'll see if I can find you a map.'

Overnight rain delayed the start and reduced the match to 45 overs per side. The little ginger fella won the toss for

England and inserted his former colleagues, five of whom were still in the opposition dressing room.

Stirlo looked good, making 33, as did Balbo until he was sent packing by a horrible piece of sharp practice by Ben Foakes. After missing a sweep, the Ireland No.3 checked the ball had been taken by the keeper and moved to get up. In doing so his back foot strayed out of the crease and Foakes whipped off the bails. The third umpire deliberated a long while before deciding that the ball hadn't been 'dead' and therefore the batsman was out stumped for 29.

I like Foakes. I saw his maiden Test century in Galle and expected him to be an automatic choice for England in all formats for a long time; I liked him a lot less after that incident. It was the sort of dismissal that leads to blows in a park game, and causes decades-long bad blood between club sides. If Balbo had stayed, the eventual Ireland total would probably have prospered by a further 12–15 runs but, as the other (updated) old saying goes, look on the scorer's computer screen.

All eyes among the travelling English press were on debutant Jofra Archer, who bowled with good pace, nudging past 90mph a couple of times, on a pitch that didn't offer him much. But it was Mark Adair who took the newbie honours with a guns-blazing 32 off 30 balls, including two powerful sixes, that helped Ireland to 198 all out. Would it be competitive, we wondered? It didn't take long to find out as a combination of Josh Little, Murtagh and Big Boyd reduced England to 66/5, including Eoin for a third-ball duck.

Inevitably it was Foakes who proved the difference with an unbeaten 61, although Timothy struck him in front on 37 and decided not to go upstairs. Poor judgement that by the bowler, and by his skipper not to risk losing the review with the game so far advanced. Little took a fourth wicket but the visitors got over the line with three overs to spare, and I suffered Namibian farmer-like emotions when the England keeper was named man of the match.

At the airport, waiting for my flight back to Leeds, I spied the man who had started me off on this journey, more than a quarter of a century ago. Someone I'd not seen since he was explaining that he liked the look of an England hopeful by the name of Collingwood.

'Excuse me, you look remarkably like John Carr!'

'David!' As ever, JC's eyebrows shot up as his face came alive. 'Vicky's sitting over there. Can I get you a drink?'

He had probably said much the same in 1993. I only had time for half a Guinness, unfortunately, and didn't think it appropriate to lay into the now senior ECB executive about this nonsense of a Hundred tournament that his organisation were planning. That could wait. Vicky was still a delight.

Bready – 1 July

It was good to be there when Shane Getkate made his ODI debut, more than a decade since first watching him as a teenager and eight years after his heart attack. If persistence ever paid off, here it was. Keep going, lad, you'll get there. He had made his full debut earlier in the year and had half a dozen T20 appearances under his belt going into the match at Magheramason, where he bowled a tidy seven overs, took two Zimbabwe wickets, and was in the middle when Ireland secured a four-wicket win.

The selectors sprung a surprise by giving the gloves to Lorcan Tucker, but it was another of the new generation who again grabbed the attention with four wickets and a brutal late cameo with the bat. If there was any doubt that Ireland had unearthed a new star during the England game, and subsequent losses to West Indies and Bangladesh, it was put to rest here.

Mark Adair was the real deal. Already dubbed 'Botham' by his coach, the all-rounder had that X-factor appeal that empties bars, especially when he has a piece of willow in his hands. A couple of his blows towards the pavilion here were enough to fill the bars again – with spectators looking to take cover.

It was generally felt that the 23-year-old Belfast man would have done better at Warwickshire if he had been more focused, and with members of the Ireland hierarchy making off-the-record comments about his 'attitude' and 'work ethic' we gathered he could be an awkward, lazy so-and-so at times – but what a talent. Not as good as Botham, Flintoff or Stokes, and never likely to be, but the sort of player and with the character to become a talisman for the team for years to come, now he realised what was required and had knuckled down a bit.

Staying with the Ardmore Express, I met up with Decker Curry the next day, still plying his trade at the age of 52 for Barry's local side. And still talking about retiring, as he was the last time I'd laid eyes on him almost exactly ten years ago. The toothy-grinned welcome was the same, the big meaty handshake and he was no doubt still strangling sheep.

When you catch up with that generation of Irish cricketers, and those older, you realise just how lucky the McCollum, Tucker and Adairs are. Decker didn't play an ODI – before his time – nor a T20 – the format first appeared two years after his international retirement.

How good would this bloke have been if he could have played now in his prime? And the others too? Simon Corlett, Ossie Colhoun, Alec O'Riordan, Monty, Dougie Goodwin, Paul Jackson and Ivan Anderson.

The new generation were walking on the shoulders of those players, and all the greats.

Lord's – 14 July

After a trio of near misses – Hendo's shout against Viv that wasn't given, Gatt's reverse sweep, another dodgy lbw escape in Melbourne – England finally won a World Cup at the 12th attempt. The coolest man on either side during a thrilling final of two ties and heartbreak for New Zealand went forward to lift the trophy. A little ginger fella who used to play for Ireland.

People have wondered how someone from such modest beginnings, with no obvious cricketing tradition, ended up captaining England to glory; they're asking the wrong question.

When I sat down to dinner with him a few months before the 2015 World Cup, he had spelled out in some detail what was wrong with his adopted country's approach to ODIs and predicted the disaster of that looming campaign. He knew how to fix it: with brave, fearless cricket of the brand he had learnt playing for Adi and Simmo. He was given the chance to fix it – and how.

So please don't ask how a Fingal man ended up as captain, ask instead how England won their first World Cup, and you'll find the answer is Eoin Morgan.

Merchant Taylors' School – 19 July

A few days before the historic first Lord's Test match, the Ireland squad were preparing diligently. With a warm-up game against one of the counties? Well, sort of: a two-day match against Middlesex Seconds on the playing fields of a posh school in north-west London.

To say it was low-key would be an understatement. As I made my way across various pitches, wondering which one contained the men who would be walking out in front of a full house at Headquarters next week, I was again reminded that this lot do things differently.

Manage was his usual helpful self. Yes, he would let the skipper know I'd like a few words. James Harris, of Middlesex, had a natter too. He would have loved to have been Irish instead of Welsh, but would never admit it.

Porty was good value. I wanted to know what it was like for the boy who grew up playing backyard cricket with his sisters on a farm in the north-west, to now be about to lead a Test team out at Lord's. He spoke about his journey, how he had first moved a few miles down the road from Killyclooney, his local side, to Donemana, helped them win the Irish Cup as a 15-year-old, and then gone south to Leinster, before spending time with the MCC Young Cricketers at Lord's and then into the county game with Gloucestershire.

The passion was there from the start – seen in an early photo of a grumpy eight-year-old who had just lost his wicket – and the ambition. But it's taken some fortitude and staying power as well to lead Ireland for 11 years without a break, during which time he has never once walked onto a cricket field without believing he could leave it victorious.

'We have to find a way to win,' he says again, looking forward to Wednesday. He worries that James Anderson with a Dukes ball in his hand could be a challenge. I tell him that Jimmy isn't fit and that his inclusion in the England squad is probably just a bit of psychological jousting ahead of the Ashes series. He assures me that, Anderson or not, Ireland will make a game of it.

I'm not so sure and neither is Gus Fraser, who I bump into on the way back to the station. Murtagh's day-job boss is worried Ireland will be steamrollered. We agree that the one good thing that might come out of it would be Timothy taking five wickets and getting his name on one of the bowling honours boards. It would be in the visiting dressing room, though, not the one that he and Gus know so well with Middlesex.

Lord's – 24 July

The big day dawned with no easing of the trepidation. At St John's Wood tube it seemed that Irish fans were in the majority, but that was probably the splashes of green everywhere. There were a good few MCC members, too, in their egg-and-bacon ties; a big, colourful crowd making their way down Wellington Road to the ground. A buzz of atmosphere, excited talk, anticipation and a song or two.

It wasn't too hard to think back to when drinks in the committee room had been the pinnacle of an Irish trip to Lord's; to remember Derek Scott and John Wright, the great former Hon. Secs. of the Irish Cricket Union, who would have loved this day; Scotty, notepad at the ready, to inform the report he would write later; Wee John shuffling through the crowd, meeting and greeting, handshakes, eyes twinkling. Lewie was there with his Hollywood smile, younger daughter in tow; the Dwyers too, Matt and Willie, Big Roy and Robin, and Larry Leprechaun.

Inside the Media Centre, the visiting press were seated along the front row, an honour granted to guests, although when the sun dropped lower in the day they would realise why the doyens of what used to be Fleet Street like to be a row or more back.

No problems with the sun in the old press box at the back of the Warner Stand when I had first covered Ireland here in 1995, and watched Ryan Eagleson and Peter Gillespie for the first time. The former now an Under-19s coach, the latter a national selector and playing his final season for Strabane, having finally reached the age he looked wearing that first cap.

The toss. Win it and bowl; lose it and bowl. Just bowl. Porty called wrong and Joe Root chose to bat. Happy days. 'We'll be here on Friday, then.'

A few minutes later Timothy was ploughing his familiar furrow from the Nursery End; the slightly angled, clenched-buttock approach that I'd seen here so many times over the years, though only once before with a shamrock on his chest. Stirlo in the cordon, also on his home ground. For the first time, the visiting side could claim more first-class appearances at Lord's than the England XI, and the pair combined for the first wicket when Jason Roy edged to slip.

Murtagh continued to probe, finding just enough wobble and nibble in the first Test-match pitch prepared by the MCC's new familiar-looking head groundsman, while Adair rose to the occasion at the other end. At seven minutes to noon, Adair had Joe Denly lbw to start a clatter of six wickets for seven runs in the space of 28 balls. England were suddenly 43/7, or (FORTY THREE FOR

SEVEN) as the old BBC *Grandstand* teleprinter would have spelt out.

And Timothy had his Michelle! Was a Ms Pfeiffer ever sweeter? When Moeen Ali nicked him behind, no bowler had earned a place on the Lord's honours board in such a short space of time, or for fewer runs. After nine overs in the heat, the old fella took a breather with figures of 5/13, leaving Adair and Big Boyd to mop up.

Callender, Ger and I had looked at each other more than once during that extraordinary two-and-a-bit hours. Joy, disbelief, incredulity, it was all there and more as England were bowled out for 85, inside the session. We had, all three of us I'm sure, worried privately that one side in this Test might have had their inadequacies sharply exposed and be rolled in an embarrassing heap – we had not for one minute considered that side would be England.

The delight on the faces of the Ireland fans who were singing their hearts out in the crowd was also tempered with a sense of 'Has that really happened?'

As Murtagh walked off smiling, ball held aloft for the cameras, he was interviewed for TV and announced that he might now treat himself to dessert with his lunch. And there, as Timothy makes his way up the pavilion steps, this journey ends.